GAME CHANGERS

GAME CHANGERS

AJ DYBANTSA, BYU, AND THE STRUGGLE FOR THE SOUL OF BASKETBALL

MATTHEW BOWMAN &
WAYNE LECHEMINANT

SIGNATURE BOOKS | 2025 | SALT LAKE CITY

For Bean, who saw it started, and for Jesse, who saw it finished—MB

For Constance, my companion heart—WL

Join our mailing list at signaturebooks.com for details on events and related titles we think you'll enjoy.

Design by Jason Francis
Cover photo by Altan Gocher, Getty Images

FIRST EDITION | 2025

Hardback ISBN: 978-1-56085-530-9
Paperback ISBN: 978-1-56085-528-6
Ebook ISBN: 978-1-56085-507-1

CONTENTS

PREFACE

Kevin Young had a lot to do. Life was coming at him pretty fast. He was an assistant coach for the National Basketball Association's Phoenix Suns, and the team was in trouble. They had what was supposed to be an outstanding roster. Three of their players had recently been All-Stars, honored among the two dozen best players in the league. Phoenix's top player, the slender seven-foot forward Kevin Durant, was regularly the subject of debate as to whether he was a top-ten or merely top-twenty player in all of NBA history. That 2023–24 season, he had scored so much that when the first game began he ranked twelfth on the NBA's all-time scoring list; by the last game he was ranked eighth. And yet, that weekend in late April 2024 when the NBA playoffs began, the Suns had woefully underperformed.

On Saturday, April 20, the Suns were walloped by the Minnesota Timberwolves, a young, untested team to whom the experienced Suns were supposed to teach a lesson. But the game had shown that while the Suns players had stellar resumes, they were also wearing down. That September, Durant had turned thirty-five, the twilight of any NBA player's career. He was not quite as nimble as he once was, having suffered a debilitating Achilles tendon tear a few years before. One of his two most acclaimed teammates was the three-time All-Star, Bradley Beal. But Beal was thirty-one and had been nursing wrist, back, and hamstring injuries for years. Surgeries, impairment, and pain had left him missing months of the NBA season over and over again and looking creaky when he made it onto the court.

On the other hand, Minnesota's young stars—Anthony Edwards, Jaden McDaniels, Karl-Anthony Towns—had never won much in the playoffs, but that night they showed up with energy. Edwards had matched Durant shot for shot. The Suns had struggled to beat the Timberwolves to rebounds. The Suns lost, 95 to 120.

Frank Vogel, head coach for the Suns, convened his staff over the next two days. He needed to game plan. He wanted to run his team through practice. They needed to batten down the hatches and figure something out.

And then Kevin Young got word. Ace and Chelsea Dybantsa were going to be visiting the Brigham Young University campus in Provo, Utah. Right away.

Not even a week earlier, on April 17, BYU had held a gala press conference in the Marriott Center, the home of the BYU Cougars men's basketball team. There were crowds; there were spotlights; there were past great BYU players like Danny Ainge, who was by then running the Utah Jazz. BYU Athletic Director Tom Holmoe introduced Kevin Young as the new head coach of the team. Young said a few words, introduced his family, basked in the applause, then flew back to Phoenix to help Vogel strategize for the Timberwolves.

This had not been what Young was planning even two weeks earlier. The BYU job had dropped into his lap with surprising speed—his predecessor's departure had been announced only five days before Young walked into the Marriott Center with his family. A whirlwind of interviews and plane flights and Zoom calls followed to seal the deal, but Young had insisted through it all that he felt obligated to stick it out through the playoffs with Phoenix. BYU had understood.

But Young could not let the Dybantsas pass him by. Their son, AJ, was the best high school basketball player in the country. The family was in Utah scouting potential high schools, not colleges. AJ was barely seventeen. But Kevin Young knew the stakes and knew he had to meet the Dybantsas.

So he went to Vogel and to James Jones, the general manager of the Suns. He begged for their blessing if he were to slip away from the playoff grind for a little while. He said he would need not even twenty-four hours.

"It was actually a crazy story," he told reporter Kevin Reynolds. "We had practice. I sprinted out of practice, jumped in an Uber, and flew on a plane to Provo."

Young frantically plotted what to say to the Dybantsas on the flight. After meeting with them late in the day on April 22, he hopped on another red-eye flight to meet the Suns in Minneapolis for their game with the Timberwolves the next day. "Got back to Minny about 3 in the morning ready to rock," Young said.[1]

Ace Dybantsa was impressed. "The man flew in from Phoenix to see us," he told Reynolds.[2]

The loss of sleep and last-minute preparation on planes would turn out to be worth it. The Dybantsas came back again later with AJ.

Eight months later, on the morning of December 10, 2024, AJ and Ace appeared on ESPN and announced that AJ would attend BYU.

* * *

By the conventional metrics of collegiate basketball in the United States, BYU's signing of Dybantsa was a triumph. The Cougars had a solid but not standout men's basketball program. BYU is a quintessential "mid-major" program, the label applied by sports journalists to schools that are good but not members of the elite college conferences. These schools don't attract the most talented or famous recruits, don't tend to get their games on national broadcasts, and don't win the biggest tournaments. BYU finally got one of those elite conferences—the Big 12—to admit them in 2023. As of the end of the 2025 men's basketball season, the school had a very respectable all-time record of 1,939 wins and 1,147 losses. Before that, BYU was in regional conferences and had never been considered a national powerhouse.

For every success, there is a qualification. As of 2025, BYU had won the championship of whichever conference it played in twenty-seven times, ranging from the now obsolete Skyline Conference in the mid-twentieth century to the powerhouse Big 12 in the early twenty-first. But in the national postseason tournaments—particularly the National Collegiate Athletic Association (NCAA) men's basketball tournament, the gold standard since the 1970s—BYU never made much noise. As of 2025, the school possessed the uneasy distinction of making the most appearances in the NCAA tournament while never making it to the tourney's Final Four.

The tournament invites only a few dozen teams from across the nation, sixty-four being the most common number over the tournament's history. BYU has been among those teams thirty-one times since its first appearance in 1950, an entirely respectable record. But in the tournament BYU has an overall record of sixteen wins and thirty-five losses—including one agonizing streak of nine appearances across the 1990s and early 2000s in which BYU was sent home in the first round of the weeks-long tournament again and again, failing to win a single game. It was not until 2010 and a gasping, exhausting double-overtime win against the University of Florida that the Cougars got that monkey off of the school's back. And then they lost the very next game.

Programs like this do not normally recruit players like AJ Dybantsa. In 2006, the NBA instituted a rule prohibiting players from joining the league until the calendar year they will turn nineteen, which must be at least a year after their high school graduation. It's come to be called the "one-and-done" rule, named for those exceptional players who because of the rule began to play a year of college before declaring their eligibility for the NBA draft. In the nineteen years between 2006 and 2025, 107 one-and-done players were taken in the top half of the NBA draft, the prized fourteen picks colloquially called "the lottery" due to the way those picks have been distributed to the worst teams in the league since 1985.

BYU had two players taken in the lottery in the forty years after 1985—the phenomenal shooter Jimmer Fredette, and center Rafael Araújo, a bruising player whose bulk and strength served him in the NCAA. Neither were one-and-done players and neither had scouts and media marking them for great things from the time they were in high school. Neither attracted much fanfare entering college. And yet both had outstanding college carreers that turned them into lottery picks.

But neither flourished in the NBA. Fredette's scoring prowess dominated the college game, but NBA players, with their superior size and speed, could contain him. And Fredette could rarely stay apace with the man he was supposed to guard. Araújo similarly had a hard time keeping up with NBA players. Neither lasted much more than a handful of years in the league.

Contrast that record with Duke, to point to one elite NCAA basketball program. Since 1985 Duke has sent thirty-one players to the lottery, and some years more than one. In 1999, four Duke players were taken in the lottery. Twenty-six of those thirty-one players were one-and-dones. Neither of BYU's lottery picks lasted past their rookie contracts in the NBA. Many Duke one-and-dones have become NBA All-Stars.

In the summer of 2024, the eighteen-year-old Russian Egor Demin committed to play at BYU for the 2024–25 season. Demin had been playing professionally in Europe and wanted to dip his toe into American basketball before entering the 2025 NBA draft. A Utah sports reporter called him "a potential one-and-done prospect," noting that Demin was perhaps the most talented player BYU had ever recruited.[3]

But he didn't hold that title for long. Six months later, AJ Dybantsa followed in Demin's footsteps.

* * *

A success, but not an uncomplicated one.

BYU announced Dybantsa's recruitment with pride but also slight annoyance at the implication that the university was descending into the glitzy, breathless, and commercialized world of modern sports. Brigham Young University is owned and operated by The Church of Jesus Christ of Latter-day Saints. The university's board of trustees, which ratifies all hirings at the university, is made up of mostly a collection of the church's highest leaders and is chaired by the president of the church. The official student newspaper estimates that only about 1 percent of the student body of more than thirty thousand are not members of the church.[4] All students are required to abide by an honor code. As with many universities, BYU's Honor Code requires academic honesty from students. And like a smaller number of religious universities, BYU's code also requires commitment to a set of behavioral standards ranging far beyond academic honesty to personal grooming; sexual abstinence outside of marriage; and abstention from alcohol, tea, coffee, and tobacco.

Such requirements have made recruiting athletes to play at BYU difficult. Gordon Monson, a columnist for *The Salt Lake Tribune*, frankly stated that BYU sports is "restricted by a recruiting base made small by the school's strict Honor Code."[5] These strictures have, at times, caused tension between the school and its athletes, particularly those who are not members of the church. One such minor incident occurred in 2004, when rumors circulated that the school's athletics publications office had removed Araújo's tattoos from photographs of him in official media guides. The guide indeed showed Araújo with bare arms, but no airbrushing was involved. The office simply selected pictures before Araújo had tattoos or from angles at which they were not visible.[6] That there was a kerfuffle over the possibility, though, is a good—if small—illustration of the tension that non-LDS athletes like Araújo endure at the school.

And yet, for many in the BYU community, the distinctiveness that the Honor Code and the school's religious affiliation confer is a good thing, a guardrail against the endless churning of the business of professional sports that has, for many critics, rendered collegiate athletics something of a farce. The NCAA has for decades scrambled to preserve the notion that these athletes are amateurs, playing solely for the love of the game and the cultivation of character. It's sometimes been a hard story to maintain. Jim Donaldson of the *Minneapolis Star-Tribune* caustically pointed out that while the NCAA's preferred term was not "players" but "student-athletes," the organization also embraced the money and publicity that followed the student-athletes, the one-and-dones in particular. "We really do want to have athletes who also are students," Donaldson wrote to an imaginary one-and-done player. He offered his best wishes but said that the very concept was "a mockery of those standards . . . a semester-and-a-half here devoted primarily to improving your basketball skills and, by extension, your marketability."[7]

For decades, the money that college athletes brought in had gone straight to the NCAA itself and to the schools the athletes played for. Student-athletes confronted strict rules designed to guard their status as "amateurs," forbidding them from receiving any sort of financial remuneration for their play—down to, quite literally, free lunches—until 2014, when the NCAA changed rules to allow schools to offer their athletes food. But regulations were still tight. In 2018, BYU received a host of penalties from the NCAA—including officially voiding dozens of wins—because BYU player Nick Emery received meals at a fancy restaurant, a car, and even at one point cash from wealthy supporters of the program.

But in the early 2020s, under immense legal pressure from current and past college athletes, the NCAA altered its rules. After 2021, players could receive payment for the use of their name, image, and likeness—what the NCAA calls "NIL." Corporations might pay athletes to put their faces on T-shirts or to appear in commercials. Schools could help athletes put together promotional packages. In 2025, ESPN reported that the University of Colorado quarterback Shedeur Sanders was making $4.7 million a year. And if Sanders's income was ranked first, far down the list of NIL contracts—even the 100th-ranked athlete—was making half a million dollars.[8]

Even before NIL money transformed the system, some at BYU were uncomfortable with the pseudo-professionalization that NCAA sports spent years inching toward. Ernest Wilkinson, the powerhouse president who reigned over BYU for twenty years in the mid-twentieth century and transformed it into a modern American university, was a staunch opponent of the slow evolution of professional sports into a business and college sports into an imitation of the pros. Early in his career, Wilkinson blasted the infamous 1919 Chicago White Sox team that stood accused of taking bribes to intentionally lose Major League Baseball's World Series. "These sinners," Wilkinson declared, "are comparable to the college that pays athletes to attend its schools in order to be on athletic teams."[9]

Of course, even during Wilkinson's tenure as president, the school took steady, incremental steps toward embracing the money that came with joining conferences, recruiting star players, and winning games. But rarely did the president seem comfortable with it. For Wilkinson, athletics were not about money. He told the people on campus lobbying him to extend scholarships to athletes—which he eventually agreed to do—that he thought athletics should be "devoted to hard work and fair play" and insisted that he "felt greater satisfaction in the team's good sportsmanship and the fact that they had group prayers" than in winning games.[10] College sports, he believed, were about character, and certainly not about income or careers.

Long after Wilkinson, even BYU coaches who might not share his sternness remained sympathetic to his determination to subordinate sports to the religious character of the university. Bronco Mendenhall, the head coach of BYU's football team from 2005 to

2015, was frank. "'Football is simply the vehicle we use to help others come to a knowledge of what really brings joy and happiness to our lives," he said. He told a reporter that "BYU's mission of spreading the church's teachings is his top priority." He told another reporter that Henry B. Eyring, a top leader of the church, told him that the church supported BYU sports in general and football in particular in order to "generate more interest in the more compelling message" of the faith.[11] Kalani Sitake, who replaced Mendenhall when the latter was hired away by the University of Virginia, was ambivalent when the NIL rule changes came down the pike. "We want to make sure that it is in line with the mission of our church and the mission of our school," Sitake said. "The key for us is to make sure our young men understand what they represent and who they represent."[12] Mark Pope, the men's basketball coach whom Kevin Young was hired to replace, agreed. "It's going to be a complicated thing here at BYU. It's not traditionally the way that we are," he said.[13]

AJ Dybantsa is certainly receiving a lot of money. So is Kevin Young, for that matter. Some initial reports pegged Dybantsa's NIL income at BYU at around $7 million and Young's compensation at $30 million for a seven-year contract.[14]

But BYU officials cast doubt on these figures. In July 2025, a reporter for the *Deseret News* (also owned by The Church of Jesus Christ of Latter-day Saints) favorably cited a report that through the work of both university and an NIL collective called The Royal Blue, Dybantsa would receive a $5 million NIL deal. Other outlets, like *Sports Illustrated*, repeated that number.[15] Such calculations are tricky because official numbers are rarely made public. But it's clear that Dybantsa's income at BYU certainly would exceed $5 million because of a number of NIL deals beyond the auspices of BYU or The Royal Blue, including with the shoe company Nike and the sports drink Red Bull.[16]

BYU has consistently emphasized the lowest possible number in order to support the assertion that at BYU, sports has more to do with character than money. Shane Reese, president of BYU, claimed that "Differentiators are what make people successful from a business perspective, and our differentiator is that we're grounded in our spiritual mission and that we are going to try to do things differently."[17]

BYU vice president Keith Vorkink, who oversees athletics at the university, told the *Deseret News* that emphasizing the money involved in BYU athletics was missing the point. "Our philosophy is to not be the highest bidder," he said. Instead the university offered people the opportunity to "contribute to the university's distinctive mission in a spiritually supportive and family friendly environment."[18] BYU's desire to be both in and not of the world, to both compete in the NCAA and hold itself distinctive from it, is reminiscent of the broader experience of the LDS Church in the twentieth and twenty-first centuries. Sociologist Armand Mauss describes the history of the LDS Church in the twentieth century as an ongoing oscillation—a desire to assimilate with the world around it giving way to a desire to emphasize distinctiveness and difference and then back again.[19] Sometimes BYU could seem to be chasing both things at the same time.

That strange struggle also gestures to the kaleidoscopic meaning of basketball itself. For many people—like James Naismith, the inventor of basketball, and the white Christians who followed in his wake—basketball was supposed to be an inherently moral sport, one that decentered the individual and built commitments to community and self-sacrifice.

But to many other people who have adopted the sport since, basketball has come to mean other things. Writer Onaje Woodbine has described basketball as a ritual of ecstatic experience for many Black players on the streets of American cities. The sport is a way to express personal autonomy, excellence, and power. At the same time, it offers an alchemy of collective identity through celebration of the sport's legacy in the Black community.[20] And for many other people—especially those who run major basketball organizations like the NCAA or the NBA—basketball is an extraordinarily profitable business.

For AJ Dybantsa, basketball sometimes means all of these things. And in his career those meanings have sometimes collided.

On the one hand, Dybantsa and his family played the NIL game adroitly from the time he was in high school. By the time he was sixteen he was blowing the doors off St. Sebastian's, a private Catholic boys' school outside Boston, where Dybantsa grew up. It had a perfectly respectable sports program and occasionally competed for championships in the independent prep school circuit. Dybantsa's parents praised the sport for teaching their son discipline and encouraging him to get up early.

But then AJ transferred to a series of private schools intensely focused on preparing young men for professional basketball careers, and there he began to earn major NIL money. Before he could vote he was earning six-figure endorsement deals. He and his parents decided to join the world of tournaments and exhibition games and public workouts for teenage players—a massive, multimillion-dollar national circuit funded and assembled by shoe companies and other corporations eager to have connections to players who might one day be as famous as LeBron James or Michael Jordan. By the time AJ was ready to let the world know where he would be attending college—for, of course, only one year—producers at ESPN were eager to have him do it on their network. He said he wanted to attend BYU because of the moves the school had made to professionalize its basketball program, particularly its recruitment of Kevin Young, a longtime NBA coach who had built warm relationships with NBA stars.

At the same time, BYU thought AJ would be a good fit for their unique campus culture. For years before Dybantsa signed, the school and the church that owned it had begun to emphasize the nuclear family in policy, rhetoric, and image. Quentin Cook, an apostle of the church, spoke on this at a university conference in August 2023. "Our commitment to education grows out of our doctrine," Cook explained. He named "uniting families" as among the most important of the church's doctrinal commitments and said this priority should receive support at BYU.[21] Clark Gilbert, LDS Church Commissioner of Education since 2021, added, "Education of the kind we're offering has not only wonderful personal benefits for individuals, but also strengthens families and the church."[22]

The notion that BYU has a special mission bound to the promotion of a particular sort of moral behavior has been a driving force behind many of the decisions of Gilbert's administration. "Religious schools must differentiate on their unique spiritual purposes, even as they strive to tie into the broader academic community," he wrote in a widely read editorial for the *Deseret News*. He tied that distinctiveness to the fostering of moral character and the family. "Where religion wanes we also see declines in social engagement, philanthropy and family stability. Thus, religious schools play a critical role in preserving civil society," his editorial said.[23] At BYU, Gilbert's administration pressed faculty to avow commitment to these ideas.

AJ Dybantsa, raised in a tight-knit immigrant family, could speak this language. "I'm a big family guy," he told a reporter for the *Deseret News*. "Now that I live here, I'm always (going to be) part of the community. I'll always come back to do community work here. I did it in Brockton."[24]

Collin Terry, an assistant coach for the BYU basketball team, was on the initial tour that Ace and Chelsea Dybantsa received, the one Kevin Young rushed to join. "I thought they were incredible people," Terry told the journalist Dave McCann. "Just like anybody else that goes to BYU, I think they realized there is way more to the university and the program than maybe you first thought there was." McCann agreed. He believed that the Dybantsa parents understood the school's values, and that, as he put it, "AJ Dybantsa's journey to BYU began with his parents."[25]

The BYU basketball program in 2025 was looking to thread the needle. On the one hand, to insist that it privileged values of family and character above those of the marketplace that American sports had full-throatedly embraced. On the other, to compete in that marketplace, to win tournament games, to join big conferences, and send graduates to professional sports leagues.

It was a challenge, perhaps an impossible one. But AJ Dybantsa seemed the school's best hope to meet it.

1

WALTER BYERS INVENTS AMATEUR BASKETBALL

In the summer of 2024, Leonard Armato made a lunch reservation at Petros, an upscale Greek restaurant four blocks from the ocean in Manhattan Beach, California. His guests were AJ Dybantsa and his father, Ace. AJ was by acclamation the best high school basketball player in the United States. Ace was a former police officer, now retired and the shrewd full-time manager for his son. Leonard Armato was once chief marketing officer of the Sketchers shoe company; an administrator who revitalized professional volleyball in the United States; and the founder of Management Plus, a heavyweight talent agency that worked with basketball superstars Shaquille O'Neal and Lisa Leslie, the boxer Oscar de la Hoya, and the musician and producer Quincy Jones.

The Dybantsas did not want Armato to be AJ's agent. Armato knew that going in.

The lunch—and its qualification—happened because the Dybantsas wanted advice on navigating a sports landscape that had utterly transformed while AJ was growing up. Traditionally, agents sought out and negotiated deals for players—endorsements of products, appearances in media, even opportunities for athletes to have their own brands of shoes or clothing, a move Michael Jordan pioneered with Nike in the 1980s. But over his career, Leonard Armato had explored something new, and the Dybantsas were intrigued.

"I'm not here to bash agents," Ace Dybantsa told a reporter. But it seemed to him that much had changed in the contemporary sports economy. "Do you really need an agent?" Ace asked.[1]

Armato had worked for years with Shaquille O'Neal, perhaps the dominant player in the NBA in the ten years after Michael

Jordan retired in 1998. Armato convinced O'Neal not to take the endorsement-for-hire route. Instead O'Neal founded his own brand, SHAQ, which licenses O'Neal's specially designed logo to companies like Reebok, Pepsi, and EA Sports. Those companies in turn make products and slap the logo on them. O'Neal runs a company that owns fast food restaurants, puts out a children's book series called *Little Shaq*, and produces reality shows for ABC and rap albums featuring O'Neal himself. O'Neal endorses products, like Papa John's pizza, that he has a financial stake in. Instead of being a freelance endorser, Shaq was consolidating a financial empire.[2]

O'Neal eventually spoke with AJ Dybantsa and offered to put him in touch with Armato. "Shaq told me that he taught [him] everything that he knew," AJ said.[3] And thus, the lunch.

AJ Dybantsa was seventeen years old when he had lunch with Armato, when he and his father asked Armato not to be an agent but to serve as an adviser as the Dybantsas navigated the new world of sports economics.

That a student not yet even in college could look at what athletes like O'Neal were doing and see possibilities for himself was a sign. For decades, all the way back to the nineteenth century, American athletics had been associated with virtue, and virtue with amateurism: the belief that people should not play sports for money. Theodore Roosevelt, the president of the United States from 1901 to 1909, was one of the key figures in the formulation of the amateur ideal. "The amateur, and not the professional, is the desirable citizen," he wrote. "Our object is to get as many of our people as possible to take part in manly, healthy, vigorous past-times, which will benefit the whole nation; it is not to produce a limited class of athletes who shall make it the business of their lives to do battle with one another for the popular amusement."[4] For Roosevelt, the purpose of sports was the development of character, and particularly the character of men, residents in a democratic republic who needed virtue to be good citizens. Injecting finances into such a system would corrupt that aim.

For years, this was the guiding assumption of high school and collegiate sports in the United States. Sports leaders extolled amateurism even as their organizations generated vast amounts of income from the performance of the athletes themselves, the only remaining amateurs in the whole business. But in the 2010s and 2020s, the presumption of amateurism finally came crashing down.

But people like Ace Dybantsa and Leonard Armato also believed that basketball could promote virtue and teach the youth who played it how to be better people. Ace Dybantsa, over and over, told his son that it did. He explained to AJ's high school coach that his son played basketball to develop a "work ethic." The coach thought Ace had taught his son to play with "really high emotional intelligence and maturity and awareness of what's going on around him." He told a reporter that AJ had "measurables and this athleticism that will blow you away, but the stuff that's allowed him to elevate is the character stuff."[5]

Was it possible to simultaneously commit to the work and the grind and the unselfishness that people from Theodore Roosevelt to Ace Dybantsa hoped athletics would teach and, at the same time, found an athletic shoe brand and take cash to endorse luxury watches, as Shaquille O'Neal does? The people who founded the NCAA, which organizes and regulates college sports, did not believe so. But beginning in the 2010s, the American judicial system began tearing the system the NCAA built to the ground. AJ Dybantsa, like many other athletes, has begun to negotiate through the rubble, trying to make money and achieve a sense of dignity at the same time.

Uncle Eddie

On April 5, 1993, Chris Webber blew it. He was a sophomore at the University of Michigan, and the cornerstone of what fans called the "Fab Five"—the five players who had signed up to play at the University of Michigan two years before. One ESPN commentator called Webber and the four other players who started each of Michigan's games the greatest recruiting class in college basketball history. It was widely agreed that Webber and his teammate Jalen Rose were two of the top-five high school basketball players in the country in 1991. The three other members of the Fab Five were also considered likely professional players—and, indeed, four of the five ended up playing in the NBA.[6]

The Fab Five were outspoken. They openly liked hip-hop music and wore black socks and baggy uniforms, which the white people who ran American mainstream media in the early nineties considered grubby and antisocial. But they also won. The 1991–92 Michigan Wolverines men's basketball team was the first team starting five freshmen ever to make the NCAA tournament's championship game. They were, it is true, soundly drubbed by a much more experienced team from the perennial powerhouse Duke University. But they had made it. And they were only freshmen. The future was bright.

The next year Michigan stormed right back to the championship game. The team went 31–4 before April 5, and Webber averaged nineteen points and ten rebounds a game. He was named a First Team All-American, one of the five best college players in the country.

In the title game on April 5, this time against the University of North Carolina, things went much better than they had against Duke the year before. The game teetered back and forth. Nobody seized the advantage. And then, with Michigan two points down and just nineteen seconds left in the game, a North Carolina player missed a free throw. Webber seized the ball and paused. His teammates galloped toward their basket on the other end of the court. Webber nearly traveled, caught himself, and dribbled his way after them. But North Carolina defenders swarmed him. Chris Webber stopped, inexplicably picked up the ball and called for a timeout that his team did not have.

Calling a timeout your team doesn't have earns a technical foul in NCAA basketball. A referee blew the whistle. He took the ball from Webber. North Carolina got more free throws and won the game, 77–71.

Webber never lived this down. He entered the NBA draft that June and was taken first overall by the Golden State Warriors. He won the Rookie of the Year award, was named an NBA All-Star five times, and by the time of his retirement had compiled a fifteen-year career that got him into the Naismith Memorial Basketball Hall of Fame. And yet, even years after he left the NBA, he still fielded questions from journalists about how many timeouts a college basketball team gets.

But Webber's botched play wasn't the worst thing that happened to the Fab Five. The worst thing happened after all of them had graduated.

At five in the morning on February 17, 1996, Maurice Taylor fell asleep while driving, lost control of his SUV, and rolled it on

Michigan State Highway 14. Taylor was a big forward for the Wolverines. In the car was another beefy Michigan player named Robert "Tractor" Traylor, a few other Wolverines, and a young man named Mateen Cleaves. Cleaves was a tremendously talented high school player deciding where he would play in college that coming fall. Tractor Traylor broke his arm, and the others were banged up.

The police wondered what the students were doing on the road so early in the morning. And University of Michigan officials wondered what they were doing with Cleaves. It turned out they were driving the forty miles back to the university campus in Ann Arbor from a party in Detroit, which was—depending on whom you asked—perhaps at the home of, or perhaps merely attended by, a man named Ed Martin. Martin was a sixty-one-year-old electrician for the Ford Motor Company. He had joined the company in the 1950s and thirty years later was a jovial, well-liked supervisor who made a lot of money on the side, organizing illegal company-wide gambling rings. He took bets on a lot of things, but mostly on the state lottery. Eventually prosecutors concluded he sometimes made as much as $100,000 in a week.

Ed Martin loved basketball. He knew the kids who grew up playing in Detroit high schools. He went to games and got familiar with coaches. The players called him "Uncle Eddie." By the late 1980s Uncle Eddie was giving talented high schoolers gifts. "Mr. Martin knew it was tough where we were coming from," Webber's Michigan teammate Jalen Rose told a reporter. One reason the Fab Five were so popular in Michigan was that both Webber and Rose were born in Detroit and grew up playing in schools in the area. They met Uncle Eddie. "He gave us what we needed to not screw it up," Rose admitted.[7] Those gifts were sometimes shoes, sometimes meals. And eventually, cash. Between 1988 and 1993, Martin gave Chris Webber more than a quarter-million dollars. When the University of Michigan coaching staff started recruiting Webber, they learned about Martin and gifted him tickets, hotel rooms on road trips, and access to the team. Martin, in turn, gave Traylor and Taylor and other players who ended up at Michigan money, too. That's why Maurice Taylor and Robert Traylor took Mateen Cleaves to meet their friend Uncle Eddie.

The summer of 1996, NCAA officials contacted people in the athletics office at the University of Michigan. They had questions. Afterward those Michigan officials sat down some of the team's players and asked them whether Martin had given them money. The players and the team's coach, Steve Fisher, said no. Some of them lied. Fisher then covertly stopped Martin from paying deposits on apartments for some of his players. Nothing was definitively proven then, but the appearance of impropriety was enough, and Fisher was fired in 1997.[8]

But Martin was not only giving money to Michigan athletes. He was, of course, running an illegal gambling ring. Eventually the investigation into Maurice Taylor's car crash turned into an investigation of white-collar crime, and the FBI caught up with Ed Martin. In 2002 he was indicted and pled guilty in exchange for leniency in his sentence. He died before he was sent to prison.

That still wasn't the end of it. Later that year, the information the FBI discovered about Martin's financial practices was reported in public. It became obvious that Martin had in fact given Michigan players money and other perks. Chris Webber pled guilty to a charge of criminal contempt for deceiving a grand jury while testifying about Martin. And the NCAA's Committee on Infractions looked like it would come down hard on Michigan.

That committee consists of roughly twenty-five officials from various universities who participate in the sports the NCAA organizes, as well as a few outside advisers, mostly lawyers. But it is guided by NCAA professionals, paid investigators, and officials who bring cases to the committee and, according to some, steer it in the direction they want it to go.[9] In 2002, the University of Michigan voluntarily gave up its eligibility to participate in postseason tournaments for the next academic year and agreed to void its postseason victories for several past years during which Martin had given money to players. Eventually, four banners came down from the rafters of the Michigan basketball arena. The names and achievements of Webber, Traylor, and Taylor were deleted from the record books of the University of Michigan and the NCAA. Webber's All-American honors were rescinded. He was ordered to have no association with the University of Michigan for ten years—not even attending a basketball game.

All of this happened because, according to NCAA regulations, college athletes were amateurs. And amateurs could accept no payment for their play.

But at the same time, National Public Radio reported that the first year the Fab Five played at the University of Michigan, the school made $4 million in basketball revenue. In 1994, coasting on the players' popularity, the school signed a fifteen-year deal with Nike, receiving $170 million from the shoe company for the rights to outfit the team and plaster the Nike logo on Michigan gear sold in the campus bookstore and across the country.[10]

For years, the NCAA allowed players to receive little more than a tuition waiver. But even as the organization was preaching the moral virtues of amateurism, it was growing wealthy. The career of Ed Martin was as much a sign of tensions growing deep within the system the NCAA built as it was of any personal corruption on the part of a player like Chris Webber. Athletes were well aware that their schools and the NCAA itself were growing rich on their images and labor, and that knowledge was as corrosive to the amateur ideal as money could be.

The Birth of a Bureaucracy

The NCAA was, in a sense, founded in the Oval Office. Long before he became president of the United States, Theodore Roosevelt was an undergraduate at Harvard University. He threw himself into collegiate sports. He boxed but most enjoyed team rowing, the dominant sport in the United States in the mid-nineteenth century. It was also the first sport colleges competed at: a two-mile race between Harvard and Yale teams on Lake Winnipesaukee in New Hampshire on August 3, 1852. The first intercollege organizations devoted to regulating eligibility and rules focused almost entirely on rowing.

In November 1904, Roosevelt, a charismatic and energetic politician, won a tremendous victory in the presidential election. He earned 56 percent of the popular vote—the most of any candidate since 1820. He was at the zenith of his fame and power and swept the progressive movement into preeminence in American politics. Progressives like Roosevelt were horrified by the problems of late nineteenth- and early twentieth-century American life—the tremendous economic impact of the Industrial Revolution, the birth of powerful large-scale corporations, the exploding populations and consequent poverty and suffering in American cities—all the way down to problems in college sports. Progressives also believed that these challenges could be dealt with. They were interested in the social sciences, like sociology and economics, and they were optimistic that competent organizations, within or without government, could apply the insights of professional experts and fix social problems.

Like many progressives, Roosevelt was a reader—he pressed Congress to pass the 1906 Pure Food and Drug Act to ensure the inspection of food and pharmaceuticals in the United States after reading exposés like Upton Sinclair's *The Jungle*, a lurid novel about the horrors of the meatpacking industry. (Sinclair hoped the book would spark sympathy for labor, but one takes what one can get.)

So when Roosevelt found an explosive two-part article called "The College Athlete," published in the spring and summer of 1905 in *McClure's Magazine*, he had reasons personal and professional to call for change. The article warned that college sports, especially football, were violent and corrupt. Players were getting hurt, and professors were going easy on athletes' grades. Universities were squandering money on stadiums, and coaches were growing unethically wealthy. Roosevelt went to Harvard to give a commencement address and spoke directly to the problem: "Brutality in playing a game," he said, "should awaken the heartiest and most plainly shown contempt."[11]

Then the president acted in a characteristically progressive way. He summoned to the White House coaches and representatives from the three most prestigious universities in the United States, Harvard, Yale, and Princeton. He told them to organize, study the problems of violence and corruption, and figure out a solution. In December of that year, representatives from sixty-two colleges and universities met in New York City and formed the Intercollegiate Athletic Association, which officially began regulating sports among member institutions in March of 1906. Four years later it was renamed the National Collegiate Athletic Association.

Initially the NCAA's ambitions were tentative. It tried only to standardize rules, focusing first on football but eventually other sports as well. In 1921 the NCAA organized its first tournament, for track and field. In 1939 it organized the first NCAA men's basketball

A political cartoon on the cover of a 1908 issue of the satirical magazine *Puck* depicts President Theodore Roosevelt at "basket ball practice in the White House gym." Roosevelt's "goal" is to get his preferred successor, William H. Taft, into the nomination basket. *Courtesy Library of Congress*

tournament. These competitions were intended as a lure. Invitations came with the expectation that schools would adopt the rules the NCAA laid out—because at this point the NCAA had little power to enforce its regulations. It could only persuade, offer, and suggest.

In part because the NCAA was largely toothless, many of the problems Roosevelt complained about were still endemic. Most of them had to do with money. In 1906 the average tuition for an Ivy League school stood at around $150, a sum that only well-to-do families like the Roosevelts could pay. Some students received scholarships.

But not, for the most part, the athletes who competed in the games governed by the NCAA. None of these students who played college sports were supposed to be reimbursed. They were doing it for the pleasure of competition. Or so college officials told themselves. The 1906 bylaws of the Intercollegiate Athletic Association declared that college athletes should be amateurs and deemed as a violation "the offering of inducements to players to enter colleges or universities because of their athletic abilities, or supporting or maintaining players while students on account of their athletic abilities." In 1916, the now-NCAA clarified the meaning of "amateur" as "one who participates in competitive physical sports only for the pleasure and the physical, mental, moral and social benefits derived therefrom."[12] These rules were intended to stop any possibility that colleges might offer players money. They were supposed to be amateurs, whether they wanted to be or not. But the NCAA, lacking much authority other than simply advisory, left enforcement of these directives to schools themselves.

It was soon clear that this simply would not work. In 1929 Howard Savage, a researcher for the Carnegie Foundation for the Advancement of Teaching, a private organization dedicated to improving education in the United States, published a report with several coauthors. It was called "American College Athletics." Savage included reports on more than one hundred colleges and universities in the United States and documented incontrovertibly that these institutions were in fact finding ways to pay players. Of 130 institutions Savage's team investigated, only twenty-eight were actually adhering to the amateur ideal. As early as 1879, university baseball coaches were finding plush summer jobs for their players at expensive resorts where they would lounge, receive cash, and occasionally play baseball with wealthy vacationers. In 1904 Yale hired investigators who determined that Harvard's Walter Clarkson, the best pitcher in college baseball, was being paid $15 a game to play at a resort in southern Massachusetts.

The report identified problems well beyond baseball. In 1922 the small Pennsylvania school Washington & Jefferson College, with 450 students, somehow fielded a football team that went undefeated and thus earned a place in the prestigious New Year's Day Rose Bowl against the University of California. Eventually an NCAA study determined that the school had put together a $50,000 pot of money from alumni and other friends of the school. The money was distributed to players who signed up with the school. And Washington & Jefferson was hardly alone. Few findings of the report attracted more attention than the evidence that many colleges had "slush funds" of thousands of dollars, mostly raised from alumni, used to lure recruits. Yale's fund exceeded $100,000, a staggering amount of money in the early twentieth century. The report accused many schools of allowing head coaches to select candidates for "subsidies," money coaches would give to certain players. Those players were in turn "expected to make good or forfeit all or part of their subsidies."[13]

Another problem was that although the NCAA instructed its member institutions that players could not be offered funding for their athletic services, colleges and universities often simply gave athletes scholarships for reasons that did not mention athletics. Savage's team noted that some schools offered dozens of athletes these sorts of scholarships. There were many other perks, too. Schools would pay "tutors" who, in practice, did athletes' homework. As the report noted, drily, "There appears to be little difference between this practice and relieving a regular salaried member of the athletic staff from some of his other duties in order that he may supervise the academic standing of athletes."[14]

The report dropped like a bomb on the small world of American higher education. But the stock market crash that triggered the Great Depression followed its publication in only a matter of weeks, giving Americans much more to worry about. It was not until 1948, after two decades of handwringing, that the NCAA attempted reform. A set of rules nicknamed the "Sanity Code" specifically forbade financial aid to athletes of any sort other than for documented financial need. But universities simply refused to abide by it. At the 1950 NCAA convention, NCAA administration found seven institutions in violation of the Sanity Code and proposed their expulsion from the organization. But the member schools did not provide the required two-thirds majority vote to expel the schools. Instead they voted to repeal the code. Darrell Royal, the football coach at the University of Texas–Austin, eventually sniffed, "I don't want Hofstra [University] telling Texas how to play football." The possibility of the NCAA wielding power over its members seemed as elusive as ever.[15]

The Ruthless Walter Byers

And there things stood. It might have seemed as though the NCAA's attempt to regulate its members was done. But in 1951 the organization divested itself from administrative entanglement with the Big Ten athletic conference, a group of midwestern schools that had been playing each other since the 1890s. For arcane reasons, through the 1930s and 1940s the Big Ten and the NCAA shared headquarters space. Many officers held jobs in both, like Kenneth Wilson, who was the commissioner of the Big Ten and the secretary-treasurer of the NCAA at the same time. This detangling necessitated a fresh staff, and the newly independent NCAA hired Walter Byers, a twenty-nine-year-old sportswriter working as Wilson's assistant sports information director, into a dizzying promotion. Byers, who had never run anything, suddenly became the first executive director of the NCAA. The organization was weak. But unlike almost everybody else in American sports, Walter Byers saw potential.

Brick by brick, through meticulous exertion of effort, persuasion, and experimentation, Byers turned the NCAA into a powerhouse. Despite his youth and inexperience, somebody who knew him well might have predicted his methodical ambition. Byers was a precise and careful introvert who for decades kept a journal documenting the daily weather and grass conditions on the Kansas ranch he had inherited from his real estate–investor father. One day early in his tenure at the NCAA, he showed up with a booklet he had written called "Office Policies and Procedures." Employees were expected to work a half-day on Saturdays. Men had to wear coats and ties, women skirts or dresses. They were penalized if they did not pull their office window drapes shut at the end of the day. Coffee cups on desks were banned. Byers announced he was giving up golf soon after taking the job to focus on his responsibilities, and he was good to his word. He never played the sport again. But he did teach his sons to play basketball.

Wayne Duke, another commissioner of the Big Ten, said that three things elevated the NCAA out of its struggling, pre–World War II era and made the organization the central locus of power in college sports: "Enforcement, football on television and the basketball tournament. And Walter was the architect of all three."[16]

With what seems like naïveté in retrospect, many sports teams in the early 1950s viewed the advent of television with worry and suspicion. Surveys showed that fewer Americans would be willing to pay ticket prices to sporting events if they could watch them on TV for free. Byers deftly seized upon that fear and turned it into power. In 1951 the annual NCAA convention, made up of representatives from every member school, voted to ban any member school from airing games—with the only exceptions a select handful that Byers and his staff would select and market to television networks. Only the University of Pennsylvania and Notre Dame seemed to see what a lost opportunity the move would be. Those two schools protested and claimed the right to sign contracts to air their own games. But Byers quickly beat them into submission, threatening penalties against any schools that played the holdouts, as well as fines for each game aired without his approval. Eventually the two schools folded, and Byers quickly turned to NBC, negotiating a deal that would authorize the network to air one college football game a week during the season. Byers suggested that for its trouble the NCAA central office should receive 60 percent of the $1.14 million contract NBC offered. The schools, which expected that the contract money would go to them, disagreed. With characteristic foresight Byers saw that as future television contracts grew, the NCAA's own cut would too, so he avoided the fight and accepted 12 percent.

Walter Byers now had the money to open a new NCAA home office. He put it in his own hometown of Kansas City, Missouri, then he turned his attention to another potential source of power.

In the 1940s and 1950s, the University of Kentucky dominated men's basketball, winning four championships between 1948 and 1959. Over these dominant years, one team stood out. The 1947–48 Wildcats amazed the basketball world with a combination of outside shooting, fast-break prowess, and a rugged frontcourt. Indeed, so enamored were fans with this group that they christened the starters the "Fabulous Five" four decades before Chris Webber and his cohort suited up for the Wolverines. This original Fab Five went 36–3, winning both the Southeastern Conference (SEC) and NCAA championships in 1948.

This dominant team was ruled by a dominant coach. Adolph Rupp, the so-called "Baron of the Bluegrass," coached the University of Kentucky men's basketball team from 1930 to his retirement in 1972, by which point he had easily secured the record as college basketball's winningest coach. Rupp motivated his team with detailed preparation, fear, and passion. As one player put it, "If you smile, you don't have your mind on the game." That player remembered that he once worked up the courage to ask Rupp, "Why don't you ever compliment a ball player, tell him he did well?" Rupp responded, "I brought you here to play a hundred percent all the time. Hell, you're not supposed to make any mistakes."[17] Rupp's rigor was legendary and spread to his players. For days before a game against College of the Holy Cross in 1948, Rupp drilled his team on defending Bob Cousy, Holy Cross's star guard, whom many fans considered the best player in the college game. Rupp assigned Kenny Rollins to guard Cousy—only to have Rollins sprain his ankle just before the game. Undaunted, Rupp assigned two assistant coaches to stay up the entire night before the game to alternate placing hot and cold towels on Rollins' ankle. The next day Rollins held Cousy to just three points.

But Rupp's stature did not save the Wildcats from scandal. In mid-1951 he proclaimed to reporters, "Fixers couldn't touch my boys with a ten-foot pole."[18] But only a few months later, three members of Rupp's Fabulous Five—Dale Barnstable, Alex Groza, and Ralph Beard—were arrested. None were still at Kentucky; Barnstable had become a high school teacher, and the other two were playing in the NBA. But all three were charged with intentionally losing a game in the 1949 National Invitation Tournament. All admitted they did so because they had made a deal with professional gamblers. They also confessed to rigging two other games. And then two more former Kentucky players acknowledged they had rigged more games. Because of the team's stature, the Kentucky arrests attracted a great deal of attention, but they were merely the conclusion of a months-long nationwide investigation. Dozens of gamblers and thirty-five players from seven schools found themselves arrested over 1950 and 1951.

Rupp denied any knowledge of or involvement with the scandal, but eventually in sworn testimony he admitted knowing his players had what he called "sponsors" in Lexington who paid them cash for made-up jobs. He also acknowledged having a friendship with

Ed Curd, a bookie who ran one of the nation's largest gambling networks. It soon came to light that the two co-owned a tobacco warehouse and that the coach sometimes invited the gambler to travel with the team on road games. After that Rupp could hardly deny accusations that he generally knew what gamblers were predicting about his games, although he strenuously denied that he ever talked to his players about such matters.

Rupp and his program were not on trial, but it sure seemed like it. When he sentenced the Kentucky players, New York judge Saul Streit said that "intercollegiate basketball and football at the University of Kentucky have become highly systemized, professionalized and commercialized." He accused the school of "the most flagrant abuse of the athletic scholarship." As for Rupp, the judge noted that he "failed in his duty to observe the amateur rules, to build character and to protect the morals and health of his charges."[19]

Streit begged for somebody, anybody, to step in. And Walter Byers was more than willing.

Quickly, Byers summoned the NCAA's Committee on Infractions, a small group of NCAA professionals and representatives from a few schools. He showed them the evidence and charged the committee to determine an appropriate penalty. The Byers-encouraged committee voted to suspend the Kentucky men's basketball team for the 1952–53 season. But of course, Byers had no real authority to enforce such a penalty beyond what the member schools were willing to vote for and cooperate with. And Byers knew that—just as with the Sanity Code—the schools in the NCAA would not rush to penalize Kentucky. Next time it might be them. So he took the committee vote and went to Kentucky's director of athletics. Byers warned the man that refusing to accept such a penalty would delegitimize not only Kentucky sports but college athletics entirely. He pointed to Streit's statement, to the torrent of negative media Kentucky and the NCAA were receiving, and stated that such a penalty would restore public trust. The university officials worried and deliberated and finally accepted Byers's arguments. They would sit out the next school year. Adolph Rupp was infuriated, but his school's administration stared him down.

Byers, in less than two years in office, had won both an independent stream of revenue and a precedent. The NCAA would indeed levy harsh penalties, and schools that wanted to keep in the good graces of the man who had negotiated the stream of television money they enjoyed would accept them.

Suddenly Byers was a man to fear. In 1952 he opened an enforcement office. Over the next three decades that office grew to a staff of more than fifty and developed a rule book of 322 pages. Technically, Byers's staff deferred to the committee on infractions, made up of a rotating cast of representatives from NCAA schools. But the committee often simply considered the evidence Byers's people laid before them. And Byers himself was known to sit in on meetings.[20]

The Rise of College Basketball

In these early years Byers's efforts—particularly those to do with money and media—had mostly to do with football. Football was the biggest sport in the United States when Byers got his job, and its popularity only grew in the second half of the twentieth century. The lucrative television deals that accelerated the NCAA's financial reach initially all depended upon football. By the 1960s, the $1.14 million deal for the television rights to the college football game of the week had risen to $3.1 million—more than the NFL's contracts were earning at the time.

But as the money increased, Byers's hold on it was growing a bit shaky. In 1981 an alliance of sixty-one schools who called themselves the College Football Association notified the NCAA they were planning on signing a $180 million, four-year deal with NBC. Byers, still only sixty years old and grown comfortable in his dominance, repeated his playbook. He made the same threats he had against Notre Dame and the University of Pennsylvania—he would fine the schools and he would penalize anybody who agreed to play them. But two members of the CFA sued, and in 1984's *NCAA v. Board of Regents of the University of Oklahoma*, the Supreme Court ruled that the NCAA's assertion of sole authority to negotiate television contracts on behalf of its member schools was an unconstitutional monopoly. Schools and conferences were now legally able to negotiate their own television deals. The 12 percent (since shrunk to 5 percent) that Byers had earned on each football television deal for thirty years was gone.

But Byers was ready. He pivoted to basketball.

The NCAA had sponsored a basketball tournament since 1939. For most of the first few decades, the NCAA invited two dozen or so teams, trying for a good mix of schools across the United States. The tournament competed with an independent event called the National Invitation Tournament, which invited eight schools every year to play for a few days in Madison Square Garden in New York City. Byers never liked affairs like the NIT. They were independent from his control and, to his way of thinking, took dollars from the NCAA's pocket.

As Byers's power over college football television contracts came under fire, the basketball tournament became more and more important. It was wholly sponsored and operated by the NCAA, and thus the NCAA controlled its revenue. So Byers did what he could to make it the center of the basketball universe. He banned any team that accepted an NIT tournament invitation from also competing in the NCAA tournament in the same year. And he began courting television deals for the tournament.

In 1969 the tournament hit the major networks for the first time. NBC paid Byers half a million dollars for the right to air it and would hold the contract for another dozen years. The tournament became increasingly popular as Byers began tweaking it to amp up the drama. The tournament had always invited the champions from various athletic conferences, but in 1975 Byers began expanding the tournament and inviting more and more schools—thirty-two in 1975, forty in 1979, forty-eight in 1980, and sixty-four in 1985. The NCAA began organizing the teams into brackets, assigning each school a seed number to indicate their strength. The number of rounds in the tournament soared from four to seven.

By 1982 Byers was looking for other possible broadcasters. NBC had cooled on sports. The network's broadcast of the 1980 Olympics had earned dismal ratings, mostly because the United States had boycotted those games. When NBC executives met with Byers and his team, they talked down sports, moaning that live coverage wasn't what it used to be. As soon as the network's opening was done, Byers did not even bother entertaining whatever offer NBC might come up with. He stood up and said, "I want to apologize to my colleagues who I brought in from around the country to listen to that."[21] Then he walked out of the room.

Byers called CBS instead and got a three-year contract, complete with a broadcast anchor team who would in effect host the tournament for viewers. CBS also agreed to a new idea Byers had—a show entirely devoted to announcing which teams would be competing in the tournament.

But neither NBC's nor CBS's coverage completely satisfied the perpetually ambitious Byers because the networks often avoided airing early rounds of the tournament. The cable network ESPN stepped in, signing a contract to snatch up the rights to games that other networks did not air. Because ESPN needed content, it would broadcast six games a night in the opening rounds. Somewhat unexpectedly, basketball fans gloried in such saturation. Small schools like St. John's College and Gonzaga University suddenly had national reputations. The value of the tournament began to skyrocket. In 1980, NBC had paid $5.2 million for the rights to the tournament. In 1982, CBS offered $48 million for three years. When that contract was up, Byers demanded CBS double their fee for three more years, and the network did, paying $96 million for the 1986, 1987, and 1988 tournaments. Ten years later, the network would pay the NCAA $6 billion to air the tournament from 1999 to 2010.[22]

Because the NCAA owned the tournament, all that money went right to the NCAA. College basketball had become lucrative in its own right. Schools noticed, and so did players.

The Persistent Dream of Amateurism

Walter Byers invented the term "student-athlete." He mandated that it be used in all NCAA publications from 1956 on. Historian Ronald Smith argues that this was central to the NCAA's strategy to present collegiate athletics as part and parcel of college education. Under a clause in Congress's Revenue Act of 1951, educational institutions were exempt from taxation. Wielding the phrase "student-athlete," Byers and the NCAA began pressing the federal government to make more and more money from college sports tax-exempt.[23]

In the 1950s, Byers, firmly convinced that it was essential to shield college athletics from the appearance of professionalism, had thrown his weight behind two Colorado schools, the University of Denver and Fort Lewis A&M College. In 1953 a Denver football player, Ernest Nemeth, hurt his back during practice severely enough that he could no longer play and had difficulty finding work. He petitioned the state government to force the university to pay him workers' compensation for being injured while on a job. The state decided to pay and ordered the University of Denver to cover the cost. The university appealed, but the state supreme court ruled that Nemeth, who received a small salary from the university to do janitorial work on top of his football commitments, was entitled to benefits.

Only two years later, Fort Lewis student Ray Dennison was killed after sustaining a skull fracture in a football game against another small Colorado school. Dennison's widow petitioned the Colorado state government to force the school to pay death benefits, arguing that Dennison was an employee killed on the job. She pointed to the fact that Dennison had received a scholarship, free food, and a trivial job from the university so long as he played football. Just as with Nemeth, the state government agreed with her and ordered the school to pay. Fort Lewis appealed, lost, and appealed again. Finally, in 1957 the Colorado Supreme Court ruled in favor of the school, relieving Walter Byers. Dennison was under no contractual obligation to play football, the court ruled. He was not an employee, and his family was entitled to no death benefits. The court said that the key difference between the Nemeth and Dennison cases was that in Dennison's case, the school's scholarship and employment offer did not make explicit reference to his playing football.

After that, Byers pulled out the NCAA constitution and personally amended it to change every appearance of the word "athlete," writing in his memoir, "We crafted the term student-athlete. Soon it was embedded in all NCAA rules and interpretations."[24]

Over and over as the decades passed, courts and legislators accepted the premise of the "student-athlete." In 1963, a California court ordered that the widow of a California State Polytechnic College football player killed when the plane bringing him home from a game crashed be paid death benefits. In 1965, after strenuous lobbying from the NCAA, the California state legislature wrote into state statute a new law excluding athletes from workers' compensation in state universities.

In 1983, the Indiana state supreme court ruled against the former Indiana State University football player Fred Rensing. In the spring of 1976 Rensing was at football practice and tackled another player. The top of his head slammed into the other player's shoulder pad, and Rensing's spine crunched. He fell to the turf and was left a quadriplegic for the rest of his life. Nonetheless, the Indiana court ruled that Rensing was not an employee of the university, since he and the school were abiding by the guidelines of the NCAA. Twenty years later, Kent Waldrep, a former player for Texas Christian University, ran into a similar wall. He had been rendered a quadriplegic during a game in 1974, eventually, through much effort, regaining some use of his arms. He pressed lawsuits and claims throughout the 1990s and eventually lost. According to Waldrep, Texas Christian University officials consistently told courts that "they recruited me as a student, not an athlete."[25]

The notion of the "student-athlete" had, then, its financial and legal upsides. But it is also worth considering that many people indeed took it seriously. Even Byers himself could wax poetic, writing wistfully at the end of his life about "the amateur status that existed before the full-ride grant was adopted in 1956" and calling for "a far more comprehensive amateur declaration before grant-in-aid money is released."[26]

Many universities took the student-athlete concept seriously as well. In 1945 the presidents of Brown, Columbia, Cornell, Dartmouth, Harvard, the University of Pennsylvania, Princeton, and Yale signed the famous "Group Agreement," establishing shared policies governing their football teams. The Ivys agreed that admissions and financial aid decisions should not be influenced by a student's athletic potential. Teams should, the presidents' statement declared, be "truly representative of the student body."[27] The 1945 agreement specified football, but a few years later the presidents extended the agreement to cover other sports as well. By 1954, the Ivy schools agreed to reject "specially recruited athletes." They affirmed that the purpose of collegiate sports wasn't financial; instead, the presidents of the various Ivy schools said, "organized athletics offers desirable development and recreation for players and a healthy focus of collegiate loyalty." By this point, the schools had formulated a league of their own, where the amateur ideal was a way of expressing hope that college sports could in fact be about moral development, not monetary gain.[28]

And yet, in 1951 the University of Pennsylvania tried to defy Walter Byers in pursuit of an independent television deal for its football team. Yale had a slush fund for athletes years before the Ivy League statements. Money was as irresistible to them as it was to Byers himself. This did not mean that the presidents' hopes for the benefits of amateur athletics were a lie or hypocritical. It did mean, though, that the cross pressures of money and character were real even on the campuses of Harvard and Yale.

NCAA Basketball '09

In 2009, Ed O'Bannon was working at a car dealership in Las Vegas. He was coaching basketball at a local high school too, but spent most of his time selling lots of cars because people recognized him. Fourteen years earlier, in 1995, he had won the NCAA's award for Most Outstanding Player in the NCAA basketball tournament. He started at power forward for the UCLA team that won the tournament that year and scored 30 points in the championship game against the University of Arkansas, a wild number for a college basketball game. O'Bannon's performance was enough to get him selected ninth in the NBA draft that year, and he went off to play for the New Jersey Nets.

Unfortunately, O'Bannon had a problem. He was a classic example of what NBA people call a "tweener." He was six-foot-eight and two hundred twenty pounds—big for college basketball but not quite big enough to really challenge NBA power forwards, who often had twenty pounds and a few inches on him. And he was also not quick enough to guard smaller players in the NBA. He struggled and by his own admission lost his confidence. He was traded twice and was out of the NBA in two years.

Fortunately, he went on to a nice career playing in the European leagues. He told the *Los Angeles Times* that he played for "12 different teams in at least six countries and for 15 different coaches" before his knees gave out and he retired in 2004.[29] Soon he made a new life for himself in Las Vegas, selling cars and coaching basketball on the side.

And then one day he noticed a character in a video game that looked a lot like him.

Beginning in the 1990s, the video game company Electronic Arts made a lot of money from its sports division. EA Sports cornered the market. It signed exclusivity agreements with the NFL, the NBA, the Professional Golfers' Association of America, and other such organizations to develop video games. In game series like *Madden NFL* (which licensed the name and image of iconic football announcer John Madden) or *NBA Live*, players could take control of actual professional teams, complete with pixelated versions of genuine players. And from 1998 to 2009, EA Sports put out a series called *NCAA Basketball*.

O'Bannon was at a friend's house when his friend's son, who was playing one of the *NCAA Basketball* games, called out to him. "Dude, you're on a video game!" Everybody gathered around the screen, where the boy was controlling that 1995 UCLA team. O'Bannon's friend turned to him and said, "You know what is crazy? EA Sports is getting all that money, and you're not getting any of it."[30]

When the NCAA sold the rights to its games, teams, and history to EA Sports, they specified that the company could not use the actual names of players, so the backs of the digital jerseys had only numbers where one might expect also to see names. This was an attempt to avoid thorny questions around the concept of "name, image, and likeness," or "NIL." For celebrities, NIL is a source of profit unto itself. It is why professional athletes and actors are paid to endorse everything from Wheaties breakfast cereal to Japanese liquor to cell phone plans. Or to appear in video games. By avoiding the names of collegiate basketball players in the video game, both the NCAA and EA Sports were attempting to duck accusations that they were profiting off of those athletes' NIL.

But to O'Bannon and his friends it was obvious. The digital figure was Black and bald, like O'Bannon. Left-handed, like O'Bannon. He even moved like O'Bannon did when he shot. O'Bannon was baffled and a little angry. He called a friend who called a friend, and he ended up speaking with Michael Hausfeld, a crusading, five-foot-six attorney.

Hausfeld knew nothing about sports. While he was preparing to sue the NCAA he admitted to colleagues he couldn't identify some of the biggest names in basketball history. But he was among the best class-action attorneys in the world. He had won more than a billion dollars from Swiss banks who had withheld assets from Holocaust victims' families and nearly two hundred million from Texaco on behalf of Black employees whom a jury agreed had suffered discrimination. A few years before, Hausfeld had met Sonny Vaccaro, a former Nike executive and legendary basketball marketer who persuaded him that the NCAA was ripe for a lawsuit. Hausfeld was intrigued, but he needed a name, an athlete willing to put himself in front of the cameras. And then Ed O'Bannon called up his old friend Vaccaro to complain about a video game.

O'Bannon agreed to be Hausfeld's client, and Hausfeld sued on behalf of O'Bannon. But the attorney also made claims far broader than O'Bannon's career. He maintained that all former players should receive compensation when the NCAA used their image. He argued that the NCAA was violating American labor law, treating players like employees when it came to profiting from their labor while simultaneously denying that they were employees when it came to matters of benefits, and colluding with its member schools to deny players just compensation. The NCAA protested, arguing that paying even former players would violate the principle of amateurism.

The case took years. Big lawsuits often do. It wasn't until June 2014 that O'Bannon took the stand, testifying that while at UCLA he spent forty hours a week on basketball and felt like he was only "masquerading as a student." Another former player, Tyrone Prothro, described how a play he made on the football field won the NCAA's "Game Changing Performance" contest, a heavily publicized competition that Pontiac paid the NCAA to sponsor. But three weeks later Prothro broke his leg, grievously, and lost any chance at a professional career. His school cut him loose, canceling his scholarship. When he wrote an autobiography in an attempt to make some money, he had to pay his former school to use pictures of himself.[31]

In August 2014, United States District Judge Claudia Wilken ruled that the NCAA's refusal to pay athletes was a violation of United States antitrust laws. She ordered that the NCAA must allow schools to offer athletes more comprehensive scholarships as well as payments for use of their images for promotional purposes. The decision did not entirely obliterate the NCAA's amateur-based restrictions on athlete compensation, but it was a crack in the armor.

If *O'Bannon v. NCAA* was a crack, *NCAA v. Alston* was a shattering. Shawne Alston and Justine Hartman were, respectively, a West Virginia University football player and University of California Berkeley basketball player. After O'Bannon's success, a host of other players and former players filed similar lawsuits. Judge Wilken combined many of these cases behind those of Alston and Hartman. Hartman testified that her daily six-hour practices and meager scholarship money meant that she often had very little food to eat, no time to get another job, and certainly little time to study for the classes that were the ostensible reason she was at Berkeley in the first place. "We don't have the means to excel at the highest level academically," Hartman said. "We go without a lot. There are many with similar experiences," athletes who were too "hungry and too tired" even to get to class.[32]

Again, Judge Wilken ruled against the NCAA. Again the NCAA appealed, and again the NCAA lost. Wilken and the judges of the Ninth District Court who rejected the NCAA's appeal decided that the NCAA was acting as a monopoly. The organization was helping schools artificially hold down the amount of compensation that athletes would receive if they were allowed to freely negotiate with schools competing for their services. This was considered a "trust in restraint of trade," illegal under the laws of the United States, going all the way back to the Sherman Anti-Trust Act of 1890.

The proof was so glaringly obvious that the NCAA did not try to deny it. NCAA lawyers admitted that they had actually created a trust. But, they said, a trust was the only way to preserve the virtues of amateurism. Wilken agreed that the amateur ideal was worth something but suggested that offering athletes more financial support would not violate it. Her March 2019 decision ordered the NCAA to allow schools to offer athletes compensation beyond simply tuition-based scholarships—money that came to be called "Alston awards" that could be used to help athletes hire tutors, pay rent, and other such academic-related expenses.

After that, the floodgates opened. In 2019 the California state legislature passed the Fair Pay to Play Act, authorizing college athletes in the state to control their own name, image, and likeness and to profit from licensing it if they chose to. In *House v. NCAA*, a case filed in May 2020, a group of former and current Division I athletes from Arizona State University, University of Oregon, and University of Illinois attacked the NCAA's rules that schools could not share any NIL money they earned with the players whose names and images were being used. The plaintiffs demanded not only just compensation but back pay and a change in NCAA rules.

This flood of cases meant it was growing obvious that the NCAA was going to have to change. In June 2021, the United States Supreme Court handed down a unanimous decision affirming Wilken's decision in *Alston*. The court seemed distinctly unpersuaded by the NCAA's appeal to amateurism, reasoning that the NCAA was certainly a "commercial enterprise" and therefore hardly a bastion of amateurism. Justice Brett Kavanaugh wrote that "the NCAA's business model would be flatly illegal in almost any other industry in America."[33]

So the NCAA began struggling to catch up. In addition to the Alston awards, the NCAA altered its rules to allow athletes to profit from their own NIL licensing, even while in school, as of July 1, 2021. An NIL industry emerged with incredible speed. Many schools organized groups called "NIL collectives." Collectives are technically independent of the schools themselves. They are usually organized and led by alumni or boosters of the school's athletic programs. By 2022, these collectives were gathering the money to offer their schools' athletes lucrative deals and figuring out how to facilitate agreements with companies to offer athletes even more money. By 2023, states like Texas and Arkansas were passing laws trying to make it easier for schools in their states to help collectives. All of this, of course, was designed to make it easier for schools to recruit star athletes.

In 2024, *Washington Post* journalists mounted an extensive investigation of the NIL boom. Dozens of schools ignored their requests for information, but despite their very incomplete records, the *Post* was able to document 22,000 NIL payments worth a total of $35 million dollars at eight schools alone. The Olympic gymnast Jordan

Chiles, a student at UCLA, seemed to have made nearly a million dollars in NIL deals with the food company Danone and the sparkling water brand BUBBL'R. She touted products from both companies on her social media channels. An unnamed athlete at the University of Kansas was paid $1.2 million in a deal with redacted details. In total, the University of Texas football team brought in nearly $21 million between 2021 and 2024.

But the vast majority of the 22,000 deals the *Post* identified were far smaller. Slightly more than half were only $100 or less. NIL collectives regularly paid players token fees to appear at events. Schools distributed royalty payments in the range of $3 or $4 to players when they sold jerseys with athletes' names on the back. Local businesses—waffle houses and yoga studios—paid players small amounts to patronize and endorse them. At the University of Minnesota, football players received free meals at a local restaurant that asked them to post about how delicious the food was on social media.[34]

In 2023 and 2024, the NCAA tried to impose some order and balance to this turbulent world. In May 2023 the NCAA decreed that collectives would be subject to the same regulations as other boosters, prohibiting them from involvement in recruiting. NCAA officials also began pursuing sanctions against schools that allowed collectives to offer special access to the team or tickets in exchange for donations. The organization also began pushing Congress to pass national NIL laws to streamline the patchwork of policies springing up in various states.[35]

By then it was becoming clear that the long-simmering resolution of *House v. NCAA* would stagger the organization. Again, Claudia Wilken was the judge, and she folded two other cases into *House*. The plaintiffs in *Hubbard v. NCAA* argued that the NCAA helped schools collude to avoid paying Alston awards. The plaintiffs in *Carter v. NCAA* argued the same but focused specifically on monies players might make beyond the Alston awards and scholarships.

The NCAA's nerve broke. In 2024, the organization offered a settlement to avoid a trial. The NCAA agreed to a massive payout to athletes and to revise its rules to allow, for the first time, players to receive direct payments from their schools beginning July 1, 2025. Judge Wilken approved the settlement on June 6, 2025.

The NCAA and the largest five athletic conferences in the country agreed to pay $2.78 billion in back pay to student-athletes who played Division I sports from June 15, 2016, to June 30, 2025. Most of the money—about 75 percent— was earmarked for football players, with 20 percent going to men's basketball and 5 percent to other athletes. On average, football and men's basketball players in those "Power Five" conferences could receive about $135,000 each, paid out over 10 years. Although not named in the lawsuit, non–Power Five schools are still expected to cover nearly $1 billion of the settlement costs.

Perhaps more importantly, the NCAA agreed to allow its schools to start paying athletes directly to play going forward. Under the terms of the agreement, schools may now opt in to a compensation model that permits them to allocate up to 22.5 percent of the NCAA's annual total revenues to their athletes. In the first year, 2025–26, this would mean roughly $21 million per school, per year, according to a letter from Charlie Baker, the former governor of Massachusetts serving as the president of the NCAA.[36] Media outlets predicted the distribution at each school to be a microcosm of the $2.78 billion payout. *The New York Times* reported that at Texas Tech University, for instance, 74 percent of the roughly $21 million would go to football players, 17 percent to men's basketball players, 2 percent to women's basketball players, and the rest to everybody else.[37] The number of tuition-based scholarships schools can offer also jumped.

In short, nearly a century of precedent and restriction collapsed. Baker's letter described a new world in which athletes would receive payments, the NCAA itself would reform governance structures, and both schools and players would benefit. It did not use the word "amateur."

Unsportsmanlike Conduct

Walter Byers retired in 1987. It was a surprise, at least in the sports world. He was only two years into a four-year renewal of his contract, and even though he had been running the NCAA for more than thirty-five years, he was only sixty-five years old.

But he was growing disillusioned, and he spent the first years of his retirement writing a book explaining why, called *Unsportsmanlike Conduct*. Byers explained that he believed the NCAA had become unmanageable. For years he had doggedly pursued the two goals that the NCAA had levied on him when it made him its executive director, even though he knew they would inevitably collide. Those goals were "keeping intercollegiate sports clean while generating millions of dollars each year as income for the colleges." The twenty-nine-year-old Walter Byers who took the job was energetic, thorough and, perhaps most touching, a fan. "In my enthusiasm for sports, I believed it possible to achieve both," he wrote.[38]

Throughout his career he was a devoted advocate of amateurism. By the 1980s he still believed in it but had become savagely self-recriminatory about his earlier naïveté. "For years I argued college teams should be made up of patriots, not mercenaries," he wrote. He wanted college athletes to be staunch supporters of school spirit, playing for their alma mater, not for money. "I believed college students playing solely for the honor and joy of it would be good for the country's future," Byers wrote regretfully. But by the 1980s all he could say was, "I suppose none of us wanted to accept what was really happening."[39]

What really happened was that the NCAA was, as Byers put it, "barely adequate in the first instance, but enormously successful in our second mission."[40] He turned the NCAA into an incredibly successful profit machine that clung to the barest husk of amateurism out of both wistful hope and base self-justification. Walter Byers was, at least, clear-eyed enough to see it.

As of 2025, much confusion remains about how *O'Bannon*, *Alston*, *House*, and the series of other cases that upended the NCAA's system in the 2010s and 2020s will actually transform college sports. In 2018 the NCAA created a "transfer portal," a central clearinghouse for players that want to move from one school to another. In 2025 the NCAA vowed to create a central NIL clearinghouse, a neutral arbiter that would ensure that NIL payments were legitimate and not simply cash transfers for no genuine business purpose. In short, the NCAA is at work turning college athletics into something more resembling professional sports: professional players sign contracts with teams and might depart when those contracts are up. Teams offer players salaries but can also facilitate other opportunities, like endorsements and licensing. Players often have agents who guide them through this maze of contracts and financial arrangements. All of these things are coming into being at the college level.

Commercialism and money beat the amateur ideal. That ideal may not be dead, but it is struggling.

In April 2022, the University of Miami basketball player Isaiah Wong's agent, Adam Papas, said that Wong would enter the transfer portal unless Miami secured more money for his NIL deals. This troubled the university because Florida law barred the school from aiding Wong to find such deals. But John Ruiz, a wealthy Miami supporter, stepped in. Wong had a NIL deal with Ruiz's company LifeWallet, and Ruiz stated he would coordinate with Papas to ensure Wong got other deals.[41] This sort of situation would have been baffling to anybody involved in college basketball ten years earlier, but it reflects the sort of negotiation characteristic of professional sports in the United States.

The change also created some chaos. In April 2025, Tom Izzo, the legendary men's basketball coach at Michigan State University, lost three players to the transfer portal and did not mince words. "We've created a bad system. The system was set up without any proper guidelines. It has not helped any players make decisions," he told a reporter. "They're getting lied to by some, and getting told the truth by others."[42] For Izzo, college basketball had become professionalized with no guardrails, and the churn of money and lobbying has done great damage to the sport.

Even more than professional sports, universities—often committed to the goals of equitable treatment of students and to offering opportunity—face a moral conundrum in situations like Wong's. For one thing, *The Washington Post* investigation of NIL contracts found that the overwhelming bulk of this money went to male athletes, particularly football and basketball players. NIL collectives tend to be men interested in male sports, and the Jordan Chileses of college athletics—female superstars capable of attracting media attention—are few and far between.

But with more money coming in, in February 2025 the Trump administration's Department of Education reversed an earlier policy. Formerly, the department's official position was that Title IX, a landmark 1972 law that prohibits sexual discrimination in educational institutions that receive federal funding, required payments from schools to athletes to be equitably distributed between male and female athletes. The new policy allowed schools to distribute money as they saw fit. Despite this reversal, many schools have worked toward equitable distribution, with some success due to collaboration with sponsors. By mid-2024, the NIL firm SponsorUnited, which matches athletes to clients, estimated that the total number of NIL agreements (though not funding amounts) were almost evenly split between women and men, a far cry from the previous year, when the balance was 66 percent men. A surge of agreements to women's basketball players tipped the balance.[43]

Another worry: Wealthy schools have the infrastructure and connections to implement revenue-sharing agreements and to recruit through the transfer portal. Other schools might struggle to keep up. Thilo Kunkel, a professor of business specializing in sports at Temple University, warned that the money will inevitably "go to revenue-generating sports, like football or basketball, and heavily favor male athletes at top institutions, creating more inequality and challenging competitive balance."[44]

Red Bull

In mid-October 2024, a few weeks after he had that lunch with Leonard Armato, AJ Dybantsa signed a deal to endorse Red Bull energy drink. It was his first NIL contract.

"I'm smart with it, my parents are smart with it: we don't want to take every deal," he told a journalist. "But, the smart ones we have to take advantage of. If I'm projected where I'm supposed to be and I keep my head down and work, I will get way bigger and better deals, so I'm not trying to take fast money right now."[45]

Both of the impulses that drove collegiate basketball are in what Dybantsa said. There is the professionalism, the cool awareness that business has thoroughly absorbed American sports and there is money to be made. More, there is the simple presumption that money should be made. But there is also Theodore Roosevelt—the hope that sports should teach young people to work, and that work will lead to success.

The weekend before he signed the deal with Red Bull, AJ Dybantsa had visited the campus of Brigham Young University. His mother had insisted to him that he attend a university for at least a year. The Dybantsas were looking for a place that could embody both impulses. And though the Dybantsas knew virtually nothing about BYU or The Church of Jesus Christ of Latter-day Saints, which owns the school, both the church and the university had spent decades wrestling for the soul of basketball themselves.

2

JAMES NAISMITH AND THE DREAM OF A MORAL SPORT

The last week of January 1940, the city of Montevideo, capital of Uruguay, hosted the eighth South American Basketball Championship tournament. That week, six teams played each other over the course of fifteen games, and it quickly became clear that the host country and Argentina were the two standouts. The Argentines hammered the poor Paraguayans 50–5. Uruguay dealt Brazil a similarly humbling loss, and the two winning teams seemed on a collision course.

The final game between the Uruguayans and the Argentinians teetered on a knife's edge all the way through. Each team played excellent defense, keeping the scores low. With only seconds left, the Uruguayans were up, 25–23. The Argentine team went on offense, drove toward their basket, and tossed the ball to their star player.

Rolf Larson, a twenty-three-year-old Mormon missionary from Snowflake, Arizona, gathered his weight and launched off the ground, back straight, eyes on the hoop, to take the final shot for Argentina.

Larson got on that court in Montevideo because his church had spent the previous three decades winding basketball into its programs for youth, education, and even theology. By 1940, basketball was central to the church's missionary operations around the world. It was integral to the church's young men's curriculum. It was woven into the church's ideas about the relationship between the body and the soul, between behavior and morality. It was even quite literally built into the church buildings—basketball courts were installed in many meetinghouses, often separated from the chapels only by a retractable dividing wall.

This project had started in earnest before World War I. "We need

God in our pleasures," observed Brigham Henry "B. H." Roberts in 1913. One of the more prominent leaders of The Church of Jesus Christ of Latter-day Saints in the early twentieth century, at this particular point he was concerned for the young people of his church, who seemed enthusiastic about sports. "Our youth need wise direction in their sports," he wrote. Sports could become a tool to "infuse pride of strength into the youth of Zion." If young people played the right sports, they could learn to "look the problems of life squarely in the face, nothing daunted, because within them is the God-given strength that belongs to their divine nature."[1]

This might seem like Roberts was asking a lot from basketball, but the sport was invented by a religious educator who thought exactly the same thing.

The Christian Origins of Basketball

James Naismith was a thirty-year-old Canadian athlete with a BA in physical education from McGill College, a Presbyterian school in Montreal, when he arrived at the YMCA Training School in Springfield, Massachusetts, in early 1890. He had long intended a career as a Presbyterian minister but was not a natural scholar.

In college at McGill, he had struggled with his Greek and Latin exams but flourished when he dabbled in the college's sports. Midway through his sophomore year, the rugby team asked him to fill in for an injured player after Naismith scrimmaged with the team during practice. He also took up boxing and played on a professional lacrosse team.

Naismith told himself he was doing this to pay for his education toward the ministry, which is also what he said to his family when he took a job as McGill's athletic director. He sternly plodded toward the ministry, dutifully studying Greek and writing sermons and playing sports in the nooks and crannies of his day. One Sunday, as a student minister, he delivered a morning sermon with two black eyes from a rough game the day before.

His friends and family protested. James seemed to be straddling the fence. Getting up at 6:00 a.m. to practice with the rugby team or spar with other amateur boxers hardly seemed what a minister who would be delivering a sermon at a 9:00 a.m. service should be doing. But James wasn't having it. Once a teammate teased him for reading the Bible while the rest of the team partied. Things escalated quickly, and James Naismith knocked the man flat. Another time a teammate apologized for swearing around him.

Events like these persuaded James to meditate on his future. The apology meant a great deal to him, and he concluded that it must have been derived from his own particular approach to playing sports. "The only reason that I could give for the guard's action was that I played the game with all my might and yet held myself under control," he wrote later, in his book explaining the origins of basketball. He thought the other player must have been impressed with Naismith's own rectitude.[2]

Eventually Naismith found a middle ground in the Young Men's Christian Association. The YMCA (and its counterpart, the Young Women's Christian Association) were founded in Great Britain in the 1840s as an outreach program to young people. The founders worried about the odd new phenomenon of the industrial city, where more and more young people were working at jobs that, unlike the farms of their ancestors, didn't provide much exercise. Coal burning and crowds meant that the air and water were bad. Taverns and brothels offered degenerate entertainment. In 1858 Oliver Wendell Holmes, a writer, doctor, and intellectual, worried about "such a set of black-coated, still-jointed, soft-muscled, paste-complexioned youth as we can boast in our Atlantic cities." Not a one of them could make it around the Boston Common within five minutes. He recommended that more young men take up boxing. "Anything is better than this white-blooded degeneration to which we all tend."[3]

Many American Christians who thought Holmes was right joined a growing movement called "muscular Christianity," which became particularly popular at universities and secondary schools among people like Naismith who were concerned about America's youth. Sports might once have been believed to be an idle waste of time in the United States. But American ministers were coming to believe that the cultivation of physical strength was a path to the cultivation of moral vigor. The YMCA offered classes in the arts, languages, and literature and provided clean, safe, cheap accommodations. They also plowed vast resources into organizing sports teams, encouraging young people to embrace calisthenics (a set of strength-building exercises similar to what would later be called aerobics) alongside Bible study. They threw open their doors in the evenings to encourage city youth to come play games instead of roaming the streets and getting up to the sort of devilry that middle-aged ministers could only imagine was happening outside.

James Naismith thought that the Y might understand him. And it did. The people who ran the Montreal branch encouraged him and sent him to Springfield, where the YMCA Training School was educating a new breed of Christian workers—not ministers exactly, but teachers and pastors who could work with young people in both body and spirit. Naismith fit right in. He quickly completed a certification program and began teaching at the school himself.

And it was there, in the winter of 1891, that he invented basketball.

Luther Gulick was the athletics director at the Training School, and he and Naismith had a lot of talks that fall. Many of the young men at the school played baseball in the summers and football in the autumn. But in the winter, the students were buried in Massachusetts snow and retreated to the dreary repetitiveness of calisthenics and weightlifting in the gymnasiums. "Distasteful work," Naismith called it, confessing he personally found all the stretching and swiveling dull. That semester, one particular class was acting up. Their original teacher departed, and Gulick asked Naismith to take charge. Most teachers are familiar with unruly, uncooperative classes, but Naismith could not quite blame these young men. Calisthenics "failed to arouse any enthusiasm," he said drily. [4]

Naismith scrambled. He tried to tweak other games for indoor usage before scrapping those plans and concluding that he had to start from the bottom up—to think about sports "from the philosophical side." He asked himself what he wanted the game to accomplish. He had a few principles from Gulick and his own beliefs. Obviously the game would have to be played inside, but there was more to the problem than simple logistics. Gulick instructed him to develop a game "requiring skill and sportsmanship," training and precision. Rather than rewarding raw athletic gifts, the game should encourage cooperation and teamwork. Gulick also said it should be "played without extreme roughness."[5]

Naismith called what he came up with "basket-ball," introducing it

Basketball inventor James Naismith poses with a peach basket and a leather-bound ball, equipment in the sport's first game, played at the YMCA academy in Springfield, Massachusetts, in 1891.

to his class on December 21, 1891. The new sport did not look exactly like what it would become. There were nine players on each side because the class had eighteen students. There was, as with so many other games, a ball. There were "goals"—actual baskets bolted to two walls on the opposite ends of the gymnasium. Naismith directed each team to try to put the ball in their own basket and stop the other team from doing the same. He decreed that moving while holding the ball would result in a foul that would stop play just as if the player had struck another. The only option once a player caught the ball was to pass. Dribbling had not yet occurred to anybody. It turned out to be quite difficult to score. The winning team scored a single goal (as they called it) and the losing team none. But the class loved it. Naismith posted rules on a bulletin board near the gym for everyone to see.

In 1910, after two decades of watching the game evolve, Naismith put to paper twelve fundamentals he hoped it would inculcate. Half were physical—skills like agility and reflexes. But the others had to do with developing the soul. Naismith said basketball was "the laboratory of ethical and moral attributes" because it, unique among sports, would force the individual to develop self-sacrifice and self-control. "In no other game is cooperation so necessary," Naismith wrote. "In basketball there is no place for the egotist. There are so few players on the team that one player not doing his best is a great reduction." To win a basketball game, a player needed to exert body and mind to the fullest, developing physical capacity and skill. And that player must also, simultaneously, learn how to subordinate personal talent to the best interests of the team, to learn how to cooperate and elevate others. Basketball, in short, was a moral university that developed multiple capacities at the same time. Naismith saw it as the ethical superior of any other sport.[6]

This was not to say that it did not require some revision and development. In that first game, the eighteen players jostled on a court significantly smaller than those in most modern arenas. Play had to stop to retrieve the ball from the basket after every goal. (Fortunately, that happened rarely.) The game officially lasted for thirty minutes, with two fifteen-minute halves. In keeping with Naismith's moralism, if a player committed a foul they were removed from play until the next goal was scored—which in practice could be quite a while.

By 1897, Naismith had decided that five was a better number of players per team than nine. The court became far less crowded and maneuvering for position far easier. Naismith also, in a forehead-slapping moment, realized that the game would work better if a hole were cut in the basket. By 1898 the basket was replaced with an iron hoop with a net. In 1896, Yale students came up with the idea of bouncing the ball off the court repeatedly while moving as a way around Naismith's strict rules against walking or running while holding the ball, and the practice of dribbling was born. This also meant that the original ball, the same sort of firm, leather-wrapped inflated pig bladder that soccer players used, gave way to a smoother ball convenient for bouncing off the ground in a relatively controlled way.

Naismith himself did not come up with all of these tweaks, but he approved of them. They were consistent with his vision for the game. He had designed basketball to require every player to play both offense and defense, to learn to cooperate in a seamless way, and settled on rules that placed far fewer players on the court than in either baseball or football. Once a hole was cut in the basket, the game began to move far more quickly than did baseball or football, requiring players to sprint up and down the court, reacting quickly and cooperatively as one.

The game placed a moral demand on each player. And Naismith hoped the players would rise to meet it.

Basketball in Zion

Basketball spread to many other cities in the country through the YMCA. In January 1892, Luther Gulick described the game in the *Triangle*, a YMCA newspaper distributed across the country. On April 23, 1892, the New York City YMCA sponsored the first game in that city. *The New York Times* reported that it was "a substitute for football, with an attempt to eliminate the roughest features of that sport." The game was played with a rough, irregular leather ball (as were the earlier games at the Springfield YMCA) between the boys who attended the 23rd Street branch of the YMCA and a team from YMCA's Students Club. The students won, 1–0, the same score in that first experimental scrimmage Naismith sponsored.[7]

Meanwhile, Gulick was receiving correspondence from all over the country asking for rules to the game. He printed and mailed out a booklet that included information not in the article—the dimensions of the court, for instance, and instructions for the size of the basket. In 1893 the game reached Texas. The next year, the first basketball game was played in India. Soon after, colleges and universities began organizing teams.

In early 1897, a team from the Salt Lake YMCA played a series of games against a team from the Hamilton School, a public school in downtown Salt Lake City. Hamilton won the last game by a score of 8–6. (Gradually, as the notions of dribbling and holes in the baskets spread, scoring crept up.) A reporter noted the crowds. "Basket-ball seems bound to be popular here," he wrote, because it appealed to the sensibilities of the community. "Little roughness was shown and the best of feelings marked the contest."[8]

The University of Utah's student athletics committee was fielding teams by then too, for both men and women. Students could play each other if no teams from other schools seemed interested. The student newspaper reported that the game attracted particular interest among women students, and many students attributed that interest to the unique spiritual meanings of the game. One male student, Chester Ames, caught the sense that basketball was something more than just another sport in a fairly strange poem he called "To the Basket-Ball Girls (At Resting Time)."

As I behold you maidens dear
In attitudes of careless grace
Reclining round about me here
There is something in each face
An absence of all worldliness
Akin to what our lives should be
That I my thoughts cannot suppress
So in these words I've set them free.[9]

Basketball, clearly, seemed to have the power to promote a sort of healthy spirituality and connectivity between a vigorous body and a clean spirit. This was the essence of muscular Christianity. The poem also pointed to the fact that the Young Women's Christian Association sponsored women's basketball leagues in the 1910s and 1920s. Senda Berenson, an educator at Smith College, developed distinctive rules for women's basketball teams, arguing that more than any other this sport could be adapted to best fit the physical and moral needs of women. So YWCA and YMCA teams would sometimes play with a different set of rules. In an era where women were assumed to be naturally spiritually gifted in ways men were not, the appeal of the game to them was taken as proof of its own moral qualities.[10]

The religion of basketball that the YMCA taught was a sort of generalized Christianity that didn't bother much with doctrinal particularities. Instead it emphasized personal moral discipline, graciousness, and honor. It didn't have much use for seemingly extraneous and esoteric religious practices like rituals or sacred clothing. It was optimistic about humanity, committed to Victorian ideals about what men and

Senda Berenson, who taught at Smith College, adapted James Naismith's rules for women's basketball in 1892. The teams have replaced Naismith's original bucket with a net but, as was common early in the sport, have yet to cut a hole in the bottom. *Courtesy Library of Congress*

women should be like, and targeted at cultivating the sorts of virtues that would lead to winning. Despite its Christian orientation, it had little space for exploring what it meant to lose or suffer. It was essentially optimistic and enthusiastic about cooperation and progress.[11]

And yet, commitment to the twin achievements of personal virtue and winning created some tension for Christian basketball players. By the turn of the twentieth century, Naismith himself was in some despair at the moral turns the game had taken, particularly in the universities. He felt shaken at a game he officiated in Kansas City, Missouri, in 1899—the first official game of the University of Kansas men's basketball team, in which the students played a team from the Kansas City YMCA. "When the Kansas City team wanted the ball they went after it without respect to the rules," he complained. "Upright aggressiveness not only got the ball but injured the players."

Naismith immediately tried to stop play, denouncing the lack of sportsmanship. But the YMCA team brushed him off. "I was informed that no foul had been committed," Naismith reported.[12] The

University of Kansas lost their first game to the rough-and-tumble YMCA players, 16–5. Naismith was working for the university by this point, and he repeatedly complained to the school's administrators and players that belligerent physical play of the sort he was seeing was not what he had imagined for a game that he hoped would teach cooperation and sportsmanship. "I have sympathy for boys who make inadvertent fouls," he told a journalist. "But I cannot stand deliberate ones."[13]

By the early decades of the twentieth century, as the game was drifting away from him Naismith was likewise drifting away from basketball, back toward the sort of moral reform work that had attracted him to the YMCA in the first place. He began spending more and more time at YMCAs around Kansas, counseling young people there. He inveighed against what he called the "commercialization" of sports in America, saying repeatedly that games should be played for moral development rather than money. He developed a stretching regimen. During World War I, he shipped out to the Mexican front, where the tumult of the ongoing Mexican Revolution spilled over into Texas, and then later to France as a member of the Kansas National Guard. There Naismith spent several years working functionally as a chaplain, trying to persuade soldiers not to patronize the local sex workers and encouraging good health.

Given his dismay with the turns the sport was taking elsewhere, the man who invented basketball might well have been encouraged by the fact that The Church of Jesus Christ of Latter-day Saints embraced his sport for the reasons he had invented it. Many early twentieth-century Mormon leaders found the gospel of basketball generalized enough to be applied within their own distinctive version of Christianity.

Of course, every generation worries that the one after it will be slack, lazy, and under-motivated, but at the turn of the twentieth century the leaders of the LDS Church were particularly concerned. In 1915 B. H. Roberts led a group of teenage boys to the exact spot where Brigham Young's first wagon train had, he believed, entered the Salt Lake Valley in 1847. Roberts—who, among other things, was an assistant in the Church Historian's Office—brought along a few diaries of members of that train, and he encouraged the boys to read them as the hike went on. He wanted them to identify with their pioneer ancestors, those who had crossed the American plains on foot and by wagon. He was quite aware that that original generation was now, seventy years later, dying off.

The hike gave "opportunity to impress the boys with the difficult labors, the determined purpose, and the noble design as well as the wisdom, faith, and hardships of the pioneers," Roberts told a church magazine.[14] He thought that the physical trials of 1847 had made the previous generation morally and physically strong and that a corresponding lack of trials was making the present generation weak. Roberts was especially attentive to young men because the church priesthood leadership was (and remains) restricted to men. Like many other Christian leaders in the United States in the early twentieth century, Roberts and his fellows in church leadership believed that women were naturally more inclined to morality and faith than men were. This was why women were entrusted with primary responsibility for childrearing. Men, on the other hand, were less inclined to faith and more inclined to wild and undisciplined behavior. Their vigor called for discipline and training.

So, like Roberts, other leaders of the LDS Church began trying to make their young men moral. Soon after World War I, church leadership mounted a campaign to encourage adherence to the Word of Wisdom, a revelation church founder Joseph Smith had handed down in 1833 that encouraged a healthy diet and avoidance of hard alcohol, tobacco, and "hot drinks." For Heber J. Grant, who became president of the church in 1918, "the law of life and health to the Latter-day Saints is to obey the Word of Wisdom." He insisted that a healthy body was necessary for a healthy spiritual life and made abstention from any alcohol, tobacco, coffee, or tea a mark of orthodoxy.[15]

The church began sponsoring Boy Scouts of America troops, and soon participation in scouting was the norm for every young man. The church also began supporting sports, including basketball.

Basketball would come to serve the church in a number of ways. Most basically, it was a way to encourage church members to understand their religion as a link between the body and the mind. Being a faithful member of the LDS Church was not merely about what you believed; it was about what you did, and what you did should be guided by the image of the pioneers. They thrived on exertion. They embraced self-discipline. And they worked together.

Similarly, basketball was a way to knit different communities together. At the most basic level, it was a game that members of any particular Mormon congregation could play with each other, and with other congregations. At the same time, missionaries could walk into a YMCA and bond with other Christians over the sport and the virtues of muscular Christianity. Congregations in Salt Lake City or California could sponsor games for the local community. Most particularly, basketball could be used to evangelize. It attracted attention to missionaries who played or sponsored games. It invited the creation of teams and leagues around which missionaries and church officials could build community. A basketball court could draw people into a meetinghouse, and perhaps could also keep them participating in the church.

By the turn of the twentieth century, LDS Church organizations were fielding basketball teams, and very quickly they reached out to other organizations. As early as 1900, the "YMCA basketballists" were playing teams from LDS College, a church-owned vocational school today called Ensign College.[16] In 1906 the game was added to an annual "field day" that church congregations sponsored every summer in the Salt Lake Valley. Over the next few years, local congregations of the church, called "wards,"began sponsoring basketball teams, and inter-ward games began popping up around Utah. Many were organized by stakes, church organizations similar to Catholic dioceses that coordinate a dozen or so wards. There were, and continue to be, teams for both young men and young women.

"Basketball is the greatest of all indoor games in the country, and especially in the state of Utah," declared an athletics director at the University of Utah in the church's largest magazine in December 1908. He then explained how each ward could cheaply build "a well-equipped game room." He said that the room should be as large as possible (up to the desired size of thirty-five by seventy feet), but that it was all right if the room was smaller than regulation because most basketball courts in Utah were. Floors were to be hardwood. The hoops should be "the size of a hay rake" and balls purchased from the Spalding company. Finally, he wisely advised that a wire frame be set over the room's electric lights.[17]

Since Mormon migrants began settling Utah in the 1840s and 1850s, they had built both chapels or slightly larger tabernacles for worship and "social halls" or "auxiliary buildings" for parties, storage, organization meetings, and so on. In 1911 the president of the church, Joseph F. Smith (the nephew of the martyred church founder) instructed his followers that they should also build gymnasiums. "We must not only provide places of worship for the youth of Zion," he said, "but also find places for the rational amusement of our children that they may be kept under proper influences."[18]

Smith was in part praising the massive Deseret Gymnasium, a hulking structure the church opened in 1910 a hundred yards from the Salt Lake Temple in downtown Salt Lake City. But he was also calling on local congregations to follow suit. By the mid-1920s more than sixty wards in Salt Lake City had built gymnasiums of their own. Yet soon, the point of building different edifices for every congregation in the church seemed obtuse for a pragmatic and increasingly cash-strapped church. Many wards began simply combining buildings. Several of those sixty gymnasiums were built in church meetinghouses—sometimes in basements or separate wings but often adjacent to the actual chapel itself, separated by only a door. By the end of the decade church periodicals referred to these spaces as "recreation halls." After World War II, the most popular design for meetinghouses installed the "recreation halls" immediately behind the chapel itself, separating the two with a removable wall that allowed for overflow chapel seating. The open flow between the secular and the sacred was quite intentional. "Church buildings have their hall for divine service," wrote church leader Levi Edgar Young, "but under the same roof is an amusement hall." For him the design revealed that his faith mingled the physical and the spiritual. "The whole scheme fosters civic, social, and ethical activity," he said. "And the people all cooperate in their work with a spirit of initiative, enterprise, and high purpose."[19]

Nearly all these recreational halls had basketball hoops installed, and the floors were hardwood.

Church Leagues

Over and over, church leaders told each other that sports would help save their young men. Youth of both genders played basketball, softball, and volleyball on church teams. Congregations sometimes fielded teams of all three if demand sufficed, and the church organized leagues and tournaments for girls' teams in softball and volleyball.

But, as the very construction of their meetinghouses indicated, basketball was the crown jewel of church sports, and basketball tournaments on a large scale were reserved for young men. Young women could and did continue to play, and individual wards and stakes continued to sponsor leagues for them. But, churchwide, basketball programs focused on men because basketball offered things church leaders believed young men especially needed. Because the church's priesthood was restricted to men, basketball was a way to preserve the future leadership of the church.

Basketball would cultivate moral fiber. Basketball brought young men into church buildings where they could be supervised and coached by adults. "Some say they do not need athletics. It seems to me all young men need them," wrote one LDS leader. "Athletics, carried on in a proper manner, will do much to increase our attendance and bring about a general moral uplift." This actually seemed to work. One congregation in Salt Lake City reported that basketball and other sports led to a 50 percent bump in attendance at youth events.[20]

The next logical step was tournaments. In 1908, the Ensign Stake of the church, taking in several wards in central Salt Lake City, began organizing formal tournaments for young men's teams. That year the 20th Ward reigned supreme, racking up a record of 10–1 in the tournament and winning the whole contest.[21] In April 1910 a stake in Millard, in rural central Utah, held a basketball tournament for young men and another for young women. By 1923, several Salt Lake area stakes agreed to stage an even larger event. By 1929, the general church leadership took over the competition and began calling it the "All-Church Basketball Tournament." As envisioned, each ward would field a team. That team would play other wards in their stake. Stake winners would play at regional levels, and these local champions would be brought to Salt Lake City every March for the finals. Eventually the tournament would pit teams from all over the world against each other.

By the time the tournament was phased out in 1971, teams from Canada, Mexico, and all over the United States were involved. That year, church magazines explained that eight thousand young men played. Three years later, they claimed it was ten thousand. More than five thousand teams—not players, but teams—participated.[22]

By the mid-twentieth century, those players were taking basketball seriously indeed. George Durrant—an excellent player whose son Devin was on some very good teams at BYU in the 1970s and 1980s and briefly played in the NBA—remembered that because ward membership is determined strictly by geography, competition for players could get fierce. "When I played for the Sixth Ward, the Third Ward was always trying to get me to move," he joked. Other players said the same. Larry Schlappi, an outstanding teenage player who ended up on the team that won the final all-church tournament, received job offers from wards in California. He turned them down but did carefully pick the Utah ward he eventually moved in to.[23]

In the 1960s the basketball program in the Edgehill Ward in Salt Lake City was run by a man named Paul Hansen, who remodeled his meetinghouse's gymnasium himself, adding locker rooms and showers. He began coaching boys as young as ten and divided them into three teams based on ability. Only the A-team was allowed to compete in the all-church tournament. It would occasionally scrimmage against local high school basketball teams for practice. Edgehill never won the tournament but was always strong. Paul Hansen's teams came in second twice, third once, and fourth once. Four trips to the final tournament, particularly when hundreds of teams were competing, was hardly shabby.

Outside of Utah, stakes would sometimes hold weekend tournaments to prepare for the big event and to select their representatives. The Cincinnati, Ohio, stake drew people from all over the region to a long weekend of game after game between various ward teams while the young people sold refreshments. In these sorts of tournaments, wards and the church as a whole could make money selling advertising space in the program as well as food and tickets. For years the final games of the tournament were hosted in Salt Lake City's

Deseret Gym, which was expanded in in 1965 to add extra basketball courts and lots of seating. By then there would be four games scheduled in a rush every evening over a long weekend in March.

In 1950, the Brigham City Fourth Ward team won the tournament and was congratulated by George Albert Smith, the president of the church, who explained why the church held a tournament in the first place. "Prize this trophy not for its intrinsic value, but rather because it stands for all that is good and righteous," he explained. "Always remember that you could not have won it except for the clean lives you have led."[24]

To drive the point home the church offered a "sportsmanship" trophy to the tournament team that best exemplified the virtues that basketball organizers all the way back to James Naismith had preached. Les Goates, a sports columnist and one of the biggest boosters of the churchwide tournament, called it "Latter-day Saint ideals as applied to athletics." Good Mormon sportsmanship, Goates claimed, required "deep fraternal feeling," "lofty ideals," and "clean living," and the award was given to the teams that best embodied these values.[25]

These were the same virtues Naismith promised. They showed that sports could be a vehicle for building good relationships with the broad swath of American Christians who also found the generalized values of James Naismith appealing. But at the same time, there was emerging in Mormon basketball something more particular, too—ways that basketball could speak to those ideals and hopes that made the church still stand apart, and Goates's language referred to both of these things. Every season Paul Hansen would divide the players in his ward into the A, B, and C teams; gather them on the basketball court in the Edgehill meetinghouse; and say, "This is a basketball. Behind me a basketball floor. Across the basketball floor is a chapel. The reason for this game is to put into practice the things you learn in that chapel."[26]

James Naismith could certainly endorse "clean living," of course, but for Latter-day Saints that phrase came to mean, in particular, adherence to the Word of Wisdom, which was required for all players who wanted to participate in the tournament. Similarly, the "fraternal feeling," cooperation, and self-sacrifice Naismith endorsed became a microcosm of the broader virtue of commitment to the church itself. Since Joseph Smith, there had always been something particularly collective about the church—on the one hand a sense of exclusivity, that salvation came only through its rites and rituals, and on the other, a broader sense of community. Smith had encouraged his followers to gather and live together, and the church's congregations were drawn with geographic lines and staffed by the members themselves. Basketball, as a congregational activity, could encourage the sort of cooperation and community building essential for the faith to survive. And that, perhaps, was one reason it became so popular in the church's missionary program.

Basketball and Missions

Joseph Smith began the Mormon movement with missionary work. After founding his new church in 1830 with only a handful of family and friends, he began sending out men (and eventually leaders began commissioning women, too) armed with little other than the Bible and the Book of Mormon to seek converts. Very quickly, these missionaries crisscrossed the United States and the world. A significant number of early converts came from the British Isles and Scandinavia. In 1845, the year after Smith died, British converts made up perhaps a quarter of the population of the church's headquarters city of Nauvoo, Illinois. And by the 1850s missionaries from the church were in Jamaica, Australia, Hong Kong, Africa, and India.

The basic parameters Smith had established for missionary work persisted through the early twentieth century. The leaders of the church summoned men—some young, some older, some single, some with families—and sometimes women (almost always younger and single) and dispatched them to a location. The missionaries would make their own way to their proving grounds. Often there would be a mission president in the area, usually a more experienced man church leaders designated to supervise and help the missionaries. The area, though, might be as large as, say, Europe, or the Eastern United States, and missionaries usually only called upon the president in cases of emergencies. Largely, the missionaries would figure out their own ways of preaching and getting around.

They had to work hard at this because in the early twentieth century Mormon missionaries still faced a great deal of suspicion. The only thing people in many countries knew about the church—if they knew anything at all—was that it had a history of polygamy. In 1890, the president of the church had officially disavowed the practice, and by the early twentieth century church leaders were beginning to excommunicate men who continued to marry multiple women. But the association between the church and the marital system was still widespread. The 1922 British silent film *Trapped by the Mormons* is a good example of the sort of worries missionaries faced. In the film, a Mormon missionary resembles nobody so much as the vampires in contemporary movies like *Dracula* (1931) and *Nosferatu* (1922). He is simultaneously intense, hypnotic, and seductive; dangerous but also somehow feminine, slender, and otherworldly. He seduces women and repels men. And in the end his attempt to waylay innocent British girls is foiled by a robust, manly set of British policemen.

This state of affairs opened the doors for improvisation. And sports, especially basketball, became a central vehicle for rehabilitating the Mormon image. Contrary to *Trapped by the Mormons*, basketball allowed Mormon men to show their vigor, strength, and masculinity. It also promoted the same sort of clean sportsmanship that James Naismith had celebrated, proving to other people that they and the missionaries actually held common values. Sometimes missionaries emphasized the virtues of the sport, as Naismith had, telling each other that the sense of cooperation and companionship that basketball could create would naturally lead people into the church. Other times, missionaries used the leagues and organized play they created as bait, treating baptism into the church as a technicality before eager players could take the court. But even in those situations, missionaries believed that basketball was serving its purpose—breaking down suspicion and social barriers, creating fellowship among previous strangers, and fostering community.

Basketball had always been a global sport. Those first eighteen players who experimented with the rules Naismith laid out at the YMCA Training School in Massachusetts were from places as far flung as Canada (including Naismith himself), the United States, Great Britain, France, and Japan. The YMCA was also a global organization. Its publications, including the newspaper article in which Luther Gulick had described the new sport, reached YMCA centers all around the world. Basketball was well-known even when Mormonism was not.

It appears that the first game that missionaries began to use for outreach was not basketball, but baseball. In 1911, some American missionaries in Japan joined the "Tokyo-American Baseball Team," a group of expatriate Americans who played against other teams in Tokyo. The next decade, missionaries in Samoa formed a team of their own to compete, as in Tokyo, with other community-based teams. One missionary declared that "our games were marked by good sportsmanship and clean playing, and they have been the means of disposing of much of that lack of understanding which formerly existed between us and our good neighbors."[27]

But by the late 1930s, basketball had supplanted baseball, and missionary teams were well established around the world. Basketball was an American sport, and though it was rapidly gaining popularity around the world, Americans drove its growth. YMCAs were the central hubs of the spread of the sport, but American soldiers in France in the waning years of World War I and across Europe after World War II also carried the game around the world. And because of their own familiarity with the game from the church's own programs, Latter-day Saint missionaries became other key transmitters of the sport to Europe and elsewhere.

For instance, there are a surprisingly large number of accounts of missionaries scrimmaging with various Olympic national teams in the mid-twentieth century. Most infamously, an official church magazine reported proudly in 1936 that a group of missionaries who regularly played basketball in Berlin were "approached by representatives of the German Olympic Association." The missionaries ended up serving as a practice squad and trainers for the German national team. "Olympic enthusiasm is promoting *Mormonismus*," one missionary crowed happily.[28] In retrospect, this delight at association with the Nazi government in Germany is embarrassing, but missionaries followed similar paths in Argentina, Finland, and other countries over the next few decades. As unlikely as these stories might seem, missionaries were a large population of young American men with familiarity with basketball, and thus, for locals interested in the sport, they were a tremendous resource.

Missionary basketball programs tended to be grassroots affairs, emerging spontaneously from the activities of missionaries themselves and encouraged by mission presidents who seized upon activities their missionaries were enthusiastic about and that gained them goodwill in the community. In the Netherlands, missionaries reached out to the Algemene Maatschappij Voor Jongeren, the Dutch branch of the YMCA, in the summer of 1937. They offered to teach Dutch youth basketball, and in return the Dutch taught the missionaries soccer. This led to what one magazine called "thorough drubbings" for both sides—each thoroughly unfamiliar with the sport they were learning.[29] But by December the Dutch had learned enough basketball that missionary teams were regularly playing competitive games against AMVJ teams before audiences of hundreds. Something similar was developing in Great Britain at the same time, again through the auspices of the YMCA. In the winter of 1937–38, missionary teams entered YMCA tournaments in Liverpool and Birmingham and did not embarrass themselves playing against German, Belgian, and British teams. Afterward the various teams gathered for drinks, and the missionaries toasted their rivals with lemonade.[30]

In Finland in the early 1930s, missionaries adopted the same strategy. The Finn Henry Matis straightforwardly confessed in his autobiography that although he wasn't interested in the religious messages the missionaries offered, he "walked even on cold stormy winter mornings over the hill from Forest Hills to Braddock to practice and be substitutes on the LDS team." Eventually he joined the church, and by the 1950s was the mission president in Finland. Remembering his own experience, Matis promoted basketball as a means to build relationships. In the early 1950s, two of his missionaries worked as coaches for the Finnish national basketball team as they prepared for the 1952 Olympic Games, held in Finland's capital, Helsinki. Matis's missionaries also served as interpreters during the Olympics. A few months before the games began, the Finnish government awarded Matis the Silver Cross, a particular national honor, commenting on the "spiritual growth of the Finnish players, as well as the growth of their physical skills, as a result of the missionaries' example."[31]

Such successes were mirrored elsewhere. In Melbourne, the second-largest city in Australia, a team of missionaries won the city's YMCA basketball championship for two years in a row, in 1939 and 1940, before the Second World War prompted the church to pull missionaries from

The 1954 "Mormon Yankees" team of missionaries became a media sensation in Australia. Team manager Loren C. Dunn had played for the BYU team that won the 1951 NIT. He later became president of the Sydney Australia Mission and a general authority of the church.

the country. After missionaries returned they went right on winning, taking titles again in 1950 and 1951. In 1954, a group of American basketball teams toured the country and garnered a great deal of publicity. The Australian mission president, Charles Liljenquist, had an idea. He called in Loren Dunn, a missionary who had been a star on the BYU basketball team, and told him, "We'll give you any missionary you want, but organize a team." Liljenquist explained this would "establish a good reputation for the church." Dunn recruited a collection of American missionaries, dubbed his team the "Mormon Yankees," and began challenging other local teams in exhibition games. At the end of that year, the Mormon Yankees won a regional tournament. And just as in Finland, in 1956 the Mormon Yankees scrimmaged against the Australian national team to help the locals prepare for the Olympics.[32]

In the late 1920s, the coach of the basketball team for a sports club in Venado Tuerto, Argentina, saw several missionaries playing basketball and invited them to try out for the team. Three of them passed muster, and one, Frederick Williams, went on to the odd situation of playing part-time professional basketball while serving a full-time mission from 1927 to 1929. When he returned to Argentina in 1938 as the mission president for the country, Williams remembered his experience vividly and set up a sports club called *Los Mormones*, staffed entirely by missionaries and local church members. In the ten years between his Argentine missions Williams had worked for the United States Department of State in Latin America, and he knew the central role that clubs like these played in Argentine culture. They offered a variety of activities, like dances and dinners, served as gathering places for communities, and also often sponsored sports teams. Williams explained in a mission newsletter that "the club is the Axle [of] Argentine social life."

Los Mormones, Williams believed, would use the club system to promote the lifestyle his church taught. Rolf Larson, a missionary, explained the philosophy of *Los Mormones*: "Often we think that sportsmanship refers only to active games where there is physical competition, but this is a grave error." Larson argued that sports would teach young people that "this generosity of soul, this willingness to cede our rights for the benefit of others, either it is an integral part of our personality or it is a grave defect."[33] Williams and the missionaries he supervised found ways to promote a certain vision of spiritual healthiness, linked to a sense of community and self-sacrifice. Through basketball and the club system, they managed to present all of this in a form that made sense to Argentines.

In October 1938, *Los Mormones* played an exhibition basketball game against a team from *Club Atlético Belgrano* and beat them soundly. Cayetano Cavelli, president of CAB, praised the missionaries anyway. "You are the best ambassadors your country has ever had," he said.[34] Over the next few years, Williams's club started softball and baseball teams, both of which won national championships. While the *Los Mormones* basketball team never won a championship, it was impressive enough that the Argentine government invited two players—including Rolf Larson—to play on the Argentine national team in the South American continental championship tournament in 1940. Larson had been in Argentina for just over two years and thus met the residency requirement.

And so it was that a Mormon missionary from Arizona took the final shot for the Argentine national team in the championship game of the 1940 South American Basketball Championships.

Rolf Larson missed, and his team lost by two. But Williams sent a letter to the president of the LDS Church gushing over the young man, who had become a national celebrity in Argentina. "He is such a gentleman—a missionary in the best sense of the word, that he has captured the hearts of the people," Williams wrote.[35] Basketball, it turned out, was a religious activity: it converted, it preached, and it promoted values.

Larson was tall—he played center on the Argentine national team—with a strong jaw, and after he returned home from his mission he taught school for a while. He moved to Washington, DC, and his command of Spanish, his religion, and, frankly, his looks, made him appealing to the Federal Bureau of Investigation. Director J. Edgar Hoover wanted agents who projected moral discipline of the sort white Christians like James Naismith preached, and that Larson fit the bill was a sign that the Mormon embrace of basketball was working. It was assimilating Latter-day Saints to American culture and to the culture of other societies that embraced basketball. It encouraged believers in muscular Christianity to see Mormons as their fellows. And it encouraged Mormons to think of their faith as something embodied, something that had to do with how they controlled and developed their bodies.[36]

Of course, Rolf Larson passed basketball on. He worked in education both in his personal life and in the church, and participated in a phenomenon that grew out of the youth programs, the All-Church Basketball Tournament, and all of the mission efforts—something modern members of the church call simply "church ball."

Church Ball

Organized missionary basketball peaked in the 1940s and 1950s and went into decline in the 1960s.[37] There were a number of reasons for this.

The '60s were the years of "correlation," the shorthand name for a large-scale overhaul of the LDS Church's bureaucracy and administration. The framers of correlation pressed for standardization of procedure and policy in a number of church departments, including the missionary program. By 1960, the highest leaders of the church were exercising greater supervision over mission activities. The expectations and permissible activities for missionaries were smoothed into churchwide standardization, and the sort of experimentation that had led to *Los Mormones* was choked off. In 1961, for instance, church leaders distributed a set of six lessons that all missionaries were told to memorize and recite in order.

Correlation signaled something else, as well. American culture was shifting in the 1960s. Clothing was becoming more casual. Second-wave feminism and the sexual revolution were changing gender norms. The counterculture movement threatened older hierarchies. One of the main reasons the church had embraced basketball—as a path to mainstream acceptance—seemed less appealing to these leaders. During the late twentieth century, they began to emphasize distinctiveness rather than accommodation and in particular grew suspicious of much popular public entertainment. The norms of behavior and policy correlation spread throughout the church often pressed back against the cultural changes of the time, emphasizing formality and solemnity (what church leaders called "reverence") in religious settings. Using sports as a missionary tool didn't quite fit anymore.

At the same time, some missionaries and mission leaders had pushed the appeal of sports far enough that it rebounded back upon them. In December 1960, Henry Moyle, a church apostle supervising missions, told other church leaders that he was planning to encourage missionaries to use sports as a recruiting tool in a way far more blunt than the public relations-centered efforts of Argentina or Australia. "In England they have used American baseball as a means of interesting the young people," he explained to a meeting of church authorities. The procedure would be to invite young people to play a sport, organizing them into leagues the missionaries would supervise, and require baptism in order to play. When the plan was implemented in Great Britain baptism numbers skyrocketed. An overjoyed Moyle spread the program to other areas of the world.[38]

But by the fall of 1963 Moyle was dead of a sudden coronary, and a number of church leaders were beginning to recognize that the vast majority of these young people were only vaguely if at all aware that they were now considered members of The Church of Jesus Christ of Latter-day Saints. New mission presidents arrived in the countries where such baptisms had taken place with instructions to clean up the church's rolls only to find thousands of young people sometimes annoyed, sometimes confused, and sometimes angry that this Utah church claimed them as members. By the end of 1965, after a round or two of purging, the number of church members living in the missions around the world was 15,000 less than it had been a year earlier.[39] Helen May Taylor Beecroft, a missionary in Chile, wrote about the visit of the apostle Spencer W. Kimball in her diary in May 1964. Kimball appeared in front of a group of missionaries and said to expect that "there would be no more basketball teams or singing groups."[40]

This was perhaps a good move for the church's broader ambitions in places outside the Western world. In 2012, Phil and Joy McMullin arrived in the Democratic Republic of the Congo to supervise the church's mission there. They found a meetinghouse built according to the plans established by the correlation movement, complete with a basketball court built behind the chapel. The court had sat utterly unused for years; grass grew through cracks in its floor. The McMullins partnered with local leaders and went back to Salt Lake City. At church headquarters they explained that in some parts of the world, basketball was utterly unappealing. The expensive materials and complicated engineering involved the creation of a gymnasium with descending hoops could be best used in other ways. By the late 2010s, new plans for meetinghouses that lacked the old familiar court were available in Africa. Basketball aided in the globalization of the church in some arenas, but church leaders did not always recognize it had its limits in others.[41]

It may not be coincidence that the All-Church Basketball Tournament wound its way to its end less than a decade after Moyle's death.

This hardly meant, though, that Mormons stopped playing basketball. Meetinghouses in the United States, at least, were still equipped with hardwood floors and hoops, and Rolf Larson and other church members like him still gathered to play—sometimes as part of official church activities, sometimes on their own. The churchwide tournament was gone, but well into the twenty-first century local areas of the church continued to sponsor small-scale tournaments. In most American meetinghouses on most Saturday mornings, men continued to play what they called "church ball."

In 2006, the Utah-based film production company HaleStorm (run, unsurprisingly, by a man named Kurt Hale) released a movie called *Church Ball.* It was the sixth in their series of low-budget comedies targeted at a Latter-day Saint audience. HaleStorm produced the film in the early 2000s, and it was less financially successful than most of those that came before. But the movie still played in theaters in Mormon-heavy areas of the United States, and Hale managed to attract well-known Hollywood comedians to appear. Fred Willard and Gary Coleman have small roles.

The movie pokes fun at the same tension that Henry Moyle, Rolf Larson, many others—all the way back to poor James Naismith, horrified at what his game had become that night in Kansas when he saw a team fouling as a strategy—felt as they mixed basketball with the practice of their faith. At one point, an athlete prays, "Bless us to play as true sportsmen and true Christians. And Lord, may we, thy best team, win."

The movie portrays how basketball is about personal development and the building of community. The bishop of the Mud Lake Ward, played by Willard, assigns a mediocre player named Dennis Buckstead to recruit a ward team. Buckstead finds only players as inadequate as himself in one way or another. Because the movie is a predictable comedy, this gang of misfits—featuring stereotypes like the foreigner with a thick accent, the overweight player, the clumsy nerd, etc.—develop values Naismith might have appreciated. They come to love each other, they stick up for each other, and they try to help each other succeed. In this way, the movie promotes the virtues that Naismith and Mormon leaders had hoped for.

Official church organizations continue to promote this mode of basketball. Periodically in the social media era of the early twenty-first century, the church's public affairs office promoted stories of church basketball binding communities and building bonds of friendship. In the Philippines a group of Mormon youth founded a regular basketball game to accompany the daily youth religion class that the church calls "seminary." The game attracted other young people who weren't in the seminary class, and friendships blossomed. "Seminary helps my life to be balanced both physically and spiritually," one player, Adryian Rumbaoa, told a church reporter.[42]

In 2009 local church leaders in Salt Lake City organized a series of workshops with two professional basketball referees who happened to be members of the church. The referees pled with their audiences to recognize the deep moral connections between basketball and Christianity. "The whole Sermon on the Mount can be seen, or at least should be seen, on the basketball floor," said one of the officials. Basketball "is still the Lord's program, and it is here for a reason. The more I watch the church sports program, the more I see the amazing venue the Lord has set out to teach his gospel."[43]

That the Salt Lake City church leaders felt they had to hold such an event points to some anxieties that the movie *Church Ball* also chronicles—the less idealistic, more aggressive side of church ball. In the world of the movie, the church has decided that the entire theory of church basketball has produced more harm than good and, thus, the gymnasiums in every chapel will soon be shut down entirely. This decree strikes anxiety into the hearts of all the game's devotees, including the bishop of the Mud Lake Ward, a longtime basketball veteran. He is missing an eye, an injury he happily attributes to his own history on the court. As the movie proceeds, bruises, bumps, tackles, cheating, and an utter torrent of profanity (the last, to ensure the movie appeals to its target audience, is almost entirely bleeped out) ensue. But beneath all the silliness, the movie puts its finger on a very real tension in the church's life: basketball could cause both harm and good.

For a time the proudly eclectic and unorthodox Mormon magazine *Sunstone* ran advertisements for a satirical "church ball"–a basketball emblazoned with the "game rules": "1. No foul language. 2. Call your own fouls. 3. Lights out and lock up."[44] The rules were widely repeated in church gymnasiums but were also widely mocked for their apparent incompatibility. As Rich Johnson, a sports columnist at a Utah newspaper, wrote, "Under this brilliant rule, you call your own fouls. Yeah, right ... I don't know how many times I've been knocked to the floor while playing church ball."[45] Dee Smith, a former All-American college athlete, reflected on the upsides and downsides of basketball courts after he became a local church leader in Cedar City, Utah. "Some people will come out to play ball that would not otherwise set foot in a church building," he said. But at the same time he had to chastise his flock for "poor sportsmanship" more than he had anticipated.[46]

Even Thurl Bailey, a professional basketball player for the Utah Jazz, was bewildered at the disjuncture between church ball's ideals and their execution. He converted to the church in 1995 and was invited to a game at a church building soon after. There, he told a reporter, he saw "someone stole the basketball from someone and they threw them to the floor and no foul was called." Bailey, the consummate professional with a well-entrenched reputation as one of the NBA's nice guys, told the reporter he "retired from church ball after one game."[47]

In 2019, the Utah Supreme Court ruled on a much-covered case that made the strain in church basketball a matter of law and media interest. A man named Judd Nixon sued his fellow Latter-day Saint Edward Clay over a 2012 game. Nixon had the ball, dribbling hard toward the basket, when he suddenly stopped fifteen feet from the basket and rose up to take a shot. Clay reached out to block the shot, hit Nixon's shoulder, and the two men went down hard. Nixon ended up with a serious knee injury that required rehabilitation.[48]

The Utah Supreme Court observed, wryly, that church basketball is often called "the brawl that begins with a prayer," pointing at the simultaneous invocation of fellowship and hospitality too often subsumed in anger, even to the point of lawsuits. Then the court ruled that the sort of contact Clay and Nixon sustained was to be expected in such a game, concluded that acceptance of such risks were implicit in stepping onto the court in the first place, and dismissed the lawsuit.[49]

The scholar Kristine Haglund has suggested that whether or not it has succeeded in inculcating the sorts of virtues people like Naismith or B. H. Roberts extolled it for, church ball does serve one purpose they expected, though did not quite articulate: It is an emotionally intense proving ground for young Mormon men, a homosocial, male-only space to create male friendships and male bonding, to express competition—often vigorous competition—in ways restricted in a church built on what's sometimes called "soft patriarchy."[50] Men lead in the church, men are in charge, but it is also

After retired Utah Jazz forward Thurl Bailey joined the LDS Church in 1995, he was invited to play in a church building but, disappointed in the lack of sportsmanship he saw, "retired from church ball after one game." *Courtesy The Salt Lake Tribune*

not uncommon to see those men cry as they talk about their families or the service they perform. This balance between the sentimental emotions of soft patriarchy and the intense competition of the male world of church basketball is another expression of the tensions that sit near the heart of church ball.

3

STAN WATTS AND THE RISE OF BYU BASKETBALL

People got killed playing football in the 1880s and 1890s. Quite a few people. So many that the journalist C. W. Whitney, a football fan, wrote huffily and perhaps unpersuasively in an 1894 book, "There have been two fatal accidents from the game in the West this season, but both came from gross carelessness." Whitney explained that the first man killed was deaf, "and of course out of his sphere, as a football player needs all his five senses." The other was a high school boy, whom, Whitney said, "was untrained and knew really nothing of the game." So, all in all, if you listened to Whitney, the deaths on the football field were not the game's fault but could be laid at the feet of the victims.[1]

This defensiveness was typical of the sport's advocates, but undeniably, the damage was typical of the sport. As with any sport, players got better, but in the case of football as their skills and tactics improved, more of them got hurt. As football evolved from rugby in the 1870s, it grew more physical. Players grew more agile, so in 1888 the great Yale football coach Walter Camp persuaded his fellow coaches to allow tackling below the waist. Metal cleats were outlawed, so players started sharpening their leather cleats. They wore virtually no other protective gear, perhaps only a padded hat or nose guard. Forward passing was illegal and teams pressed forward en masse, so players sometimes got crushed. As blocking tactics grew more ambitious, coaches drove players to grow stronger and designed tactics to leverage more force. In the 1904–05 season alone, eighteen players across the United States were killed playing football. And that was a good year. Fifteen years earlier, in 1890, the death toll was twenty-three; the year after twenty-two; the year after that, twenty-six.[2]

In 1894, at the annual Harvard-Yale game, the trouble started when a Harvard player's leg snapped. So, by way of vengeance, another Harvard player jabbed a Yale player in the eye, after which a different Yale player hammered yet another Harvard player so hard that his collarbone snapped. There were two broken noses, a bleeding eye, a coma, and two concussions before the game collapsed into a fistfight. After the so-called "Bloodbath at Hampden Park," Harvard and Yale refused to play each other again for years. Three years later, the University of Virginia team killed a University of Georgia player when their offensive line crashed into Georgia's defensive line, crushing Richard Gammon in the middle. After his death the Georgia legislature passed a law banning football at any university that received state funds, but the governor refused to sign it. Later, New York State banned the game at its schools.

So rumors flew when The Church of Jesus Christ of Latter-day Saints' board of education met in October 1901 to issue an edict banning football at church schools—particularly at Brigham Young Academy (BYA), which would be renamed Brigham Young University two years later. One writer speculated that the son of a trustee had, like Gammon, been killed in a game. Another pointed to other football deaths in the state.[3] After all, in 1885 an Ogden, Utah, newspaper announced a local high school football game by assuring readers that the team had "a carpenter busily engaged in manufacturing crutches. Several competent surgeons have been retained for the occasion."[4]

Students at BYA had been playing football on their own since 1892, mostly in Provo's Pioneer Park. In 1896, the school formally sponsored the game—but fairly quickly, trustees began fielding complaints. In December 1897 a Brigham Young student team played Salt Lake City's Crescent School. George Goddard, the superintendent of the church's Sunday School, dropped in to see how the sport worked and was horrified. He went home and wrote an outraged letter to church president Wilford Woodruff urging him to do something, for heaven's sake. "I cannot conceive of one particle of good arising from indulgences in either Yells or football games, but I can see a great amount of evil," Goddard wrote. He complained about "profanity" and "fighting" both on the field and off.[5]

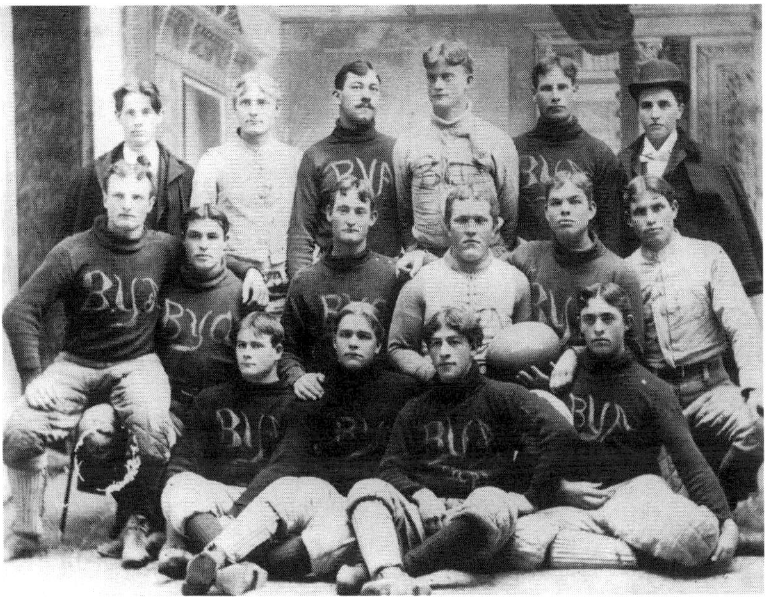

Brigham Young Academy's football team, 1896. After church leaders banned football at BYA in 1901 because of its "brutality," men's basketball slipped into the breach. *Courtesy University Archives, Harold B. Lee Library, BYU*

Other church leaders agreed. Legendary educator Karl Maeser was hired to teach at Brigham Young Academy at the time of its founding in 1875 and ended up running it for nearly two decades. During his lifetime he was widely regarded as the greatest teacher in the church, known for his strict moral code and insistence that ethical discipline was central to the educational process. It was then unsurprising that he had little use for football. By the end of the nineteenth century he had been promoted to the general superintendency of the church's educational system, but he still took an interest in what was happening on his old stomping grounds. In 1899 he wrote an appalled letter to Benjamin Cluff, who had replaced him as president of the academy. Maeser was well aware that BYA students were playing football and professed horror at the thought. "I can not believe that you would permit such things to be carried on," he wrote to Cluff. Later he declared himself "strongly opposed to foot ball."[6]

Rather than any particular crisis, it was these broader moral arguments that church leaders marshaled when they halted football at Brigham Young Academy. As one Provo newspaper put it, "Our young men are not barbarians."[7] Dr. J. H. Paul, a senior educator for the church, appeared in front of a crowd of unruly students to defend the ban. The young people were grousing. One sneered that he supposed now "marbles" or "tag would be the chief sports of the LDS in the future." Others declared they would leave the school for a place where they could play what they wanted.[8]

But Paul was unmoved. He calmly explained that football stood contrary to everything church leadership believed a sport should be, morally, physically, and spiritually. He pointed to Columbia, which had recently banned the sport, and Charles Eliot, president of Harvard, who praised the actions of his sister school in New York City. And Paul denounced the very soul of football. "The spirit of low cunning and brutality which is behind it is as repugnant to the honor as it is destructive to the culture of men who should be eminent in both," he read from a *New York World* editorial, before endorsing the sentiment.[9] Paul and other leaders of the church condemned football as uncivilized, privileging brute force over cooperation and impulse over discipline.

The students protested. The administration held firm. And thus, into the breach slipped basketball, which was supposed to be everything football was not.

Eugene Roberts Invents the Cougars

By the mid-twentieth century it was common wisdom on BYU campus that the administration and student body had turned to basketball in earnest because football was banned. Ernest Wilkinson, an acerbic and ambitious attorney, reigned over the university as president from 1951 to 1971 and transformed it from a sleepy parochial college into a sprawling research university. He said it frankly. "Since football was banned," he wrote in his centennial history of the university, "the school focused its energies on basketball."[10] The English professor J. Marinus Jensen, another historian of the school, was teaching on campus when football was banned. He said, "Football having been banned from the Church school system, basketball was adopted as a substitute."[11]

The shift was both a matter of practicality and of moral ambition. In 1902, BYA (a year away from becoming Brigham Young

University) opened the Training School Building, a headquarters for the training of teachers. The building's top floor was entirely open, with metal girders and a hardwood floor. The space was sixty feet wide and ninety-three feet long—barely large enough to accommodate what would soon become the official college basketball dimensions of fifty feet by ninety feet (since lengthened by four more feet).

A court was available, and Brigham Young students soon started to use it. Since the mid-1890s the students had been running an "Athletic Association," pooling funds to buy equipment and arrange their own intramural sports competitions. Both men and women were in the association, which selected officers to organize a variety of games—baseball, track, and football (before it was banned), among others. They approached other organizations, like the YMCA and YWCA, to schedule games.[12] Then they began mounting basketball teams. The Athletic Association sponsored basketball games against intramural teams from other schools, some in-state like LDS College in Salt Lake City, and even some that traveled quite a way to get to Provo. In 1903, the University of Colorado men's basketball team swept through Utah, defeating every college team it played, including the hapless Brigham Young team, which lost 23–15.[13]

Initially, more women than men played basketball. As Marinus Jensen described male students' initial reaction to the sport, "basketball had been introduced as a girl's game," not for "red-blooded young huskies."[14] The Athletic Association organized regular games among women students at the academy, and the BYA women often played other teams as well. Regularly the Athletic Association sponsored field days, in which athletes from the University of Utah or LDS College traveled to Provo for a whole series of games and the "lady teams" would compete.[15] When football was struck by the ban, however, men soon rediscovered the masculine potential of basketball.

In 1910, when he hired Eugene Roberts as director of BYU athletics, George Brimhall had been running BYU for ten years. Brimhall had stepped in as acting president in 1900. His predecessor, the impulsive and charismatic young Benjamin Cluff, had taken leave to travel to South America in search of archaeological evidence he believed would prove the historicity of the Book of Mormon, against the advice of church leaders who thought Cluff ill-prepared

The first official basketball team to take the court for
Brigham Young Academy was the women's team, in 1900.
Courtesy University Archives, Harold B. Lee Library, BYU

for a dangerous venture. Cluff returned in 1902, battered and unsuccessful, and stepped down for good. Brimhall took up the permanent position and held it until 1921.

Cluff had been an enthusiastic and inventive educator, a native of Provo and graduate of the academy himself. He had also earned a bachelor's degree from the University of Michigan. When he took over Brigham Young Academy, he guided its transformation from something like a high school to a true institution of higher education. Under his leadership the school introduced new subjects and curricula, founded a "normal school" for the training of teachers, and regularized an academic calendar. Cluff also encouraged students to participate in school governance and threw official support behind the Athletic Association.

Though Brimhall was not so inventive, he was a warm personality, solid, cautious, and capable. He raised the money to build the Training School Building, reorganized the university into the departmental model that continues today, and approved the painting of the letter Y on the Wasatch Mountains near the university. He also worked hard, perhaps more than Cluff, at promoting the school's religious character. Brimhall lobbied for several faculty members who were teaching liberal religious ideas popular in eastern schools to be pushed out of the school, and the BYU board agreed.

Brimhall's decision to hire thirty-year-old Eugene Roberts as athletic director was characteristic of both his eagerness to transform BYU into a modern university and his desire to ensure that process would retain a moral and religious character. Like Brimhall and Cluff, Roberts had attended BYA, but also sought education outside Utah. He earned a physical education degree at Yale in 1910. He, like Benjamin Cluff, was of an optimistic, adventurous younger generation of Mormons. Cluff had taken Roberts with him on the doomed trip to South America. The two were enthusiastic about their faith and the national culture that surrounded it, and both felt that these two communities could have a warm and mutually enriching relationship.

Roberts thought James Naismith was right—sports, and particularly basketball, were powerful vehicles for inculcating morality into young people, especially young men. Roberts had served a mission for his church in Switzerland, where he absorbed mountaineering and muscular Christianity alike. When he returned he went to Yale, which one American minister called "the seminary for muscular Christianity." Yale inculcated in students like Roberts the intimate connection between the body and the spirit; the notion that physical discipline generated moral discipline; the execution of duty and service to others; and, in particular, a form of masculine Christianity that located male spiritual virtue in strength, competition, and accomplishment.[16]

These were the virtues Roberts brought to BYU sports when he moved into his office in Provo. After World War I, the heyday of muscular Christianity passed, but it had left a lingering mark on what historian Paul Putz calls the "middlebrow Protestant ethos" of organized sports in the United States. As sports gradually professionalized, its American exponents insisted it was an ideal vehicle for personal moral development. Universities, professional leagues, and informal organizations like the Fellowship of Christian Athletes promoted this connection, using it to justify the expansion of organized sports in the United States.[17]

Roberts shared this commitment to sports as a means for developing character. So in the temporary absence of football (which Roberts brought back in 1922, once the equipment and rules caught up to the physicality of the game, although injuries still happened and continue to happen today), he turned to basketball. He hired a women's director and charged her with overseeing the women's basketball team, which he himself took very little personal interest in. He decided to make basketball a men's sport on BYU campus and began promoting the ways in which it would cultivate a particularly Mormon way of being a man.

Roberts thought basketball cultivated individual virtue but also fostered cooperation for young men, a virtue particularly significant to Latter-day Saints, whose religion stressed community. This was true both in the historic sense—unlike most Protestant denominations, Mormons built cities from the ground up, and in Utah, one's neighbors sat next to you in the pews—but also in the religious sense. Mormons had long stressed that salvation came through being sacramentally bonded to each other through religious rituals, and Roberts pointed to these ideas as he celebrated the importance of sports at BYU.

Roberts believed athletics was important because he, like a lot of other Americans, believed that modern urban life was draining the vigor from the young men of the United States. And his own people, increasingly integrated into the modern world, were not excepted from this trend. Sports, though, might be a way to preserve their values. Roberts was certainly not alone here; these impulses were shared with Protestants like Naismith and Roman Catholics like Knute Rockne, the famous football coach at the University of Notre Dame. Rockne and Roberts enjoyed a cordial correspondence in the 1920s, after Roberts brought Rockne to Utah to teach a workshop on coaching in the summer of 1923. After that visit Mormons often held Rockne up as an icon of muscular Christianity. The story circulated on BYU campus, for instance, that Rockne refused to endorse cigarettes even after being offered the princely sum of $2,000 by a tobacco company.[18]

Roberts said he was "not primarily interested in the star athlete or the Olympic hero. Our primary objective is not to turn out winning athletic teams." This seemed to some at BYU an odd thing to say. But Roberts was clear. He was "concerned about the physical and social welfare of every student." He refused to recruit athletes who would boost the team. Instead, he wanted to attract regular BYU students to experiment with sports, certain that they would grow a great deal from the experience. He also wanted to emphasize the collective benefits that sports could bring.[19]

But that general conviction came with caveats. In one article extolling the virtues of sports as a means for moral discipline, Roberts warned other Latter-day Saints about "race deterioration." This was a common fear among white Americans in the early twentieth century. From presidents to university professors to famous writers, white Americans had learned the wrong lessons from the theory of evolution and had come to believe that not simply species but also nations and races were in competition for survival and dominance. To be clear, Charles Darwin insisted that his theory worked on a far slower time than even centuries and on the level of species rather than countries, but most people didn't grasp this. Theodore Roosevelt, president of the United States during Roberts's young adulthood, wrote, "If a race is weak, if it is lacking in the physical and moral traits which go to the makeup of a conquering people, it cannot succeed."[20]

Eugene Roberts wasn't unusual in warning that the comforts and leisure of modern life were weakening the vigor of white Americans or in linking that warning to racialized fears. Roberts said that without wholesome physical activities like sports, young white Americans might be lured by the "savage rhythm, the barbaric movements" of a "vulgar" jazz club.[21] He did not use the word "Black"; he did not have to. And though Roberts believed women could gain from sports, he was particularly concerned that they benefit men—because male virtues were those under greatest pressure. For him, basketball was just the ticket to keep the young white men of BYU in vigorous pursuit of the virtues that would keep white American civilization strong.

Once Roberts took over BYU athletics he absorbed the students' Athletic Association into the university proper. He organized faculty basketball teams and reached out to local high schools in order to field other teams of teachers the BYU squad could play. And when Henry Rose, the popular basketball coach Roberts had appointed, quit, Roberts began coaching basketball himself. He didn't consider himself a very good in-game tactician. Instead he called the team into his office and told them that he would implement a set of what he called "drills"—organized strategies for getting the ball in the basket that basketball players today would call "plays." Roberts promised the team that if they would master these drills, sink them deep into their bones so they could execute them like clockwork, they would win. They did, and they won.

The BYU team began playing in the Utah Basketball League, an intramural league of a variety of schools in the area, including some high schools and various colleges. With discipline, the BYU squad won the league's title four of the six years that Roberts coached the team. After one particularly notable championship run, one of Roberts's players wrote in the BYU newspaper that the "brilliant record" of the team shouldn't be credited to Roberts's basketball mind. The player explained that Roberts "regards basketball epidemics like the one recently experienced as a sort of necessary evil to be tolerated in order to get people interested in the real thing: PHYSICAL EDUCATION."[22]

Roberts wanted to teach discipline, moral and physical. That's what he believed his drills to be: a way of exercising spiritual power over the flesh. Basketball was a tool—a means, not an end. But in the meantime, BYU's basketball team got quite good at the means.

In 1918, Roberts took on a challenge. BYU joined the Rocky Mountain Athletic Conference, a group of institutions of higher education based primarily in Colorado. They set up regular matches among themselves and coordinated a conference tournament every spring. After 1918 the BYU squad still occasionally played high schools and local junior colleges for practice, but from here on out, the real games were against universities. The logistics were challenging. Early on, BYU mostly played the University of Utah and Utah State Agricultural College (later Utah State University), who had also recently joined the conference. By the 1920s the schools were getting the hang of traveling and schedules and BYU was playing schools in Wyoming, Colorado, and Montana, as well as hosting visiting teams in the gymnasium in the Training School Building. Roberts alternated coaching for the next few years with Alvin Twitchell.

The conference offered much more competent competition than did the high schools of the Wasatch Front, and BYU initially lost a lot more. But eventually the team rallied. By the late 1920s they had taken second place in the conference twice.

In 1928, Roberts took a job teaching at the University of Southern California, another indication of how athletics had opened doors for Mormons nationwide. And though the departure of such a dominant figure as Roberts might seem to have boded badly for the team, the coach had set BYU basketball up for success.

He also left the team with one more bequest. He suggested that the cougar would be an appropriate mascot for the university's sports teams. They were native to Utah, powerful, agile, and self-sufficient, Roberts said. The school took him up on it.

The Rise of Stan Watts

Stan Watts, the seventh of eleven children of Eugene and Gertrude Watts, was born in 1911. He grew up working on a farm in Murray, a small town just south of Salt Lake City. The Watts family grew sugar beets, and Stan and his siblings spent every morning hoeing and weeding before rushing off to school. They also played sports—baseball and backyard football. When Stan was six years old his father gave him a basketball for Christmas. By the time he entered high school, Stan was hooked. He and his brothers dominated the Murray High School sports teams.

The Great Depression descended on the nation in 1929, and it was only a year or two before Utah was suffering unemployment rates of 33 percent—one of the worst in the country. Their farm provided food, but the Watts sons were growing up, and they were having trouble finding jobs. Stan wanted to go to college to develop skills that would make him more competitive in the market, but couldn't afford it. He caught a break when James Henager, who operated a business college in Salt Lake City, offered him free tuition if he would play on the school's basketball team. So Stan took classes in typing, accounting, and filing while playing for the Henager team.

The Depression wasn't over by the time he graduated, and he spent two more years working odd jobs until the coach at Weber Junior

College in Ogden, Utah, offered him a similar deal. Weber had gotten money from a federal grant that allowed it to offer students part-time jobs, and Stan began working in the college kitchen and on the janitorial staff. He also starred on the Weber basketball team for the two years he studied there, getting named to two all-conference teams. One day, he attended a state high school basketball tournament, and saw Vadal Peterson, the head coach of the University of Utah men's basketball team. Stan's time at Weber was done and he wanted to move on to a four-year university. He screwed up his courage and walked up to Peterson, who apparently didn't recognize the young man and brushed him off.

Stan took it as a sign, and he was about ready to give up sports entirely when a family friend he hadn't seen for a while knocked on the Watts front door. Edwin Kimball—or Eddie, as the Watts family knew him—was on the athletic staff at BYU.

Stan got the same deal Weber Junior College had given him—a campus job and a place on the sports teams. The BYU athletic staff wanted him for both football and basketball, and he played both in his two years in classes, starting at quarterback on the football team and playing on the basketball team from 1936 to 1938.

Stan's time as a student was marred by a damaging knee injury and two nasty bouts with tonsilitis, but he played well. The BYU teams were flourishing under a series of competent coaches who followed in Eugene Roberts's footsteps. When Watts entered the university in 1936, the basketball team hadn't had a losing season in ten years. In 1933, Elwood Romney was one of the best college basketball players in the country and named the team's first All-American player. But Watts's second year was the first losing season in more than a decade, and the school promptly replaced hapless head coach Fred Dixon with Watts's friend Eddie Kimball, who coached the team while also serving as the school's athletic director. The Cougars had a winning record for the next ten years.

When Watts graduated in 1938 he was nursing hopes for a position on Kimball's staff, but nothing was available. Instead he ended up coaching high schools. In 1947, Eddie Kimball again tracked Stan down—this time catching him shopping for a suit in a Salt Lake City store—and told him that BYU finally wanted him back. Kimball first put him on the job of resuscitating the college's baseball team, which had been moribund for decades. But Kimball couldn't keep Stan Watts away from basketball. Stan coached the freshman team until 1949 when the head coach of the varsity team resigned to work for his father-in-law's house-painting business. Stan Watts took over.

His first full year coaching the team, 1949–50, was a time of wild disjuncture. That Watts's predecessor resigned because he thought he could make more money painting houses spoke to how rickety, and distinctly amateur, BYU college athletics still was. The team still practiced upstairs in the old Training School Building, on a worn wooden floor with barely enough room between the lines of the court and the wall for anybody to stand. Stan had practiced there himself when he was on the team. The players called the place the "attic," and BYU's coaches were so embarrassed that they avoided showing it to prospective students. The team played its competitive games at a local high school. Eventually the University of Utah allowed BYU to use its fieldhouse in Salt Lake City, the same place where the U's own teams played.

However, Watts's tenure at BYU marked the university's basketball program's transition toward the high level of competition and systematization that Walter Byers, who was just then taking over the NCAA, was dreaming of. In the spring of 1950, Watts took the team through a shaky start—at one point losing four games in a row—before rallying and winning the last three games of the season in a dominating fashion (for instance, beating the University of Denver 75–50) and claiming the championship of the Skyline Conference, a group of Western universities the Cougars had joined in 1937. By virtue of winning that title, BYU earned its first appearance in the NCAA men's basketball tournament. Suddenly BYU was entering a world in which basketball got media coverage, made money, and was thoroughly professional.

The NCAA tournament had existed for only eleven years but was already among the most prestigious events in national college basketball. By the 1960s it was widely considered the best tournament for the best teams from the best schools in the country. But in the spring of 1950 only eight teams were invited to participate, far from the sixty-eight that became standard by the 2010s. The tournament was intended for conference champions, and BYU got in by virtue of winning the Skyline Conference.

The invitation was intimidating. In late March, the team traveled to Kansas City, Missouri, for the four-game tournament of the Western half of the NCAA bracket along with the other contenders—Baylor, UCLA, and Bradley University. BYU was matched up first with Baylor, and the betting line favored the Cougars. But the game turned out to be a grind: low scoring, hard defense, sloppy play. With twenty seconds left, BYU was four points ahead—and then completely fell apart. Baylor scored the last five points of the game and won, 56–55.

Watts was devastated. A tide of telegrams was waiting for him when he and his team dragged into the hotel that night. Watts gathered his team, offered some consolation, then took the stack of messages to his room. Some congratulated the new coach on making it as far as he did. Others were disappointed. One was particularly nasty. Watts had "let them down," the fan wrote. He went on to accuse Watts of being entirely unqualified for Division I college athletics. Stunned, Watts left his room and wandered the streets for several hours. He returned to the hotel, knocked on Eddie Kimball's door, and offered his resignation.

Kimball refused. He told Watts, "We think you're ready," and sent him to bed.[23] The next day, the two losers of the first round played for third place in the Western bracket, and BYU thumped UCLA 83–62. Stan Watts shook the hand of his fellow novice head coach, UCLA's John Wooden. Then he took his team back to Provo, where the team's boosters, wealthy fans simply excited that the team had made the trip to Kansas City, had already begun raising money to build a real basketball arena on campus.

There was a fine consolation waiting for Watts the next year. In the early years of college basketball, the National Invitation Tournament (NIT) attracted a great deal of media attention, not the least because it was held every year in New York City. It was regarded as particularly prestigious because, while the NCAA tournament was made up of the winners of conference championships, the NIT's organizers hand-picked their competitors. The teams all flew to New York, where the tournament was held on the floor of Madison Square Garden, the court the professional New York Knickerbockers had just begun to use.

In 1951, a year after being knocked out in the first round of the NCAA tournament, Stan Watts's BYU team won the National Invitation Tournament. The win changed his life. It also changed the course of basketball at BYU.

The team came to the tournament ranked third out of twelve—strong, but by no means the favorite. And then they simply romped. In their first game they trounced St. Louis University by seventeen, then Wednesday night made the championship game by beating Seton Hall University by ten. Hy Turkin, sportswriter for the *New York Daily News*, offered praise. "This a smooth, professional looking club," he wrote, and marveled that the Cougars were as well disciplined as they were despite having "no home gym." Word about the embarrassing Training School Building had made it all the way to New York. The Cougars were "the travelingest team in college basketball" and "getting a little weary," said Turkin. But he still thought Watts had them playing sharp.[24]

The star of the team was Mel Hutchins, a center from Arcadia, California, outside Los Angeles. He was relatively short for a center—only six-foot-five at BYU (he grew an inch in the NBA)—but was a gritty defender and outstanding rebounder. Hack Miller, a sportswriter for the LDS Church-owned *Deseret News*, wrote that in part because of Hutchins, "The Cougars are running red hot defensively—just warm offensively."[25] He predicted that if BYU won, it would be because Hutchins managed to stifle the Dayton offense.

Saturday afternoon, only a few hours before the championship game, they got a telegram from George Albert Smith, president of The Church of Jesus Christ of Latter-day Saints. "Many thousands share my pride in your record. I have faith in your abilities. Play clean. Play hard. Play to win. May God bless you."[26]

Stan Watts took his team to the arena and hammered the University of Dayton. BYU won 62–43. Hutchins indeed controlled the basket. It was the school's first national championship. Two months later, propelled by his good press, Hutchins went second overall in the fifth-ever NBA draft. He went on to play seven years professionally and became the first Latter-day Saint and first BYU alumnus to be named an NBA All-Star. The next year, 1952, his sister Colleen, the former BYU homecoming queen and reigning

Miss Utah, won the Miss America beauty pageant. The year after that she married the New York Knicks guard Ernie Vandeweghe, whom she met through her brother. The two had six children and were married for nearly sixty years. Colleen attended LDS services throughout her life, the children—including NBA All-Star, coach, and executive Kiki VanDeWeghe (who changed the capitalization of his last name)—were raised in the church, and Ernie was eventually baptized in 2010. The marriage, which perhaps ultimately owed its origins to Stan Watts and that triumph over Dayton in Madison Square Garden, shows how basketball was facilitating Mormon integration into American culture.[27]

This cascade of accomplishments—the success of making the NCAA tournament and the shocking dominance in Madison Square Garden—set Stan Watts's reputation. Few expected this from a regional religious school out of Utah.

Watts coached BYU for twenty-three seasons, finally retiring to the comparatively lighter job of university athletic director at the end of the 1972 season. His all-time record at BYU stood at 371–254. He took his teams to the NCAA tournament seven times and to the NIT four times, winning the whole thing again fifteen years later in 1966. BYU won their conference eight times while he coached. Stan Watts became famous as one of American basketball's great theorists.

In fall 1951, the Cougars began playing in a new fieldhouse on BYU's campus—funded in large part by excited fans. Mel Hutchins was playing for the Tri-Cities Blackhawks, a short-lived NBA team that eventually moved to Atlanta and was redubbed the Hawks. Mormon basketball had arrived. But its arrival also signaled BYU's enmeshment in the big business basketball would soon become.

Stan Watts's Game

In the mid-twentieth century, The Church of Jesus Christ of Latter-day Saints was rapidly expanding both overseas and in the United States. David O. McKay served as president of the church for nearly twenty years, from 1951 to 1970. When he became president there were just over a million members of the church; when he died in 1970 that number had tripled. In particular, growth outside the United States had skyrocketed: 15 percent of the approximately three million Latter-day Saints in 1970 lived outside the United States.

The Cougars hoist coach Stan Watts on their shoulders in celebration of their win over New York University in the 1966 National Invitation Tournament. It was Watts's second NIT championship. *Courtesy University Archives, Harold B. Lee Library, BYU*

This growing church became somewhat unwieldy. Its leadership in Salt Lake City was facing pressures from around the world. In the 1930s and early 1940s, a sizable group of church members in Mexico claimed autonomy from Salt Lake's leadership, demanding materials in Spanish and greater native oversight—a ten-year schism that required the intervention of church president George Albert Smith to resolve. In West Africa the decolonization movement saw dozens of nations gaining their independence from European governments in thc 1950s and 1960s. Groups of Nigerians and Ghanaians began discovering LDS Church materials in those years and using them to worship. The church could not establish itself in those countries because of its long-standing policy preventing people of African descent from participating in the church's priestly leadership or worshipping in temples. Nigeria, for instance, would not issue Latter-day Saint missionaries visas to enter the country. The racism that Eugene Roberts had nurtured still sat comfortably in the church. Church leaders simply watched as groups that claimed the title "Mormon" began to spring up across West Africa.

In the early 1950s, the building department of the church, pursuing a policy of awe, spent vast amounts of money on impressive new meetinghouses in places where the faith hoped such things might attract converts. The campaign nearly bankrupted the church. Over the same years, a small group of members who insisted that the church's abandonment of polygamy at the turn of the twentieth century was a mistake were organizing and attracting media attention. Referred to as "Mormon fundamentalists," they managed to draw several thousand adherents from the LDS Church, which began excommunicating them in force in the 1930s.

By the 1960s, church leaders determined something had to be done. Thus, the correlation campaign. The program aimed at centralizing oversight and authority in the hands of the church's top leaders: its three-man First Presidency and the Quorum of the Twelve Apostles. It also stripped away independence from various other church entities like the Sunday School program and the women's organization, the Relief Society. All spending, all publications, and all decision-making in the church now required the approval of committees led by those top fifteen leaders.

The movement also promoted a culture of uniformity and orthodoxy among church members. Whereas once local wards would build their own meetinghouses, now meetinghouses were designed by a centralized church committee that issued lists of approved art that might hang on walls and approved furniture that would sit in buildings. It became the stated norm for worshippers in Mormon chapels on Sunday to wear what white-collar workers in American business would wear to the office—white shirts and ties for men, formal dresses for women. Statistics of Sunday attendance and participation in church activities went to Salt Lake City to be reviewed by a host of committees that oversaw everything from hymns to missionary work. And at church-owned employers, leaders began to implement certain standards of orthodoxy and behavior for employees, and at church-owned schools, for students.

In 1951, the First Presidency and Quorum of the Twelve, acting as the trustees of BYU, installed an attorney named Ernest Wilkinson as president. Wilkinson was gruff and seemed perpetually convinced that other people were wasting his time. He was equally as strong-willed as many of the high ecclesiastical leaders who put him in the post and frequently butted heads with them. But he shared many of the aims of the correlation movement. He served until 1971.

Wilkinson wanted BYU to become a world-class university. He sent recruiters to church gatherings. He watched as the GI Bill, national legislation that paid college tuition for World War II veterans, and the baby boom of those veterans' children, spurred massive growth in the nation's universities from the 1940s to the 1970s. He imitated what other universities were doing at BYU: raising faculty salaries in order to recruit graduates of nationally prestigious doctoral programs, launching a massive fundraising and building campaign, and coordinating all of this effort to vastly expand BYU's undergraduate population. During his tenure the number of students more than sextupled, from four thousand to twenty-five thousand. The faculty population nearly quadrupled, from 244 to more than 900. Campus grew from six buildings to more than 250.

But at the same time, Wilkinson wanted to promote uniformity and adherence to church expectations. During his administration the number of non-LDS students, though never large, steadily decreased.[28] He pursued faculty with prestigious educations and instituted the expectation that new hires hold a PhD. But he also ensured those faculty members were members of the church and pushed church leadership to allow him access to records indicating whether his faculty paid tithing to the church or not. (At that he failed.) Late in his term of office he gained permission to distribute questionnaires to the ecclesiastical leaders of students and faculty, asking about their regular attendance at services. BYU had long had an honor code similar to that of other universities, providing penalties for academic dishonesty. Over the course of the late 1960s, Wilkinson added a new code of student conduct. It included precise dress specifications, church standards on sexual practices, adherence to the Word of Wisdom, and a general ban on "immoral" behavior. Wilkinson also seized control of enforcement of these codes from a student-run honor council. Under Wilkinson, an office of professional administrators began investigating and enforcing code violations.

And thus, it should have been no surprise that early in Stan Watts's tenure, Wilkinson summoned the coach to his office and said, "Stan, there is no reason that you should not be active in the Church. You have no bad habits, your sister holds a key position as a leader in the church, and it just doesn't look right for a non-Melchizedek priesthood holder to be coaching these boys."[29]

Watts's oldest sister, LaVern, had just become president of the churchwide children's program called Primary. She would run it for two decades, leaving a lasting imprint on the church's education of youth. But her brother was not a regular church attender, never really had been, and as such had not been ordained to the Melchizedek priesthood, an office all practicing adult men in the church held.

Wilkinson, in his usual blunt way, later told a journalist that Stan Watts "took the hint."[30] Watts began attending Sunday services and was ordained to the priesthood. He later told his biographer he had considered himself a faithful member even before Wilkinson's nudge. This sort of situation was a common one in the mid-twentieth-century church. As the correlation movement took hold, attendance at Sunday meetings steadily rose. When Watts was born in the 1910s, hardly one in five church members regularly attended Sunday services, even though far more than that number considered themselves faithful to the church, paid tithes, and volunteered in its organizations. But a hundred years later, surveys showed somewhere between two-thirds and three-quarters of people who identified themselves as Latter-day Saints in a national survey said they attended services every week.[31] Regular attendance was among the behaviors promoted in the new curriculum and programming emerging from correlation, and many, like Stan Watts, followed suit.

Stan Watts's life gestures to a paradox. As the church became more modern in the mid-twentieth century—mass-produced curriculum manuals, statistics tracking, business dress—it also began to emphasize its distinctiveness. Church leaders wanted members and non-members alike to know what made its people different from other Americans. Ernest Wilkinson wanted BYU to be both things:

an outstanding modern American university and a shining symbol of Mormon particularity.

For Wilkinson, there was no tension there. But for Stan Watts, there was. The two began to butt heads over exactly what Mormon basketball should be.

Just as Wilkinson was urging Watts to be a good role model for the young men he coached by attending church regularly, Watts was pressing Wilkinson to make BYU basketball more like that of other NCAA schools. For years the president of the university, and many of its athletic staff, had held firm to the position that BYU's teams should be recruited from the students who were already attending the school and should receive no benefits other than those the sport itself offered. Students should play for the moral virtues of the game, not for any sort of compensation.

Many in BYU administration understood sports the same way, and they had allies. What historian Kurt Kemper calls the "liberal arts agenda" had some support in the NCAA in the early 1950s. Newly installed executive director Walter Byers was pushing the organization to commercialize sports, selling television rights to games and trying to market college sports to potential sponsors. But some schools—mostly small colleges, academic powerhouses like the Ivy League, and religious schools like BYU—championed instead a model of integrating athletics into education. They rejected the notion of competitive recruitment of student-athletes and warned that universities should not come to depend on athletic revenue. Instead, universities should encourage as many students as possible to participate in athletics to some degree, with the aim being the cultivation of character, not winning.[32]

Wilkinson thought this model mirrored the church itself, which operated at the local level entirely as a volunteer institution. There was no paid ministry in any ward; its administration and teaching and ministering were done entirely by the members themselves. Church leadership explained that lay government offered moral benefits. "Officers in the Church of Jesus Christ are called," wrote the apostle John Widtsoe, "to gain the development and enlarged understanding which always follow earnest service in a responsible position."[33]

Parley Christensen, an English professor and ally of Ernest Wilkinson, served for years as the chair of the university's athletics committee. At a 1950 meeting of the NCAA, Christensen spoke up in favor of the liberal arts agenda, arguing that schools with strategically designed curricula like BYU should find ways to integrate sports into the broader project of the university rather than walling off specially recruited athletes. "The value of competition certainly lay not so much in scores or ratings or physical benefits," he said of the history of sports at his university, but in "the larger life of the campus," the moral purpose of education at a Mormon university.[34]

What Christensen and Wilkinson worried about most was the growing practice of recruitment. As far back as the 1930s, the Southeastern Conference schools, where football was booming, had agreed all participating schools could offer athletes full scholarships, which covered room and board as well as tuition.[35] As competition in the NCAA tournament and the NIT grew more intense, universities began seeking out athletes and pelting them with benefits in return for their enrollment. Financial benefits were first and foremost among these, but athletes were also sometimes promised special tutoring or looser academic standards. By the 1940s and 1950s the Ivy League was regularizing its policies against such practices precisely because other schools headed in the opposite direction.

Wilkinson fully believed in what the Ivies were doing. "In college athletics, the winning of games must never be the predominant motive," he said in his inaugural address as president of BYU, six years after the Ivy League schools had signed the Group Agreement. "Athletes should neither be given special favors nor be discriminated against. Unfortunately in some universities," he went on, "there has been a double standard."[36]

Watts didn't necessarily disagree. He also believed that athletics could inculcate moral virtue. But at the same time he wanted to win, and the nation was moving with him and against Wilkinson. In 1957 the NCAA agreed that universities could offer full scholarships of the Southeastern Conference sort. And thus emerged the great conundrum that Watts struggled to balance in his two decades as head basketball coach at Brigham Young University.

A couple of years after both he and Wilkinson moved into their offices on campus, Watts wrote the president pleading letters. "Unless we have similar opportunity to attract the outstanding athletes and to have an equal chance with our opponents our athletic program will decline rapidly," he said. He hastened to clarify that he was still seeking young men who were members of the church who would abide by the Honor Code and receive ecclesiastical endorsements, but he worried about losing those players to the University of Utah or Utah State University. Eventually Wilkinson grumpily acceded and extended the athletic scholarship program, authorizing more than a hundred grants to student-athletes.

That surrender was substantive but also symbolic. It meant not only that athletes at BYU would be treated like athletes at any other university in the country, but also that the ideal Christensen and Roberts had insisted upon—that winning was secondary to the cultivation of souls—was growing increasingly difficult to maintain. But Stan Watts insisted it was still there. "The kids stuck with their principles and in no way made any compromise of them," he said, reflecting upon the hundreds of players he had coached after announcing his retirement in 1972.[37]

Watts's efforts to balance idealism and ambition made him in demand among members of the national basketball community. For ten years he served on the board of directors of the National Association of Basketball Coaches and was the organization's president in 1970. In 1972 he was the chair of the United States Olympic Committee for men's basketball, charged with guiding the selection of the team and coaches who would represent the country at the 1976 Olympic Games. Over the course of his career he was invited to give basketball clinics in Brazil, Turkey, Yugoslavia, and across the United States and Europe.

After a decade at BYU, Watts tried to distill thoughts on basketball into a book for a general audience. *Developing an Offensive Attack in Basketball* was published by Prentice Hall in 1959. Watts had cultivated a reputation for an aggressive, scoring-centric style of play based on what he and other coaches began to call the fast break—an attempt to rush the ball up the court and score very quickly before the opposing team could get its defense ready. His teams were renowned for their offense.

Yet Watts insisted that though the system prioritized scoring, it was a mistake to think it elevated individual players. Instead, winning came through moral commitment to community. "Basketball, probably more than any other sport, requires teamwork of the highest degree," he explained, closely echoing James Naismith. "Individualists," unfortunately, "will in most cases never experience the thrills that accompany a team championship."[38] And in addition to pages diagramming various sorts of fast breaks and the many forms a defense might take, Watts devoted an entire chapter to the morality a coach should try to instill in his players.

Some of those values were imported from his faith. Many basketball coaches undoubtedly counseled their players to not smoke cigarettes, but Watts went further. He recommended "refraining from the use of alcohol, tobacco, and harmful drugs. It is our opinion that young athletes will also be better off without the use of tea and coffee."[39] As did many Latter-day Saints in the mid- and late-twentieth century, Watts couched this counsel in vaguely medical terms, worrying about "extra strain," but the particulars were drawn directly from the Word of Wisdom, the dietary code of his church.

In a media guide he wrote introducing BYU basketball to the press, Watts was even more explicit. He claimed that BYU had a distinct "philosophy of basketball." He began the guide with a condemnation of "the mad rush of the population today" and a promise that basketball could alleviate such moral disorder. In Watts's estimation, mid-twentieth-century American society encouraged young people to pursue bad habits of consumption, pleasure-seeking, selfishness, and self-indulgence. He worried about young people staying up too late, going to too many parties, and sacrificing self-discipline on the altar of laziness.[40]

Instead, Watts said that success on the court and in life generally occurred only when a player decided to "place certain values in life on a higher plane." He explained that BYU sponsored a basketball team mainly to help its players "prepare for experiences of later life." He put them on a strict regimen of physical care—no juices (too much sugar); ten hours of sleep a night (as many as possible before midnight); regular "elimination"; and, of course, no coffee, tea, alcohol, or tobacco.

But more than that, Watts tried to inculcate in his players

self-sacrifice, not simply as an ideology, but as a practice. He told his players to raise their hands every time they committed a foul or other violation on the court, even before the referee might blow the whistle. He coached them to help opposing players up when they fell down. He told his assistant coaches that their role was not simply to teach young men how to play basketball but also, analogous to the job of older men in any ward, to inculcate in them moral virtue through modeling behavior as well as through instruction in activities. That virtue was centered, ultimately, around the idea of respect—for oneself, to be sure, but mainly for others on the court, both teammates and opponents. "This is the philosophy we have tried to instill in our athletes at Brigham Young University," Watts wrote in an essay to the young men of the church. "The same things may be applied to our everyday living in helping to serve God."[41]

In a sense, Stan Watts was always coaching church ball.

Ćosić

The pride and joy of Stan Watts's career at BYU—and really of Mormon basketball to that point—was Krešimir Ćosić, the first in a long string of players that by the early twenty-first century made the Balkans a basketball powerhouse. By the 2020s, the Serbian Nikola Jokić was generally considered the greatest basketball player in the world, closely followed by the Slovenian Luka Dončić. Before them there was the center Vlade Divac and the offensive wizard Dražen Petrović, and before them, Krešimir Ćosić, a Croatian who became the third non-American to be inducted into the Basketball Hall of Fame. The championship trophy in the Croatian professional league is named after him. And he played for Stan Watts at BYU.

To Watts and other Mormon leaders, Ćosić and his story embodied all the values they hoped basketball would inculcate. He also happened to be probably the best player Stan Watts ever coached.

In 1958, BYU became the first Division I basketball program to have a foreign-born basketball player join its team, a native Finn named Timo Lampén. The church missionary program's fostering of basketball in Finland had paid off handsomely. A few years later, another Finn, Veikko Vainio, was starring on his national team and followed Lampén to BYU.

Krešimir Ćosić was named to the Communist Yugoslavian national team as a teenager. He later fled Yugoslavia, played for BYU from 1970 to 1973, and was twice drafted by NBA teams. He returned to his native country and became a central figure in the development and spread of both basketball and his adopted church in his homeland. *Courtesy BYU Photo*

In fall 1967, Vainio met Krešimir Ćosić at the International Basketball Federation's European tournament in Helsinki, Finland. Ćosić, who would turn nineteen that fall, was playing for Yugoslavia, an amalgamated country created in the wake of World War I that incorporated Croatia, Slovenia, and several other Balkan nations. By the 1960s the communist dictatorship of Marshal Josip Tito had controlled the country for years. Ćosić had been a long-time celebrity in Yugoslavia, playing basketball professionally and for the national team since he was sixteen. Vainio's Finland team took silver in that tournament, but the next year Yugoslavia won silver at the Summer Olympics in Mexico City. Ćosić, still young, played a bit on that team.

Vainio met Ćosić when their basketball paths crossed here and there across Europe. Once in Paris, they were roommates. Vainio told Ćosić about playing basketball in the United States, BYU, and Stan Watts. Ćosić knew about American college basketball. He had been following John Wooden's powerhouse UCLA teams for a decade by then, like just about anybody else who enjoyed basketball. And like many of the people under the Yugoslavian regime, he bristled at Marshal Tito's brutality. He decided that at a tournament in Italy the next year, he would flee to the United States and attend either BYU or UCLA.

By that point he had been writing letters to both schools and there were officials at each working on visas and the red tape of international travel during the Cold War. But neither school was expecting him imminently. Ćosić simply took matters into his own hands. He slipped away during the closing party for the tournament, took a cab to the airport, and decided on the spot that he would go to Salt Lake City. On a layover in New York City, he called the number he had for BYU's athletics department and left a message on the answering machine in broken English. "In New York. Be there soon. Collect me please."

Stan Watts and his staff were stunned. It was early October 1969; school had already begun. Ćosić spoke very little English. Fortunately there was another Croatian on campus—Zdravko Mincek, a tennis player—and Watts sent him and an assistant coach to the airport to fetch Ćosić. He assigned Mincek to be Ćosić's roommate and began working to integrate the young Croat player into campus.

It was a rough go. Ćosić had somehow missed that BYU was a religious school. He was not aware that Wilkinson's rigorous Honor Code forbade alcohol or tobacco, not to mention premarital sex. Ćosić was a big personality who enjoyed beer and had a reputation on the Yugoslavian team as a partier. By early 1970, he was stuck on BYU's freshman team, not even coached by Stan Watts himself. He didn't like the atmosphere of the school and was ready to head home. He told Mincek's girlfriend, Christina, that he was going back to Yugoslavia over the summer and was so annoyed he planned on simply vanishing, the same way he had in Italy. "Nobody knows, because I'm not coming back," she remembered him saying.[42]

The next day, Ćosić was back in Christina's rooms complaining that Stan Watts's staff had discovered his plans. He felt trapped. In frustration, he told her that he had even been dreaming about BYU's mountains. He was rather stunned when she told him her father would say that the dream was a sign from God.

So Ćosić showed up at Christina Nibley's father's office on campus.

Hugh Nibley turned sixty that spring. He had earned a PhD from the University of California, Berkeley, writing a dissertation on religion in ancient Rome and picking up several languages. He served in the US Army during World War II, and afterward returned to Utah, where he paid his Ukrainian roommate for every word of English his roommate heard him say. Nibley wanted to teach himself Russian. In 1946 he became a professor of history and religion at BYU. He published a number of significant articles on early Christianity, and after Berkeley offered him a professorship in 1960, BYU scrambled to keep him, giving him more research funds and freedom from teaching classes he found dull.

By the time he met Krešimir Ćosić, Nibley was writing less and less for scholars and more and more for his church community, theorizing on the Book of Mormon and what ancient Christianity might mean for contemporary Christians.. He earned a reputation as the church's greatest intellectual. On an increasingly conservative campus he was famous for his outspoken pacifism, belief in Christian socialism, and disdain for the obsession with conventional middle-class respectability that he felt was driving the correlation movement. He was a mystic, a prototypical absent-minded professor (stories circulated about the legendary disarray of his front yard), and a legend in the church.

Ćosić knew none of this when he knocked on Nibley's office door. But the two men ended up talking for several hours about dreams and visions and God. Ćosić was delighted when Nibley spoke Russian; the émigré had learned the language in school as a boy, and his Russian was better than his English. Nibley fully concurred with Ćosić's frustrations about the Honor Code and took out a Book of Mormon. He opened it up and read a passage. Ćosić didn't understand it. Nibley read it again, but this time used the Russian word "radost"—joy, in English. Ćosić understood that. Nibley told Ćosić that the fluid, physical, unconscious collaborations with his teammates that made Ćosić feel alive on the basketball court created joy, and that was what religion really was.

Ćosić was fascinated. He came back, and Nibley took him to lunch. Over the next few weeks the sight of the six-foot-eleven Croatian and the five-foot-seven professor wandering campus deep in conversation became common. Ćosić became a regular visitor at the Nibley home, and in November 1971 he asked Nibley to baptize him. To avoid publicity the ritual was done in secret at Temple Square in Salt Lake City. Ćosić skipped basketball practice to do it; the coaches didn't know where their player was until they saw him the next day.

After his baptism, Ćosić did not simply become a Latter-day Saint but an enthusiastic, devoted Latter-day Saint. His faith orbited around what Nibley had put his finger on—a sense of joy in communion with others, in cooperation, in building something together. As Nibley recalled later, Ćosić's joy was "the spontaneous childlike happiness of sharing an eager awareness of each other," the sort of joy that manifested when he and a teammate completed a fast break with no communication other than eye contact, or that followed a no-look pass turning into an assisted basket.[43] Ćosić himself said that after his conversations with Nibley, "I realized I was not alone."[44]

Meanwhile, Ćosić moved to the varsity team and was flourishing on the court. He was a natural fit for Watts's fast-break offense. At six-eleven, he was the height of a center, the sort of player that generally hangs around the basket to rebound missed shots and get easy dunks. But he was also a gifted dribbler and passer, with deft coordination despite his gangling height. He liked to catch a rebound and simply turn and drive headlong for the opposite basket, perhaps tossing a pass at the very last moment. Or he would simply stop and take a deep jump shot, which players his size were definitely not supposed to do. It sometimes frustrated the guards on his team who were used to handling the ball for most of the time and passing it to big players like Ćosić.

One former teammate remembered a particular play in December 1971, a month after Ćosić's baptism. "Ćosić took a long rebound and drove the ball the length of the court, took the ball around his back, faked a pass to the right and then threw a behind-the-back bounce pass to a streaking player on the left for a layup."[45]

During timeouts he would wander back toward his team's bench singing loudly in Croatian, cracking jokes, clapping hands, waving fists in the air, laughing. Joy. By the time he graduated he was BYU's all-time leading scorer and rebounder. He still holds the school's record for most double-doubles and most games with more than 15 rebounds. By the end of the 1971–72 school year, he was averaging 22.3 points—the most in the Western Athletic Conference, which BYU had joined in 1962—and 12.8 rebounds per game. He was named WAC player of the year. That summer the Portland Trail Blazers selected him with the 10th overall pick in the NBA draft.

Ćosić decided to spend another year at BYU instead of joining the NBA. The next summer, the Los Angeles Lakers tried drafting him. But he declined to move to Los Angeles. Instead he wanted to go back to Croatia and play for Zadar, the hometown team he had played for as a teenager. He was homesick, but he also wanted to bring the message of joy back to Croatia. He translated the Book of Mormon into Croatian, pressured the Yugoslavian government to allow missionaries, and smuggled religious tracts into the country. Because he was so gifted, the government forgave his desertion, and Ćosić played in four straight Olympic Games for Yugoslavia, finally winning a gold medal in 1980. After that he coached the national team for a decade. When the Yugoslavian government collapsed in 1992, Croatia became an independent nation, and Ćosić became his country's deputy ambassador to the United States. He died of cancer in that job in 1995.

While reporting on his sickness, a Utah newspaper called Ćosić a "modern-day pioneer" in more ways than one. He helped open the American college game to foreign players. He took his newfound faith to Croatia. But, as Stan Watts told *The Boston Globe*, Ćosić really understood what Watts was trying to do. "He was so much fun" to play with, to coach, to watch. He brought joy to his teammates and his audience. He understood the "joie de vivre" of the game. "Basketball, to him, was an art form," the *Globe* wrote, and he made it an art for others too.[46]

In 1971, the Marriott Center opened on BYU campus. The new basketball arena funded by the wealthy hotelier family it was named for sat 23,000—far from the Training School Building's narrow margins around the court and the most of any college basketball arena in the country. The saying went on campus: Stan Watts built it, the Marriotts paid for it, and Krešimir Ćosić filled it.

Protest

Krešimir Ćosić's ecstatic embrace of a communitarian, joyful, physical faith, embodied as much in what he did on the court as in the chapel he worshipped in, represented the apex of Stan Watts's fusion of basketball and Mormonism. Even better, Ćosić showed that a religious understanding of basketball could coexist with the emerging professionalization of the game. By the early 1970s college teams were recruiting players from around the globe and competing furiously in conference tournaments, all with an eye to potential careers with a professional team or in the international apparatus that governed the game. Ćosić's career seemed to show that BYU could do all of these things.

And yet at the same time, Stan Watts was feeling the tension between the growing professionalization of the game and the particularities of the Mormon community. Eventually, despite all his efforts, that tension burst onto the court.

The igniting issue was race. For more than a hundred years by that point, the leaders of The Church of Jesus Christ of Latter-day Saints had elaborated on a policy first publicly enunciated by Brigham Young, the second president of the church, in 1852. Reversing the church's practice under founder Joseph Smith, Young declared that men of Black African descent were ineligible to hold the church's priesthood. Subsequent church leaders concluded Young also meant people of African descent could not fully participate in the church's temples, where an initiation rite called the endowment was given to all adult members of the church and where marriages between church members were solemnized, or "sealed," for eternity.

So over the next few decades church leaders told missionaries not to seek out Black people in the United States and did not attempt to send missionaries to Black African countries, due both to hesitance on their part and the policies of those nations restricting missionary work. Brigham Young had said that Black people were cursed because they were descended from Cain, and that belief was widespread in the church in the mid-twentieth century, repeated by white church members and leaders alike.

In 1966, the church-owned publisher Deseret Book put out *Mormon Doctrine*, a new edition of a book originally published in 1958. It would sell thousands of copies and receive a third edition in 1978. The author, Bruce R. McConkie, was a prominent church leader and a son-in-law of Joseph Fielding Smith, who became president of the church in 1970. McConkie bluntly claimed that "The whole negro race have been cursed with a black skin, the mark of Cain, so they can be identified as a caste apart, a people with whom the other descendants of Adam should not intermarry," and who were "barred from holding the priesthood."[47]

Despite these restrictions, by the time Stan Watts was coaching at BYU dozens of Black members had joined or even been born into the church. Black students came to BYU and succeeded. BYU's first Black student, Norman Wilson, earned a master's degree in agricultural economics in 1939. He was not a member of The Church of Jesus Christ of Latter-day Saints, but others who followed him were. By the 1950s and 1960s a number of African American and African students had enrolled at the university. They were welcomed, in part, because church leaders hoped to explore the possibility of future conversions in Africa.

At the same time, the growing Black freedom movement in the United States was drawing attention to the church's restrictions and the racist rationales behind them. A week after the Supreme Court's 1954 *Brown v. Board of Education* decision, BYU president Wilkinson wrote to a high church leader that the student body was very interested in the debate. "The Negro Question," Wilkinson wrote, "arises more frequently and gives us more trouble than any other."[48]

The students seemed generally sympathetic to the decision, Wilkinson thought. But he also knew that many of the church's top leaders were, like himself, wary of the movement, worried that social tumult was fomenting, and believed that American society would be much more stable if Black Americans simply accepted second-class status.

Because of those beliefs, Wilkinson and his administrators became very cautious about sports. Basketball was particularly dangerous because the audience was so close to the court and the players' expressions were not obscured by masks or hats. Emotions rode close to the surface.

On February 4, 1961, a tussle broke out among the players in a BYU road game against Utah State University. USU was winning easily when a frustrated BYU player, Bob Wilson, fouled out of the game. Wilson blamed the call on Utah State player Max Perry and rushed at him. The two threw punches. Other players entered the fray. According to newspapers, BYU center Dave Eustis, who was white, confronted Utah State forward Darnel Haney, who was Black. Haney threw a punch at Eustis, who did not respond in kind. Students poured onto the floor, and the game was paused until the arena could be cleared.[49]

Wilkinson saw what might be coming. Late that night he desperately pulled together a meeting with the USU president, Stan Watts, and the Utah State coach. The next day the men issued a statement claiming remarkable insight into the minds of the players. It stated that the fracas "was not triggered by any racial animosity on the part of the players, but was a case of individual controversy between certain players."[50] But regardless of this effort, as the 1960s went on the number of voices critical of the church's racial restrictions and promoting social equality increased, including nationally prominent members of the church like George Romney, governor of Michigan, and Sterling McMurrin, John F. Kennedy's commissioner of education. Romney strongly endorsed strengthened civil rights laws and received a letter from an LDS apostle admonishing him for doing so; McMurrin publicly criticized the restrictions.

The church's racist policies were increasingly well-known, and BYU sports was perhaps the major public venue where disputes were aired. In April 1968, only nine days after the assassination of Martin Luther King, Jr., seven Black athletes from the University of Texas at El Paso refused to participate in a track meet against BYU. They said it was because BYU's athletes believed Black people "are inferior and that we are disciples of the devil."[51] By October of that year, several members of the San Jose State College football team made it known that they would be boycotting their November 30 game against BYU. They had a series of concerns, for instance, wanting San Jose to hire a Black coach. But they also did not want to play BYU.

Wilkinson agonized. He and the trustees of BYU considered canceling the game but decided not to because it would look like backing down and hence an admission of guilt. When the game went forward, seven Black players refused to take the field for San Jose State, and protestors wielded signs outside. Newspapers noted the low attendance.[52]

By this point the *Daily Universe*, BYU's student newspaper, was roiling. A survey showed that 65 percent of the students wanted BYU to recruit Black athletes. The article quoted a student saying that Wilkinson and his team "don't want negroes to socialize with our girls."[53] Students organized a "Brotherhood Week" with faculty panels on racism, but the administration blocked several speakers students wanted to bring to campus. Other students told the paper they backed the church and BYU administration. Wilkinson angrily informed the newspaper that any articles dealing with race had to be cleared by his office before publication. He went to the Quorum of the Twelve and First Presidency, asking permission to issue a statement on BYU's policy on recruitment. The church's top leaders fell into disputes among themselves and finally concluded no statement should be issued.

By the next fall, students at other institutions in the Western Athletic Conference, particularly at the University of New Mexico, were pressuring their administrations to refuse to play BYU and even to drop the school from the conference. The football games that fall were rough. In October 1969, hundreds of student protestors heckled BYU players as they walked into the Arizona State University stadium. A few weeks later, fourteen players on the University of Wyoming team told their coach they wanted to wear black armbands during a game against BYU. The coach removed the players from the team. At a game against the University of Texas at El Paso on October 25, fights broke out between protestors and fans, leading to five arrests. Two weeks later, the entire San Jose State team wore black armbands to their game against BYU. Then Stanford University announced it would no longer play BYU.

And then basketball season began.

For many opposing teams, Eugene Roberts's legacy of imagining basketball as a tightly regimented team sport that deemphasized the individual and elevated community—and particularly as a vehicle for cultivating the virtues of young white men—was a profound misinterpretation of basketball. For them, it had become a vehicle to express their desires for social change. On January 8, 1970, the University of Arizona rejected a petition from civil rights organizations to cancel a game against BYU. Coach Bruce Larson summoned a meeting of the Arizona team—which had three Black players in its starting five—and asked the players what they wanted to do. According to Larson, they told him "they wanted to play the game but expressed sympathy for the protest." They asked Larson if they could wear black armbands, and Larson said, "That would be all right." He told the media, "They feel they have to do something to show their support." Eddie Myers, the Black starting center for Arizona, emerged from the meeting and told the media, "We will play the game." And they wore black armbands.[54]

Bruce Larson was a Latter-day Saint, and that he understood the game in a somewhat different way than Eugene Roberts or Ernest Wilkinson was a sign of basketball's malleability.

A month later at Colorado State University, the BYU team took the court to the sight of a banner that read "Bigot Young University." The BYU team and cheerleaders endured screamed profanities, thrown food and raw eggs, and threats. Fights broke out when more than a hundred protestors commandeered the floor during a BYU cheerleader routine at halftime, and a newspaper photographer was knocked out by a thrown tire iron. Someone tossed a Molotov cocktail that burst into flames. Police arrested seven people.

Stan Watts was furious. We shouldn't get him entirely wrong. His beliefs about decency and good sportsmanship had long led him to endorse the notion that his players should treat all people with respect. All the way back in 1950, Watts lavished glowing praise on Jim Richey, a BYU player who stopped a fast break in a game against the City College of New York. Richey had collided with Ed Warner, a Black player, who fell to the ground. Richey noticed the fall, turned, and helped Warner up, sacrificing an easy bucket to do so. Watts said that Richey had done the right thing and that he hoped his players would show such respect to anybody they played against.

But Watts missed how such gentlemanly personal behavior did little to address the very real injustices that Black people in America

Student protestors swarm the court during a 1970 basketball game between Colorado State University and BYU. They denounced the LDS Church's policy restricting Black people's full participation in the church. *Courtesy Colorado State University Libraries*

faced. Like many of the LDS leaders he followed, Watts was in the abstract sympathetic to discrimination and suffering, but in practical terms prized social order and respectability to such a degree that he recoiled from any sort of disturbance of the peace. As he saw it, there was nothing valuable or useful in the protests that made that 1970 season so terrible for him. He sneered at the protestors, labeling them "trained militants" who didn't truly represent the communities they claimed to advocate for. "It's deeper than BYU or the Mormon church," he told a group of BYU faculty. "These people aren't after us. They're after America."[55]

These sorts of accusations were common among white conservatives, and most leadership in the LDS Church fit that category. The sort of lawbreaking Martin Luther King, Jr., mounted was strictly pacifist; King called it passive resistance. He and his followers would sit in places where Black people were forbidden, march in peaceful protest, and occupy public spaces. But to many white people, even these careful actions were too disruptive and radical. The protests in

Colorado went far beyond anything King would have sanctioned, and yet Watts's accusations were the same. The notion that Black people on the streets were "trained," not sincerely seeking equality but rather out to disrupt society, was the sort of thing that the deeply reactionary director of the FBI, J. Edgar Hoover, believed. He accused Martin Luther King of being a communist out to undermine American democracy and indulged in secretive wiretapping and harassment of the civil rights leader.

Some LDS leaders, like Wilkinson and the apostle Ezra Taft Benson, agreed with Hoover. It is not surprising that Stan Watts, close to Wilkinson, shared their paranoia.

As the 1970 season limped to a close, Stan Watts's team played the University of Wyoming in a deeply awkward game at which ten uniformed policemen surrounded the court. Then the Cougars finally visited the University of New Mexico, where the same student protestors who had urged the administration to get BYU thrown out of the Western Athletic Conference pelted the court with eggs and other raw food. The game was delayed forty minutes for cleanup.

The team ended the year with a record of 8–18, seventh in the Western Athletic Conference. It was the worst season of Watts's career. Only once before had he failed to win at least ten games. He wasn't sleeping well; several times during the season the assistant coach who shared a hotel room with Stan when the team traveled woke up to find the head coach sitting on the side of the bed grimacing with stomach pain. His doctor told him that he was on the verge of an ulcer. He had been coaching the team for two decades, was nearly sixty, and was exhausted. On March 27, three weeks after the end of the season, the BYU newspaper announced that Watts had retired.

It was a close thing. Two weeks later, the newspaper reversed itself, announcing that Watts would stay. Wilkinson had appointed a committee to interview potential replacements, but the administration was also leaning on Watts to change his mind, and he finally agreed. The school also hired the first Black professor, made a determined effort to recruit Black students for the 1971–72 school year, and, to Watts's relief, the protests of the previous season died down. In February 1971, the team bid farewell to the old fieldhouse in favor of the magnificent new Marriott Center, and Watts confessed he was glad to be the head coach when the building was inaugurated.

Only a few days later, though, he entered the hospital for surgery. For the entire season Watts had been fighting prostate cancer. He did not accompany teams on road trips so that he could have regular radiation treatment, but it turned out the surgery had been too long postponed. Over fourteen hours of surgery the surgeons removed his bladder, prostate, appendix, and several inches of colon, fearing the spread of the cancer.

Watts rehabilitated for the next six months and returned for one more season, in part for the joy of coaching Krešimir Ćosić. In the 1971–72 season the Cougars won twenty-one games and lost only five, winning the Western Athletic Conference championship and gaining a berth in the NCAA tournament. And then Stan Watts was truly done.

He would live nearly another thirty years. After stepping down as coach he moved into BYU administration, working as the university's athletic director until 1976. Ten years later he was inducted into the Naismith Memorial Basketball Hall of Fame.

Two years before he left BYU for good, Watts and Glenn Potter, his replacement as head coach, recruited Gary Batiste to play on the BYU team. A six-foot-three guard who transferred to BYU from a California community college, Batiste became the first Black player on BYU's team. He lasted less than one school year before leaving. He and Potter butted heads in practice, after which Potter suspended Batiste, who decided that BYU wasn't for him. "Things just didn't work out," Batiste told a Provo reporter.[56] By the 1977–78 school year, two more Black players were on the team. Keith Rice, another transfer from a California community college, played two years as a solid starter. Danny Frazier attended BYU on a football scholarship but played basketball that year because the team needed a big forward.[57]

In June 1978, Spencer W. Kimball, the president of the church, announced that policies barring Black people from priesthood office and temple attendance would be immediately reversed. Danny Frazier, who had joined the church with his family in 1974, was delighted.[58] He was ordained to the priesthood and eventually served a mission for the church.

The disjuncture between Batiste's experience and Frazier's lays bare the tensions Stan Watts managed better than most: the balance between Mormons' sense of their own particularity and the centrifugal forces of national culture. Sometimes that particularity strengthened the church in general and BYU basketball in particular, as when its promises brought Krešimir Ćosić joy; sometimes, as with the painful issues of race, it handicapped the church and BYU with it. Those tensions only increased as the twentieth century went on. That BYU was celebrating one or two Black players at a time when many other universities were starting five Black players on the court was telling. BYU didn't manage that until 2022.

4

AINGE, JIMMER, AND THE PRESSURE OF THE SPOTLIGHT

On December 17, 1996, the administration at Brigham Young University ruined Roger Reid's Christmas. Reid, who was the men's basketball coach, claimed later that his abrupt firing that day, midway through the season, was a shock. It did seem like a confusing decision. Reid was homegrown. Like Stan Watts, he had risen through the ranks of Utah high school coaching before finding his way onto the coaching staff at BYU and finally being handed the top job in 1989. And he was undoubtedly the most successful coach since Watts himself. The team had drifted a bit, going through three coaches in only a few years before hitting upon Reid, who stayed a while. Even though the team kept winning at a decent clip, its coaches kept leaving, retiring, resigning, or being fired. Reid finally seemed like a steady hand. He had won 152 games and lost only 77—an even higher percentage than Watts. He took the team to five appearances in the NCAA men's basketball tournament in the seven years before December 1996.

But the team was off to a pretty poor start that season—in fact, the worst in years. They'd lost their first four games before barely edging out a decent Utah State team. Whatever relief that earned, though, was quickly dashed. The next weekend, December 13–14, the team suffered two embarrassing home losses. On Saturday the 14th, the University of Houston whomped the Cougars by twenty points in the Marriott Center, and university officials did not miss that attendance was pretty meager. A lot of people thought it was Houston that killed Reid's career. "It's as obvious as the Cougars' 1–6 record that Reid, despite his protestations otherwise, was in trouble," wrote local sports columnist Steve Cameron.[1]

Reid could, and did, point to the fact that by December his team's guard line was decimated by injuries. But it was true also that his success had always been trailed by criticism. In particular, Reid struggled with problems similar to those that had bedeviled Stan Watts. He understood BYU basketball as more than merely another college program—he understood it as a manifestation of the community of The Church of Jesus Christ of Latter-day Saints. And as BYU basketball became ever more integrated into the brutal world of NCAA competition and media, that became a problem.

Reid grew up in Springville, Utah, a small town eight miles south of Provo, and virtually his entire career unfolded within ten miles of his hometown. He played on the Springville High School basketball team, earning all-state honors that got him scholarship offers at two Utah universities. By the early 1970s he was twenty-five and coaching at Payson High School, ten miles south of Springville. After a few years coaching in the Salt Lake City suburbs, he got the assistant coaching job at BYU in 1978. He would live in Spanish Fork, Utah, just south of campus, for the next twenty years. Reid's sons Randy and Robbie played on the Spanish Fork High School team and, like their father, earned all-state honors. Roger Reid grew up and raised his family in a small-town, community-oriented, tightly knit basketball world of the sort church ball fostered.

From a certain angle, it looked like he ran BYU the same way. By the early 1990s, both Randy and Robbie were playing for their father. Randy started games at guard for BYU teams from 1992 to 1996. Robbie joined in 1993 and was starting alongside his brother by his second year.

This was not nepotism. The Reid boys were good. A far cry from stars, to be sure. Neither would ever have any hope of playing in the NBA. But at the time of his graduation from Spanish Fork High, Randy had scored more points than any other player in recorded Utah high school history. Both Reid boys picked BYU over offers from national basketball powerhouses like the University of North Carolina and UCLA. Both were pesky defenders—they each made the all-defensive teams in the Western Athletic Conference. So Roger was hardly committing malpractice when he put them on the court. In fact, when his father was fired, Robbie transferred to

Michigan, where he played a healthy number of minutes for a nationally ranked college team.

And yet there was some grumbling. *Sports Illustrated* (in a story on BYU basketball in, ironically, the magazine's annual "swimsuit issue," which featured photographs of models in bikinis alongside stories about football or the NCAA) reported the Reid boys often heard fans yell some version of "I'd be starting too if my old man ran the program!" This was not an unheard-of taunt in the college game. A number of successful college coaches sent their own sons onto the court. Bobby Knight, whose Indiana teams won three NCAA national championships, was giving playing time to his son Pat at the same time Roger was coaching Randy and Robbie. Nonetheless, even in Utah there were rumblings that the Reid family proved that BYU basketball was irrevocably parochial.[2]

And then Roger Reid blundered in a way that confirmed these fears.

Six-foot-ten, two hundred and forty pounds, Chris Burgess dominated high school basketball in Southern California in the mid-1990s at Woodbridge High School in Irvine. In 1997 he was named the National High School Player of the Year by the *Sporting News*. Burgess was born in Provo and was a member of The Church of Jesus Christ of Latter-day Saints. While coaches from Kentucky and UCLA and Kansas and Duke—all nationally contending programs—flew to Irvine to meet the Burgesses and lure Chris to their schools, all of them suspected that Chris would choose BYU. Kentucky coach Rick Pitino tried to convince Burgess that he'd play against better competition on another team but told a local reporter he thought the tactic had failed.[3] Roger Reid likewise thought he had Burgess locked up. He had spent three years getting to know the young man. So when Burgess called him on November 18, 1996, to tell him that he was going to attend Duke, Reid was crushed.

After the phone call, several newspapers reported that Burgess said Reid had hurt his feelings. According to Burgess, the BYU coach, smarting from rejection, told the young man he had "let 9 million people down"—those nine million being the members of the church. Reid also said, "I was letting down the prophets and apostles," Burgess told a reporter.[4] When the journalists turned their microphones to Reid, the coach admitted he had told Burgess he was letting down the members of the church. "I didn't mention he'd let the prophet down," Reid said, trying to save some face.[5]

After a meeting with BYU administration, Reid called the Burgess family to apologize. A month later, he was fired.

The leadership at the university denied that Reid was canned because of the Burgess affair. The school's athletic director pointed to the disappointing season. But newspapers around the country insisted on bringing up Burgess. *Salt Lake Tribune* columnist Dick Rosetta thought that Reid "sealed his fate with LDS Church leaders through his misguided, sour grapes broadside." BYU had its work cut out for it, Rosetta said, because of Reid's "public relations failings."[6]

These were the same tensions Stan Watts faced in the unpleasant final years of his tenure. BYU's basketball success drew the spotlight to Provo more and more. And more and more, coaches and players alike had to negotiate two worlds at once. On the one hand, the small world of the church featured tightly knit communities, practices, and beliefs that sometimes appalled outsiders—as with the racist restrictions that had invited protests twenty years before—and sometimes simply bemused them, as with its dietary code that forbade coffee. But on the other hand, the world of NCAA basketball was increasingly consumed with celebrity players and character coaches who could sell copies of *Sports Illustrated* and add to the vast rivers of money sluicing through the game. These two worlds often seemed at odds.

Roger Reid was a victim of their collision. His appeal to Burgess was not so far from the kind of language that any ward coach might use to straighten out a player cursing during a church ball game. But to the American sports media, it was baffling and provincial. And BYU administrators knew it. Over and over, BYU basketball had to take a side.

The two greatest BYU players after Krešimir Ćosić were Danny Ainge and Jimmer Fredette. Both won the John R. Wooden Award, which the NCAA began in 1977. Named for Wooden, Stan Watts's friend and widely considered the greatest college basketball coach of all time, the award honors the best college player in the country. Ainge won it in 1981, the spring of his senior year. Fredette won it thirty years later in 2011, his senior year. The years between the awards marked, in some ways, the maturation of BYU basketball as a national force. But those years also saw a school still figuring out what the relationship between religion and basketball should be.

Danny Ainge

In 1977, Danny Ainge accomplished something never done before or since. Every year the NCAA collates votes from a number of journalism and coaching organizations to name outstanding college players to "All-America" teams. Since the 1950s other organizations, like *Parade* magazine and national high school coaching organizations, have done the same for high school players. That year Danny Ainge became the only high school athlete in American history named a First Team All-American in three different sports—baseball, basketball, and football. He did it while playing for the relatively obscure North Eugene High School in Eugene, Oregon, a logging town and home to the University of Oregon. Danny's father, Don, a talented athlete himself, had moved to Oregon to play football at the university and had never left. The family joined the LDS Church in the early 1960s, when Danny was four. Despite its obscurity, during Danny Ainge's junior and senior years, North Eugene High School's basketball team won fifty-one games and lost one. They took the state championship both years.

All the Ainge boys (there were three) were good at sports. Danny's older brother Doug played basketball at BYU in the 1973–1974 season, but the school's Honor Code wasn't for him, and he transferred to Linfield College, a couple hours up Interstate 5 from Eugene. The family therefore hardly had an ironclad commitment to BYU, so when it came time for Danny to pick a university, he was torn. He couldn't decide which sport to play, or if he should go to college or simply become a professional athlete right away. Danny hoped he could play two sports at the same time, which might mean college. And then in January of 1977, before Danny graduated from high school, Major League Baseball's Toronto Blue Jays selected him in the annual MLB draft. This meant that they had the exclusive rights to sign him if he wanted to play professional baseball. They were offering him around $100,000 a year.

That was tempting. But at the same time, as Ainge remembered later, "a lot of people said football was my best sport," and a good number of college football coaches were calling the Ainge house.[7] After some deliberation, though, the Ainges decided that Danny, even though he was six-foot-four, was probably too skinny to survive the bruising he would take in college football. He settled on basketball, and the Ainges politely told the football recruiters they could stop calling.

Several college teams sniffed around. UCLA coach Gene Bartow met with Danny. Dick Harter, the coach at the University of Oregon, offered him a scholarship, and Don Ainge pushed his son to take it. But then Frank Arnold, now coaching BYU, came to Eugene and told Danny that he'd give him a scholarship but that Danny would have to earn playing time on the team. Danny said he was revved up by the challenge, and when he visited Provo he liked the school far more than the Oregon campus. He told reporter Peter May that at Oregon "there were all these parties with booze and pot and I didn't feel comfortable."[8]

So he picked BYU. Then his family started getting angry letters and late-night phone calls from Oregon fans, so Don Ainge moved them to California. The move signaled that the Ainges were convinced that Danny's career would be promising. The Ainges found a loophole in NCAA rules—Danny could indeed play college basketball at BYU while also taking a contract from the Toronto Blue Jays because they weren't the same sport and because Danny would be playing baseball outside the school year. For the next four years, Danny played college basketball in the winter and professional baseball in the summer.

And he attracted media attention.

Part of the reason was that despite Frank Arnold's try at curbing Ainge's confidence, it was clear the young man was the best player BYU had from the moment he joined the team.

He averaged twenty-one points a game his freshman year, starting as the lead scoring guard in BYU's backcourt. He was in a neck-and-neck race for the freshman scoring title across all of college basketball that year and lost it only when he slumped a bit at the end of that first season. Alan Taylor, a center and BYU's second-leading scorer, averaged fourteen points per game. But the team was not good—they won twelve games and lost eighteen.

It's a cliché of sorts—a team with a single offensive wizard who scores at will but can't help his woeful squad to victories. Coaches know why. Teams like that are predictable. Their opponents know who will be getting the ball. They also know it's impossible for a single player to score every point needed for the team to win. Danny Ainge could put up thirty points (as he did several times), but if the opposing team could keep everybody else on the team from playing well, BYU would lose. This was precisely the sort of basketball James Naismith shook his head over. From the very beginning of the sport, if a team wanted to win, it had to figure out how to maximize the talents of all five players and to weave their skills together. That was what Eugene Roberts had meant when he said he didn't care if BYU won games so long as his players learned how to work together. Krešimir Ćosić had understood this too—the Croatian was a magnificent scorer, of course, but his real joy on the court was making the right pass and maximizing his teammates' potential.

The next season, 1978–79, two talented freshman forwards, Devin Durrant and Fred Roberts, joined the team, and Frank Arnold and Danny Ainge started figuring things out. Arnold began drawing up more plays to get Ainge's teammates involved in the offense. Ainge's scoring average dropped to just over 18 points a game, but his percentages went up. He was taking two fewer shots per game than he had his freshman season, but he was making nearly the same number. He wasn't dribbling and holding the ball as much as he used to, but he was doing better things with it when he had it. Ainge was playing smarter basketball.

But he could still simply score, apparently whenever he wanted to. Two days before Christmas 1978, Oral Roberts University's basketball team visited Provo and was run out of the Marriott Center, losing 120–104. Danny Ainge scored forty points. Though he had two years left at BYU, he would never score that many points again. He made fifteen of his nineteen shot attempts—the sort of shooting percentage one would expect from a big center who had only to stand near the basket and dunk the ball whenever he caught it. But Ainge was mostly shooting jump shots and driving to the basket. After the game, Lake Kelly, the coach for Oral Roberts University, simply sighed. "Ainge is the best white player I have ever seen," he said.[9]

The game was a useful microcosm of how Ainge was beginning to play. "Our defense allowed me to score as much as I did," he said.

"It's never intentional when I score that many points."[10] Reporters credited his success to taking good, open shots, mostly layups under the basket and jump shots with no defender trying to stop him. And he got those sorts of shots for two reasons—because of BYU's excellent passing and because BYU's defense stopped the Oral Roberts offense and moved the ball back to their own basket fast, before Oral Roberts could set up its defense. It was a fast-break offense, the sort that Stan Watts had perfected, designed to get as many players as possible involved and confuse the opposing defense. Danny Ainge was wide open, over and over again, but he was wide open because of Fred Roberts and Steve Trumbo and Steve Craig. He was open because of his teammates.

Jerry Pimm, coach of BYU's Western Athletic Conference rival, the University of Utah, summed it up. His team had thumped BYU in the last game of the Cougars' disappointing 1977–78 season. But the next year, a month after Ainge wreaked havoc against Oral Roberts, the Cougars visited the Utah team on their own court in Salt Lake City and walked out with a win. A month later Utah came to the Marriott Center and was beaten by 26 points, 76–50. Pimm shook his head. "Ainge could be the most prolific career scorer in WAC history," he said, "if he wasn't such a terrific team player."[11]

It was not as though Utah's players were pushovers. BYU finished that season with twenty wins and seven losses and had the best record of all the teams in the Western Athletic Conference. But Utah was only a game behind in conference play and two games behind overall, at 20–10. Yet the Cougars routed them. That year, Danny Ainge made it to his first NCAA tournament. They lost in the first game they played, but it was clear the team was on its way.

The next year, 1979–80, the Cougars were even better. The team was nearly identical, anchored by Danny Ainge, Devin Durrant, and Fred Roberts, but all three were older and more experienced. Ainge's statistics were nearly identical, but the team had settled into a humming buzzsaw. They won twenty-three games and lost five, ending the season at twelfth in the national Associated Press college basketball rankings. Of 265 American college basketball teams, the Cougar offense averaged the tenth-most points.

But then they lost in the first game they played in the NCAA tournament. Again. And Danny Ainge didn't seem to show up. He played badly, and Marion Dunn, the sports editor for the *Provo Daily Herald*, BYU's hometown paper, threw down the gauntlet.

"You can carry this sportsmanship thing a bit too far," he complained. "This is, after all, a capitalist country."[12]

Dunn's protest was tongue-in-cheek, but his grievance was serious. BYU lost to Clemson University, 71–66. Though the South Carolina school would become a basketball power to be reckoned with over the next two decades, in 1980 Clemson was not terribly well-known. It was a regional agricultural college, not even the state's flagship institution. In 1980 it enrolled ten thousand students, many into its notable forestry program. That was the first year Clemson appeared in the NCAA tournament. Coach Bill Foster, ran the team from 1975 to 1984, slowly amassing a track record of finding outstanding players other college programs had overlooked. In the next few years he discovered the Grant brothers, Horace and Harvey, who were unheralded out of high school. The two eventually played in the NBA, and Horace won three championships as Michael Jordan's bruising enforcer on the Chicago Bulls in the early 1990s.

The Clemson team Danny Ainge ran into was built around two similar players. Neither Larry Nance nor Billy Williams had received much attention from college recruiters, but both would end up drafted by NBA teams after Bill Foster got through with them. They carved up the Cougars in the tournament. Foster told a reporter for *The Salt Lake Tribune* that "we wanted to go with either Billy outside or Nance inside down the stretch," and it worked.[13] The Cougars could not stop the two stars. Nance scored sixteen points and Williams twenty-four. Both made well over half the shots they took, and between the two of them they scored more than half their team's total points. Danny Ainge, on the other hand, made five of his twelve shots and scored only thirteen points. Devin Durrant and Fred Roberts, his two running mates, performed even worse. Alan Taylor, the center who had been with Ainge since the guard was drafted, stepped up and scored twenty-seven points, but it was a losing effort.

Frank Arnold complained that his team was "a dead, listless group of players."[14] They weren't doing the hard work of running the plays he wanted them to run, they were not playing cooperative defense, they weren't working together. What had worked for Danny Ainge in the past—the team basketball, clever offense, and fast breaks that were the legacy of Stan Watts's team-first approach—had been overwhelmed by Foster's surprising stars.

Perhaps all this emphasis on teamwork and discipline wasn't cutting it.

Six Seed

In March 1981, the Cougars made it to the Elite Eight. By the twenty-first century the NCAA tournament would feature more than sixty teams playing each other in a brutal and unpredictable single-elimination tournament. But even in the 1980s the tournament was earning a reputation as the most riveting sports event in the United States. NCAA executive director Walter Byers was happy with expansion. In 1981, he ensured forty-eight teams were invited. Sixteen of those forty-eight teams got to skip the first round, which meant that the second round was made up of thirty-two teams. Thirty-two to sixteen. Sixteen to the Elite Eight, to the Final Four, to the championship game. It took six games to win the championship. The Cougars won three.

BYU had never made it that far before. Stan Watts was generally proud simply to make the tournament, though he did win a game or two in it. As of 2025, the Cougars had never made it to the Elite Eight again. They did it in 1981 because of Danny Ainge—but not only because of him.

That season Ainge reverted to the form of his freshman year. His scoring jumped to twenty-four points per game. His shooting efficiency dropped, but he was still making 51 percent of his baskets, quite good for a guard. And he began taking more shots, an average of eighteen and a half a game, three more than he took his freshman year.

But even with Ainge playing like he had three years prior, the team was still very, very good. He had managed to blend his old style into BYU's team-first approach. Their record was only a tick behind the 1980 season; they lost two more games and finished second in the Western Athletic Conference. They were ranked the sixteenth-best team in the country instead of the twelfth. They were scoring the twenty-third-most points in NCAA men's basketball, down thirteen slots from the prior year. But many fans and journalists think that the 1980–81 team was the best of all Ainge's college teams. Ainge himself said, "That team was just a really well-balanced team of size and speed and shooting and skill."[15] Alan Taylor had been replaced with Greg Kite, another big center who would eventually play in the NBA. Fred Roberts had blossomed, putting up nineteen points and eight rebounds a game. The core of the team had been playing together for years by that point, and Ainge had found a way to mesh his one-man heroics into the talents of his teammates.

The bit of slippage, then, is misleading. Five days before Christmas, the team dropped its second game of the year, losing 81–65 to the University of Tennessee. At that point BYU's record was 6–2. They went 16–4 the rest of the way, and of the four remaining losses, one was by 4 points, one was by 2 points, and the others were by a single point. The team put up decisive wins against three teams ranked above them in NCAA polls, including drubbing the University of Utah team by 21 points, 96–75, in the last game of the season. The day of that game BYU was ranked sixteenth in the country, and Utah (featuring the future NBA All-Star Tom Chambers, a worthy rival of Danny Ainge), was ranked ninth.

All this is to say that the machine of BYU basketball was humming by the time the Cougars hit the tournament, and it was the machine, not merely Ainge's own brilliance, that took them as far as they got.

The first game of the tournament was against Princeton. Ainge was hurting. Three years of basketball in the winters and baseball in the summers were catching up to him. He had back spasms the day of the game, and pain showed in his play. He scored 21 points, the most on the team, but shot the ball poorly. It was Fred Roberts who stepped up, making two-thirds of his shots and single-handedly grabbing seven of his team's twenty-three rebounds. BYU won 60–51.

That was expected. BYU was a six seed in the tournament; Princeton was an eleven. From then on the tournament bracket was tougher. The next game was against UCLA. John Wooden had been retired for six years by 1981, but UCLA's basketball heritage still cast a long shadow. They finished second in the previous year's tournament. The tournament's bracket makers favored UCLA over BYU, making them a third seed. UCLA was tenth-ranked in the country overall. It didn't matter. Ainge erupted, scoring 37 points and making 14 of his 22 shots, a brilliant performance. And yet, as Ainge himself often said, he scored because Greg Kite and Fred Roberts did their jobs. UCLA coach Larry Brown said that his team lost "mostly due to BYU's defense."[16] Kite and Roberts stopped UCLA from getting easy shots at the basket. UCLA made only a third of their shots. BYU won easily, 78–55.

Notre Dame would be harder. Since taking over in 1971, coach Digger Phelps had spent a decade turning the Catholic school into a national basketball powerhouse. The Fighting Irish had made the NCAA tournament for ten years straight and had a good record, advancing past the first round every year but one. In 1978 they had been to the Final Four. In 1981 they were a second seed in the tournament and had been ranked seventh in the final Associated Press poll. Six of their players would eventually make it into the NBA, and four of those were seniors who would be selected in the NBA draft three months after the game with BYU. Danny Ainge would be drafted too, of course, but three of Notre Dame's players—Orlando Woolridge, Kelly Tripucka, and Tracy Jackson—would hear their names called before Ainge. All three had long NBA careers, and Tripucka ended up an NBA All-Star as a rookie.

All of these Fighting Irish were big and agile, from the six-six Jackson to the six-nine Woolridge. The shortest player Notre Dame started was the six-two John Paxson, who was, like his bigger teammates, a stout defender. All of the players could shoot, pass, and dribble. They threw opposing teams for a loop—no one could predict who would be doing what. BYU Coach Frank Arnold called them a "very complex club" and said that Phelps "does a lot of changing defenses," taking advantage of his players' versatility.[17]

From all apparent metrics, Phelps's strategy worked. Notre Dame controlled the game. Their defense was stifling. As they had planned, Notre Dame got Fred Roberts in foul trouble, and Ainge's beefy second fiddle played barely two-thirds of the game. Even worse, as Notre Dame player Tom Sluby remembered, the Irish "shut Ainge down the whole game."[18] John Paxson and Tracy Jackson alternated defensive responsibility for Ainge, who made only 4 shots the entire game. But even more significant, Ainge only took 10, not even half of the number he had tried against UCLA. Notre Dame kept forcing him to pass, and he scored only 12 points. Steve Trumbo, BYU's other forward, shot 1 for 8. Overall, BYU made not quite 44 percent of the shots they took—if not dire, not the percentage a winning team usually achieves.

But under those seemingly dismal numbers something else was going on. Even with Roberts in foul trouble, BYU was working together. They got more rebounds than Notre Dame. They stole the ball twice as many times. Their defense forced Notre Dame into giving up more turnovers. Woolridge and Tripucka were brilliant—the former scored 17 points on 8 for 10 shooting; the latter 14 points on 7 for 12 shooting—and overall the Fighting Irish shot 55 percent. But because BYU kept scrapping to get the ball back, even though Notre Dame's shooting percentage was ten points higher than BYU's, over the entire game both teams made the same number of shots—21.

That meant the game came down to the final possession. With ten seconds left in the game, Kelly Tripucka's jump shot put Notre Dame up a single point. Danny Ainge then grabbed the ball and without bothering to call a timeout to set up a final play rushed the entire length of the court, cut between two surprised Notre Dame defenders with a behind-the-back dribble, and went straight for Orlando Woolridge under the basket. He leapt into the air and stretched out to gently scoop the ball into the basket. The big forward had a hurt calf—he played with a tight bandage around his leg—and though he jumped and reached, his fingers were two inches short of the ball. Ainge made the layup, and the Cougars won, 51–50.

The shot was extraordinary, the sort of heroic play that made the NCAA tournament incredible television and turned Danny Ainge into a national star. A month later, Ainge won the John R. Wooden Award, naming him the best men's college basketball player in the country, and that night the Cougars celebrated madly.

And yet, there was just a hint of tension. Frank Arnold, Ainge's coach, told the reporter Marion Dunn that he was frustrated when Ainge simply took off without bothering to see if his coach wanted to organize a play. In the first half of the game, frustrated by Notre Dame's suffocating defense, Ainge tried what his coach called a "360-degree shot." With Tracy Jackson draped all over him, Ainge leapt up facing away from the basket and tried to twist around in the

Danny Ainge taking the buzzer-beating shot that sealed a victory over Notre Dame for BYU in the NCAA tournament. That basket sent his team to the tournament's Elite Eight for the first time in school history. *Courtesy BYU Photo/Doug Martin*

air to get an open look at the rim. It didn't work. Arnold told Dunn, "I was thinking, I hope Danny doesn't try that" again.[19]

The reporter observed that Arnold could laugh about the shot in the aftermath of a win. But two days later, BYU played the University of Virginia in the Elite Eight. Virginia was led by the gigantic Ralph Sampson, a seven-foot-four center who would win the Wooden award himself both of the next two years. And BYU and Ainge got frustrated. Early in the second half, the Sampson-led defense began choking off BYU's offense. Ainge started forcing it. He demanded the ball and took bad shots, making only four of his thirteen attempts. And then, after Sampson caught and dunked a missed shot, Ainge began yelling at the referees. "I thought he grabbed the rim," Ainge told a reporter afterward. That's an illegal move in college basketball. But a referee turned back to Ainge, who had been grumbling about the officiating the entire game just loud enough to be heard. The referee "thought I was complaining too much and maybe he was right," Ainge conceded afterward. Ainge was called for a technical foul. According to Frank Arnold, it "was a turning point."[20] The Virginia team pulled away and won easily, 74–60.

The NBA and Danny Ainge

And just like that, Danny Ainge's time as a Cougar was over. His career there showed the legacy of what BYU basketball as Eugene Roberts and Stan Watts imagined it might be—elevating teams over stars and prioritizing cooperation, self-sacrifice, and moral discipline—but also the frustration that some individual players could feel in such a system. His career in the NBA illustrated how that tension could accelerate the transformation that a modern commercial economy was already bringing to professional basketball in the United States.

David Stern, a lifelong New Yorker, a bulldog of an attorney, and a basketball fan from childhood, took the reins as NBA commissioner in 1984. He held the job for thirty years. When he took over the league, even its playoff games were only irregularly broadcast on national television, and professional basketball languished far behind football and baseball in the race for most popular American sport. David Stern would do for the NBA what Walter Byers did for the NCAA.[21]

By the time of Stern's retirement in 2014, the NBA trailed only professional football in popularity, and its revenue had skyrocketed. Stern personally mailed tapes of NBA games to China and Argentina, and he eventually orchestrated NBA media deals in foreign countries and recruited foreign players to join the American league. If Krešimir Ćosić had been born ten years later, David Stern would have had him playing in New York, Chicago, or another city with a lot of Croatian immigrants.

In 1990, Stern brokered a massive new television deal, preying on networks awed by the amount of attention the NCAA men's basketball tournament had received. Stern's deal moved the National Basketball Association to NBC from CBS because CBS divided its professional sports coverage between basketball and baseball. In part because it was hungry for sports, NBC promised to broadcast far more games than the fifteen per season that CBS offered. The initial contract paid the NBA $125 million a year. In 2007, Stern negotiated a new contract with Disney, which by then owned the networks ABC and ESPN. The contract paid the NBA nearly a billion dollars per year and broadcast games on both of Disney's major networks. By the 2020s, the NBA earned $3 billion per year from its television partners. That money was split nearly down the middle between the NBA's team owners and players, and they were all getting quite rich.

Every few years the players and owners negotiated a new contract and hammered out how to split that television revenue. In 2005, the players secured 57 percent of total basketball-related revenue on the basis that they had a lot to do with this surge in popularity. In 1979, Larry Bird and Magic Johnson had entered the league and quickly established themselves as two of the greatest players of all time, certainly the best of the 1980s. Their outsized personalities made them perfect tools for Stern's visions of a new way the NBA might be covered in the media. Johnson was Black, a charismatic, ebullient guard, and the embodiment of the glitz of Los Angeles, where he played for the Lakers. Bird was white, an intense, driven forward from rural Indiana who seemed to characterize working-class Boston, where he played with the Celtics. The two faced each other three times in the NBA Finals in the 1980s, and even in the other seven years, one or the other of them was in the finals. Johnson won five NBA championships; Bird won three. Every time the two teams played, Stern made sure the NBA marketing pushed not simply the game but also the clash of cultures, personalities, and stories that Johnson and Bird, in his telling, represented. Commercials touted Magic versus Larry. He put their faces on magazines and media guides. He made them stars.

And then, in June 1984, the Chicago Bulls drafted a young guard from the University of North Carolina named Michael Jordan. He won six titles in the 1990s and retired as the undisputed greatest basketball player of all time.

While earlier NBA leaders had encouraged fans to focus on their loyalties to their teams, Stern, well aware of how television had changed the landscape, saw an opportunity. Unlike baseball, basketball is fast-paced, with only five players on the court. Unlike football, basketball players wear no helmets, and television could easily broadcast players' faces and emotional responses during swiftly tilting games. Stern encouraged this. He saw the players not simply as great athletes but as celebrities and potential corporate endorsers. He wanted McDonald's and Ford and Coke to want NBA players to appear in their commercials.

To do this Stern had to change the image of the league, which advertising agencies and corporate liaisons told Stern time and time again, was simply too Black. That meant racist stereotypes: drugs, hip-hop music, and crime. In the 1970s and 1980s cocaine was rampant in Hollywood and the New York financial industry, but the media fixated on cases like that of Len Bias, a promising college player who died of an overdose only hours after the Celtics selected him in the 1986 NBA draft, or Spencer Haywood, who was tossed from the Los Angeles Lakers in 1980 because of his addictions.

Stern took cold-blooded action. He sold the players' union on a drug-testing policy and brought down the hammer, banning several players from the league. He convinced the union to accept a salary cap, limiting the amount of money players could be paid. And he worked very hard to turn players into celebrities, personalities that could be marketed to potential advertisers. He gently guided companies to seek the endorsements not of teams (as often happened in the 1960s and 1970s) but of individual players. In particular he supported the efforts of shoe companies to associate its brands with players. Stern enabled the unprecedented rise of Nike, a small northwestern athletic clothing company that began growing by 20 percent every year after it signed Michael Jordan to endorse a new line of basketball shoes the company called Air Jordans.

Stern negotiated with the United States Olympic & Paralympic Committee, persuading them to form the American basketball team not of amateurs, as the Olympics had always done, but with professional players. The resulting coverage of the 1992 "Dream Team" that stormed through the Barcelona Summer Olympics was unprecedented. Led by Johnson, Bird, and Jordan, among other NBA stars, Stern credited the Dream Team with a surge in NBA ratings the following season and growing interest in basketball overseas. Stern even talked NBC into putting together a half-hour Saturday morning show called *NBA Inside Stuff* targeted at the same young audience that watched cartoons.

Jordan's older brother once told *Sports Illustrated* that one day during a game of driveway basketball, Michael looked at his brother's feet, smiled and said, "Just remember whose name is on your shoes."[22]

And yet, amidst the flood of cash and media coverage, Stern's focus on marketing stars rather than teams drew criticism, too—often from old-line basketball purists who worried that a focus on stars would change how the game was played. Chuck Daly, the legendary coach of the Detroit Pistons and that first Dream Team, said "I'm not dealing with just 12 men out there. I'm dealing with 12 corporations."[23] By the late 1990s, the sentiment that a game that had once been premised on teamwork had become a vehicle for personal advancement was widespread.

Danny Ainge joined the Boston Celtics in the fall of 1981, two years into Larry Bird's tenure. After a bit of agonizing and a legal struggle between the Celtics (who had drafted him) and the Blue Jays (who had also drafted him, albeit several years prior), he decided to walk away from professional baseball for the NBA. He later told a reporter that he might have stayed in baseball if the team involved wasn't the Celtics—but the lure of playing with Larry Bird for a franchise that had for years been one of the best was a temptation. That said, the rookie had a rocky first couple of years. The team had won its first championship several months before, management and coaches were comfortable with its players and hierarchy, and there was little space for a rookie who wanted to play. Ainge's mood and involvement with the team were up and down for the first couple of years. Sometimes he started games and sometimes he played backup. Sometimes he played lots of minutes and sometimes few. He never felt he got much of a rhythm. His father said that "early on, he didn't fit in well at all."[24] He wasn't shooting the ball particularly well. Ainge had to figure out something that tripped up many college stars. He had to adapt to being a supplementary player. In a way, it was the same task he had faced at BYU: He had to learn how to make his talents mesh with other players. It was just that in this case, some of those other players—Larry Bird, Kevin McHale, Robert Parish—were better at basketball than he was.

Ainge was also a curiosity. He was certainly the highest-profile Mormon athlete of the 1970s and the 1980s, and his religion was a point of curiosity for nearly every journalist who covered him. They often contrasted his affable, soft-spoken demeanor with what quickly became his legendary ruthlessness on the court. "Ainge is not a big holler guy and he doesn't swear," observed the *Syracuse Herald-Journal*, who covered Ainge while he was playing baseball in the Blue Jays system. But, observed the reporter, Danny "with some pride" confessed, "I had my troubles with referees. I got some technicals," for unsportsmanlike behavior.[25] Another reporter noted with amusement that Ainge seemed shocked and "[shook] his head vigorously" when a teammate offered him some chewing tobacco.[26]

Eventually, Ainge balanced the paradox. Celtics forward Cedric Maxwell summarized the situation succinctly when he said, "We accepted him quickly when we found out he was a card-playing Mormon."[27] Ainge could be as competitive as the rest of them. By the mid-1980s he hit his groove as the starting shooting guard. He didn't handle the ball much but was content with taking open three-pointers, passing, playing aggressive defense, and vigorously mocking the opposing team. He averaged ten points a game, only fifth highest on the team, but was fine with that. His natural athletic gifts and the paradoxes of his demeanor allowed him to glide between being the sort of clutch star that the NCAA tournament was delighted to publicize and the sort of team-first player orbiting the sun of Larry Bird that the Boston Celtics needed. The best teams of the 1980s—Bird's Celtics, Johnson's Lakers, and the Detroit Pistons featuring point guard Isiah Thomas—all had charismatic superstars that David Stern's NBA put front and center. But these teams also figured out how to balance those stars with a harmonious supporting cast. They were able to persuade players with great talents like Ainge, perhaps capable of scoring more points or seizing the spotlight if given the opportunity, to take a step back and do the things necessary for a Larry Bird to succeed.

So Danny Ainge won two NBA championships.

A Family in Glens Falls

Glens Falls, New York, is a small town on the Hudson River in the northern part of the state, about fifty miles north of Albany and some ninety miles west of Sharon, Vermont, the birthplace of Joseph Smith Jr. Mormon missionaries baptized people in the area soon after Smith founded his new church in 1830 in Fayette, New York. By 1839 there was a thriving congregation in Albany. It was called a branch, the name the church uses for congregations with only a couple dozen members. But the Albany branch and other congregations in the region closed down in the late 1840s after Smith's murder. Brigham Young, Smith's successor, called for all faithful members to move west to the valley of the Great Salt Lake.

What followed was a long period of tension between the church and the United States, mostly centered on the issue of polygamy. After the church officially abandoned that practice in 1890, congregations began to appear east of the Mississippi River again. By 1901 the Albany branch was reborn. It served as the headquarters for the church's mission work in the entire region. In 1906, five residents of Glens Falls were baptized, and by 1960 that small nucleus had slowly grown into a community of twenty-two. The church turned it into a branch in its own right.

In 1969, the Glens Falls branch picked up a new member named Al Fredette. His older brother Dennis had joined the church while in the army and brought a convert's enthusiasm home to Glens Falls. Al watched as some of his siblings straightened their lives out after they joined the church and quit drinking. In early 1969, he met a young missionary with the thoroughly Mormon name of Kimball Young. The two were the same age—eighteen—and they both loved basketball. They would shoot hoops and talk about religion in the Fredette family driveway. That summer, Dennis baptized his younger brother Al.

The Glens Falls branch grew, and in 1973 it became a full-fledged ward, with several hundred members. A few years later officials in church headquarters in Salt Lake City decided to stop renting space in Glens Falls and built a new meetinghouse in the town, complete with a basketball court. Al became a mainstay. He taught Sunday school, served as the president of the ward's young men's organization, and drove people to and from church on Sunday. For the gregarious, outgoing Al Fredette, church was a social haven.

Al married the daughter of Clinton Taft, his coach at Whitehall High School. The Tafts, including Al's new wife, Kay, were Catholics. But she and Al navigated their mixed-faith marriage by finding the things in their respective faiths that could bring them together. Kay attended Sunday meetings with her husband, particularly after their children—Lindsay, TJ, and James, nicknamed Jimmer—were born. She didn't object to their kids being raised Mormons because she knew what was happening in the Glens Falls meetinghouse. "I knew my kids would get a good idea who Jesus Christ is," she said. And Al agreed. "The most important thing you're ever going to do in this life is be a good person," he would tell the kids. "If your role model is Christ you're going to follow his example."[28]

Two of the three Fredette kids were athletes at BYU, and all three grew up that way. That was in part simply because Kay and Al loved sports. (There's a family story about Clint Taft finding his daughter in the high school gymnasium arm wrestling the boys he was coaching.) But it's also because sports, especially basketball, were a place where they could build the sort of relationships with each other they believed Jesus wanted for them. Physical competition, exertion, and good sportsmanship had been bridging the gaps between Christianity for years, after all.

Calling sports a space where a Catholic and Mormon family could come together is a metaphor, but it also is a reference to actual spaces. At their home, Al and Kay put up lights in the front yard so their kids could play football. They called it Fredette Field. They poured concrete over half the backyard to build a basketball court and let their kids dribble the ball in the house. In the winter the Fredettes would go to the church meetinghouse and use the basketball court there.

TJ Fredette was seven years older than his little brother and took a special interest in teaching Jimmer how to play. He invented the "church hallway drill," a practice routine in which TJ would turn off the lights in a long, dim hallway at the Mormon meetinghouse and command Jimmer to dribble from one end of the carpeted corridor to the next while TJ would burst out of the Sunday school classrooms on either side to shake his little brother's handle on the ball. TJ had grown up playing basketball himself, but in puberty he was stricken with depression and panic attacks that crippled his performance at school and made it impossible for him to go away to college. So he poured his energies into training and supporting his little brother.

The Tafts found themselves at the Mormon meetinghouse because of basketball too. Jimmer and TJ's uncle Lee appeared at those training sessions. Lee was a three-sport high school athlete, coach, and trainer whose most important clients in those days were his Fredette nephews. He was a Catholic like his sister Kay, but he spent hours in the Glens Falls Mormon chapel, teaching Jimmer and TJ how to play basketball.

Jimmer Fredette did not have Danny Ainge's lanky, almost balletic athleticism. Ainge's long reach, excellent balance, and grace made him both a natural baseball second baseman as well as the sort of basketball player who could snake through defenses and twist his body while driving to the basket. Jimmer's other sport was football. He was stocky and strong, six-foot-two and two hundred pounds, with a linebacker's shoulders. But he loved basketball, and the Fredette family rallied around him to make him great.

Lee zeroed in on what seemed to him Jimmer's best advantages. He told Jimmer that he was not going to be the tallest or quickest player on a basketball court, so he had to master precise bodily control: stopping suddenly, pivoting just so, changing direction in order to throw off a defender and get enough space to shoot the ball. "It's not about being the most athletic, quickest, or fastest but knowing how to use your body to your advantage," Jimmer said. "Getting your shot off is about understanding how to get enough space."[29] He returned to Lee for advice and counsel throughout his life.

For Jimmer Fredette, basketball was about family and about church, and how those relationships helped him become the best that he could be. When basketball made him famous it brought with it other expectations, of fame and stardom, and he always wore those a bit uncomfortably, like a jersey that didn't quite fit. That was why it was hard for him to leave for Provo.

He was a great high school player. When he graduated in 2007 he ranked sixth on the list of New York State's all-time men's high school basketball scorers. And yet, many college scouts saw what was missing instead of what was there. They saw Jimmer's chunky body and short arms and doubted his ability to thrive on a court with taller and longer players. Syracuse University, the closest university with a powerhouse basketball program, never paid much attention. He got some offers from smaller schools with smaller programs, generally considered a middling recruit.

But his sister Lindsay—nine years older—had graduated from BYU four years earlier and was still living in Utah. She kept encouraging him to consider BYU. And BYU wanted him.

Coach Dave Rose had taken over the team in 2005, inheriting a program both successful and frustrating. Ever since Danny Ainge had graduated in 1981, the Cougars had made the NCAA tournament as often as not and had a reasonable share of strong players. Devin Durrant and Michael Smith were both named to national All-American teams and played in the NBA in the 1980s.

But the team kept bumping its head against a ceiling. In the ten years before Jimmer Fredette joined the team in 2007, the Cougars had made the NCAA tournament six times but had never won a game. Their last victories there had come in the early 1990s. In the 1991 tournament, the towering freshman Shawn Bradley, a seven-foot-six center whose size and strength made him among the most dominant defensive players in American college basketball history, set a record for most blocked shots in a game, leading BYU to a first-round victory over Virginia. The Cougars lost their second game, when Bradley was outplayed by the University of Arizona's center Bison Dele. Bradley then served a mission for the church and entered the NBA immediately upon his return. Two years later, a scrappy BYU team led by Roger Reid's son Randy edged out one win in the conference before falling to national powerhouse Kansas.

The next ten years saw first-round loss after first-round loss. Halfway through the first game of the tournament on March 15, 2007, Dave Rose had high hopes. His team was six points up on Xavier University at halftime, but fell apart in the second half, letting Xavier back in the game and getting outscored by eight. The Cougars lost by 2 points, 79–77, upset by a lower seed. A Provo *Daily Herald* sports columnist was blunt. "This program cannot win a tournament game," he wrote.[30] The way Dave Rose saw it, if his team was going to be competitive, it needed offense. Journalist after journalist observed that the BYU team that lost to Xavier couldn't score in the final minutes of the game when it really counted. "When it came down to crunch time, Xavier got clutch shots," wrote Provo reporter Darnell Dickson. "BYU had two opportunities to tie but [none of its players] could convert."[31]

After that defeat, Rose went back to his office in Provo and thought about Jimmer Fredette. The young New Yorker had been on Rose's radar for two years by that point. Always on the lookout for LDS high schoolers who could play, Rose had first noticed Jimmer at a BYU summer camp for high school players two years before. The coach told the reporter Pat Forde that he saw both Jimmer's limitations but also the years of discipline and training. Jimmer was "occasionally awkward" but had "a limitless repertoire of unorthodox moves and ways to score." In September 2006, Rose and an assistant coach flew to Glens Falls, paid for a dinner at a local Italian restaurant run by friends of the Fredettes, and laid out a plan. Rose said he thought Jimmer would eventually be "running the show" for Cougar basketball, the focus of the team's offense. He asked Jimmer to commit to attending BYU.[32]

Jimmer hesitated. He wanted to talk to his uncle Lee, who was running late. It wasn't until Lee arrived and the family conferred that Jimmer told Rose he would sign.

Rose wanted Jimmer to run the show. He needed a star. Jimmer wanted his people involved. Basketball was something he did with his family and friends. He was ambitious—no mistaking that. He wanted to be great, and he was a great player. He was also, though, not the sort of player David Stern saw standing astride the modern NBA.

The Contract

Jimmer struggled a bit his first year at BYU, both in terms of basketball and because he missed his people. One Sunday afternoon in early fall he called home and told his dad that he didn't have anything to eat. He didn't have a car. Campus was closed. He didn't have much cash. "He was really down," Al remembered. "He was alone, beat up, tired, hungry." Jimmer was naturally shy and hadn't made close friends yet. "It was tough on him," Kay told a journalist, those first few months. It wasn't until his uncle Dennis and sister Lindsay, both of whom lived in Salt Lake City, about forty-five minutes north of BYU campus, began making a concerted effort to reach out to Jimmer that he began to feel more comfortable on campus and able to make friends with some of his teammates. By the end of his freshman year, three of them were close and watched sitcoms together every evening.[33]

That growth began to show on the court. When Fredette arrived, BYU's team was built around the guard Lee Cummard and the big forwards Trent Plaisted and Jonathan Tavernari. Plaisted was a rock-solid post player from Texas who would skip his senior season to try his luck in the pros; he ended up with a respectable ten-year career in Europe. Cummard was the team's best player and spent most of the game with the ball in his hands. In Jimmer's freshman year, Cummard ended up leading the team in points and assists. Tavernari was a streaky gunner who had won the Mountain West Conference Freshman of the Year award the year before Jimmer showed up. Tavernari frustrated Rose to no end—he could score in bunches when he was having a good night, but when he was off, he was way off. And he didn't always seem able to tell the difference.

This team was good. They won the Mountain West Conference. Jimmer came off the bench, because like Tavernari, he was streaky. He didn't shoot well that season. His ankle gave him problems toward the end of the year, and he closed out the season with a 39.8 shooting percentage, a fairly dire number for a kid who was supposed to be able to score.

More dangerous for his potential future prospects, Jimmer didn't seem to fit into Rose's game plan. Rose held to BYU's long tradition of a democratic offense built around the fast break and running and gunning. He didn't want any single player to hold the ball too long. It was supposed to bounce around, from the guards on the perimeter of the court to the bigger forwards closer to the basket and back. But Jimmer's game was built around the inches that his uncle had taught him: dribbling, maneuvering, clearing space, taking the shot that nobody thought he could find, let alone make. "We had to figure out whether Jimmer would be a better shooting guard or point guard," Rose said. He played Jimmer as a backup to start the season, while player and coach figured each other out.[34]

But despite the awkwardness of Jimmer's initial fit, there was something about him that caught attention.

Mostly, it was his grinding relentlessness. He just kept on coming. His long years of drills meant he was always steady. His nerve never failed him, even when his team was floundering or the situation was desperate.

The Cougars went to the NCAA tournament after Jimmer's freshman season, and, yet again, lost in the first round. They were an eighth seed and lost to the ninth seed, Texas A&M. Seeding aside, BYU was playing catchup the entire game. They fell behind by double digits almost immediately and scrambled the rest of the way. And just as a quarter-century earlier, before Danny Ainge put it all together, local journalists complained that it was because BYU lacked a star to step up and bend the game to his will. Darnell Dickson of the Provo *Daily Herald* wryly complained that he would have given any of A&M's fans "100 dollars if they would have picked out Lee Cummard as the team's best player. Not to knock Cummard; he's a fine player. [But] we already knew that BYU will never have the size and athleticism of a major Division I program."[35]

The one hope Dickson and other beat writers saw was Fredette, who calmly stepped off the bench and onto the court when the team needed him most. In fact, the day after the game, Dickson and his fellow basketball writer Jason Franchuk put Fredette in a headline: "Fredette Gives Fans, Team, Glimpse of Future." Fredette's play in that elimination game seemed to be BYU's only bright spot. He entered the game and scored quickly. He single-handedly pulled BYU out of an eleven-point deficit in the first half and gave BYU its first lead of the game by hitting a three-point shot—the shot that would eventually become his trademark. BYU couldn't keep that lead, but spectators saw a flash of possibility. After the game Coach Rose pointed to two things. Jimmer "came in with a lot of confidence," Rose said. And second: "We hadn't scored for a while and we were looking for a little bit of a lift."[36] Jimmer might be BYU's future. Jimmer might make BYU the sort of team that, by the twenty-first century, Americans had come to expect from basketball.

Even before the legal earthquakes like *O'Bannon v. NCAA* opened the way for more money in the college game, the revolution that David

Stern brought to the NBA had by the twenty-first century made its way down to college basketball. In 2002 a young forward from Baltimore named Carmelo Anthony landed at Syracuse University. Nearly every ranking of high school players that spring put him in the top five, often first or second. He had to take the American College Testing standardized test multiple times before earning the minimum score of nineteen required by Syracuse, but he wanted to go. Anthony wrote in his memoir that—just as Jimmer heard a few years later— "I would get to run the show. I wasn't coming through to back up a senior or learn a system behind somebody else."[37]

Anthony was an overwhelming college player. He averaged twenty-two points and ten rebounds a game, both in the top twenty in all of college basketball in the 2002–03 season. He could score like a polished professional player at age eighteen, with multiple moves and good form: jump shots, driving, posting up. He took Syracuse to its first-ever NCAA tournament championship. And then he declared he would leave college and announced himself eligible for the NBA draft. In June 2003, less than a year after he enrolled as a freshman at Syracuse, the Denver Nuggets took him third overall. The departure was a bittersweet decision for him. Anthony thoroughly enjoyed Syracuse. But, as he told a reporter ten years later when Syracuse retired his jersey number, he "accomplished everything" that freshman year.[38] After all, as he wrote, "The NBA isn't promised, and it waits for no man."[39] He ultimately knew what he wanted, and he shaped his college experience in the image of David Stern's NBA.

Though he perhaps exemplifies it better than any other player of his era, Carmelo Anthony didn't carve out that path. By the early twenty-first century, the best teams in college basketball were built around great players, players who came to campus because it would be a good launching pad for an NBA career. They would stay one year, perhaps two, then leave; leave with no degree, but hopefully with a tournament victory or two under their belts; leave with thc expectation of hearing their names called in the NBA draft. For these players, the tournament and college season were a thrill but also mostly a showcase. And, like it or not, that was how the Utah media, the BYU community, and Jimmer Fredette started to perceive himself.

In 2007, as his little brother was preparing to head to BYU, TJ had scribbled a contract that Jimmer signed. Then they taped it to the wall above Jimmer's bed.

> "I, James T. Fredette, agree on this day, January 27, 2007, to do the work and make the necessary sacrifices to be able to reach my ultimate goal of playing in the NBA."[40]

Jimmer and the rest of the Fredettes loved BYU, but their sights were set higher.

Jimmermania

It wasn't as though Jimmer yanked BYU basketball off of its track. Ever since BYU began playing in tournaments, ever since Stan Watts persuaded Ernest Wilkinson to start giving prospective basketball players scholarships, BYU had begun thinking of basketball in the same ways that David Stern and the American sports media did: it was a source of community pride and entertainment and, frankly, money, and all of those things came from winning. The meanings that James Naismith and the church tournaments wanted to inscribe on the sport had begun to fade when Wilkinson conceded that not only was it perhaps unrealistic to expect that the teams would draw equally from across the student body and still win, but that winning should be the primary goal.

That was not to say that there were not vestiges of the older way of imagining sports at BYU. At many schools the athletes live in special dorms separated from the regular student body. While Jimmer was there, this wasn't the case, and he was grateful. By the end of his freshman year he had made a much wider circle of friends than he thought would have been the case otherwise. He also loved the tight-knit community that basketball created, both on campus and back in Glens Falls. His brother TJ and other members of his family would head over to their local LDS meetinghouse, which was equipped with a satellite hookup to watch Jimmer's games.

By his sophomore year, Jimmer's particular offensive gifts were becoming undeniable, and BYU began, slowly, to look more and more like Carmelo Anthony's Syracuse team. Tavernari and Cummard were still around, but Fredette began to assert himself, and Rose gradually gave him more leash. In Fredette's freshman and sophomore years, the coach engineered a set of home and away games against Wake Forest University's team, the Demon Deacons. Wake Forest had a basketball program to be reckoned with. There were several future NBA players on those teams, including future All-Star point guard Jeff Teague. In both games, Fredette went toe to toe with Teague, trying to answer each of Teague's baskets with one of his own. The Cougars lost both games, but in the second, when Wake Forest was ranked sixth in the country, the Cougars pulled off a respectable performance. Reporters noted that Jimmer was fearless. "Sure, the Cougars were blown out," one reporter observed. But "Fredette doesn't mind where the games are played ... [he] had one of his best games as a freshman at Wake Forest."[41]

On January 31, 2009, Fredette scored twenty-eight points, his career high, against the University of Wyoming. He did it again three weeks later against San Diego State University. In March, BYU played the University of Utah, led by the towering center Luke Nevill, and reporters applauded Fredette's iron will. After his team fell behind in the first half, Jimmer "was nothing short of huge, unflinching while taking the ball at the massive Nevill," wrote the *Daily Herald*. The Cougars won the game because of "Jimmer Fredette, whose ability to make individual plays ...sparked the Cougars on offense early in the second half."[42]

Jimmer, as a sophomore, was named one of the Mountain West Conference's five best players a few days after that game. The Provo newspaper declared that the award was not only well-earned but of critical importance to BYU because Lee Cummard was graduating. When Jimmer became a junior, he would "be a focal point from Day 1." The team would rest "on his broad shoulders."[43]

And it did. By the time the team was preparing for the 2009–10 season, headlines read "BYU To Test Out Different Player Combos," and "Rose Planning to Shake Up Rosters." With Cummard gone, Rose finally took the plunge and built the team entirely around Fredette. It worked. Jimmer began winning even more awards, and the team thrived. They won thirty games, lost only six, and closed the year ranked seventeenth in the country by the Associated Press. By Fredette's senior year, the success was even clearer. "As Jimmer Fredette goes, so does this team. Fredette is the heart, soul, spirit, and everything else," wrote Utah sports reporter Paul Delos Santos in November 2010.[44]

Jimmer's usage rate steadily climbed. The statistic measures one player's possession of the ball as a proportion of his team's total time with it. In Jimmer's junior year he held the ball for 25.2 percent of BYU's possessions, a number not unusual for a point guard. By his senior season that percentage had climbed to a whopping 37.8 percent, the second highest in NCAA men's basketball. He averaged 28.9 points per game that year, leading the NCAA in both average and total points scored. He won the John R. Wooden Award and the Associated Press College Basketball Player of the Year awards. He became the most decorated BYU player since Danny Ainge. But more than Ainge, Jimmer was not just a player but a star, in a very modern sense of the term

BYU's approach seemed to pay off. In March 2010, to everybody's deep relief, Dave Rose and Jimmer Fredette threw the monkey off the school's back and won an NCAA tournament game. It took double overtime to do it, but BYU edged a good University of Florida team, 99–92. Even though they lost in the next round to a Kansas State team that ultimately made it to the Elite Eight, the Cougars wrapped up their season with a feeling of relief. Jimmer told *The Salt Lake Tribune*, "We had a great season."[45]

Again, much of the focus fell on Jimmer himself. The *Tribune* complimented the team on its chemistry, a somewhat backhanded compliment. The reporter explained that "Fredette emerged as a superstar" while other players who might have expected to play a bigger role, like Tavernari or the talented shooting guard Jackson Emery "were relegated to support roles." Emery acknowledged, "Lots of guys that have the talent that Jimmer has, they can let it go to their head and think about themselves and about their personal future."[46] Jimmer tried not to let that happen.

But the entire college basketball ecosystem was pulling him in that direction. In that win against Florida, Jimmer scored thirty-seven points and took 40 percent of his team's shots, and almost immediately reporters began to speculate he would leave BYU after his junior year in order to enter the NBA draft. His parents confirmed that he would declare himself eligible to be drafted, mainly to assess how interested NBA teams might be in him. It was the logical thing to do, even if, as Dave Rose acknowledged, it put the team in an awkward spot. "He's a good player. It doesn't take too many people to see a tape or film or a game live to understand that he's a really versatile guy," Rose shrugged when a reporter asked him what he thought about whether Jimmer should take the plunge. The tantalizing possibility of even more fame and more money left BYU and its fans on edge, even as it seemed Jimmer might only be going through the motions. Toying with the possibility of the NBA was what a famous college player did in the 2010s, and the team and fans felt proud even if the possibility would hurt the team's prospects.[47]

Ultimately, Jimmer stayed for one more year at BYU, and things went wild. "Jimmermania is reaching a new level of crazy," wrote the Associated Press reporter Lynn DeBruin on January 28, 2011.[48] The night before, Jimmer scored 43 points against San Diego State University in the Marriott Center. At that point in the season the AP had SDSU ranked fourth in the nation. They had not yet lost a game, and they were led by Kawhi Leonard, a six-foot-seven forward with octopus arms who three years later would win back-to-back awards as the best defensive player in the NBA. But not even Kawhi Leonard could slow down Jimmer that night. SDSU went down.

Halfway through the game, Kevin Durant, who was enjoying a three-year reign as the leading scorer in the NBA, posted in awe on Twitter. "Jimmer Fredette is the best scorer in the world!!"

When the final buzzer sounded and BYU officially claimed victory, the crowds in the Marriott Center surged onto the court and surrounded Fredette, trying to lift him into the air before security managed to surround him.

Meanwhile two dozen NBA scouts sat in the stands, frantically taking notes.[49]

Over the next few weeks, newspaper reporters began to use the word "Jimmered" as a noun and a verb. As Kate Fagan of *The Philadelphia Inquirer* parsed the term, "The Jimmer. You've been Jimmered." A Jimmer happened when a team might indulge a brief lapse of focus and defensive intensity and look up to notice that Jimmer had hit seven 3-pointers and scored 52 points, which is what happened to the University of New Mexico Lobos on March 11 during the Mountain West Conference tournament.[50] When the NCAA tournament bracket was announced a few days later, BYU was designated a third seed—its highest seeding ever. They would play Wofford College, a small liberal arts school in South Carolina. A South Carolina reporter told Jamar Diggs with a straight face that "Dozens of defenders this season have been Jimmered." Diggs was the ace defender on the Wofford Terriers. "I'm not saying I can stop him," Diggs said. "But I am looking forward to the opportunity."[51]

As it turned out, Diggs couldn't stop him. The teams played on St. Patrick's Day, 2011, and Jimmer scored 32 points. BYU won, 74–66. At the same time, Jimmer was on the cover of a *Sports Illustrated* issue devoted to the tournament.[52] After beating Wofford, BYU trounced Gonzaga University, and Jimmer upped his game, scoring 34 points and hitting seven of his twelve 3-point shots. He personally scored 40 percent of BYU's points in the two wins and had taken 40 percent of his team's shots.

Jim Meehan, a reporter for Gonzaga's home paper, observed that the crowd in Denver's Pepsi Center where the game was played began chanting "You Got Jimmered" as BYU was pulling away. Jackson Emery, BYU's second-leading scorer, told Meehan that "Jimmer is going to demand so much attention because of the player he is," and a Gonzaga player marveled, "They were hitting 3's like crazy and we just surrendered."[53] Jimmer took BYU to the Sweet Sixteen—the furthest in the tournament the Cougars had gotten since Danny Ainge's 1981 team thirty years before.

The March 28, 2011, cover of *Sports Illustrated* carried a photo of Jimmer launching a shot over a Gonzaga defender—but the story *SI* published the next day was not one BYU would have preferred. It described BYU's loss in the Sweet Sixteen to Florida four days before. The game was a heartbreaker. One year earlier, Jimmer had beaten this team in the first round of the tournament in double overtime. This time, the Cougars lost in overtime, and the *SI* reporter Kelli Anderson thought she knew why. Jimmer again scored 32 points, but "Fredette and his teammates, none of whom broke into double figures, fell victim to a far more balanced offense." Four Florida players scored between 16 and 19 points, and Florida guard Kenny Boynton pulled off what Jamar Diggs couldn't. Even though

Jimmer again put points on the board, he did it inefficiently. He made only eleven of his twenty-nine shots, and under Boynton's pressuring defense, didn't score for the first fourteen minutes of a forty-minute game.

"I know when he goes to the hole he does a lot of faking up," Boynton told Anderson. He had caught on to the trickery that Uncle Lee had drilled into Jimmer all the way back in the Glens Falls LDS meetinghouse.[54]

The cracks had been there for a while for those who were paying attention. John Blanchette, who covered the Gonzaga basketball team that lost to BYU a few days earlier, said that the "Zags didn't get Jimmered. They got grimmered." No matter how well Fredette played, BYU's reliance on him left some openings. If Gonzaga wasn't mired in its own "grim offense and grimmer defense," they could have taken advantage. Blanchette also made a prediction—sooner or later, "Jimmer Fredette, in all likelihood, joins the human race again."[55]

Despite the loss, a week later Jimmer received the John R. Wooden Award. It was clear he was headed to the NBA. But there were some like Blanchette who worried that the hype of Jimmermania was actually unfair to Jimmer himself. The style of play BYU had fallen into, the star-centric model, placed too much pressure on him and set up expectations that he, through no fault of his own, could not possibly meet.

And that, unfortunately, is what happened. Despite Jimmermania, despite the gravitational pull of star-driven basketball, Jimmer wasn't Carmelo Anthony. But he never claimed to be.

The Lonely Master

In March 2018, journalist Jesse Hyde published a feature story in the *Deseret News* titled, "The Lonely Master: from March Madness to Shanghai, the Unlikely Journey of Jimmer Fredette."[56] It opened with a stark image: Jimmer Fredette, alone in an apartment in Shanghai, China, building a Nativity scene out of Legos on Christmas Eve, 2017.

It was a long road to Shanghai. On June 23, 2011, the Sacramento Kings drafted him tenth overall in the 2011 NBA draft. He went five picks ahead of Kawhi Leonard, whom he had embarrassed on the Marriott Center court a few months earlier. As with all players selected in the first round of the NBA draft, the league's policies guaranteed Jimmer a contract for at least three seasons. The rookie scale salary for the tenth pick would start at $1,865,300 per season. If the Kings chose, they could extend that contract for a fourth and fifth season, but Jimmer would receive a pay bump if they did.

The choice was not universally acclaimed. A few days earlier Chris Mannix of *Sports Illustrated* mused about what he called "the Jimmer dilemma." Mannix called team managers around the NBA and concluded that "in a draft loaded with question marks, Fredette is one of the biggest." Jimmer was a "folk hero." He would guarantee media attention and probably sell memorabilia. He was, at least at that point, a star. But he might also be a bust. Team managers worried whether he was fast enough and athletic enough to hang with professional basketball players. He was strong enough to overpower other college players, but his size—six-two, two hundred pounds—that made him a bull on the college court was below average for a scoring guard in the pros.[57]

After he was drafted the Sacramento media wondered, too. "Did the Kings select Jimmer more for his skills or for his fan base?" *Sacramento Bee* columnist Ailene Voisin mused. She was a bit equivocal. "They love the marketing," she observed. But she also thought that Jimmer was an ideal player for Sacramento coach Paul Westphal, who pushed a running, fast-break style straight out of BYU's playbook. "Westphal signed on for Jimmermania when the BYU star completed his pre-draft workout at the Kings' practice facility," she wrote. Westphal thought that Jimmer's ability to score at any point, from anywhere, would make Sacramento's offense unstoppable.[58]

Unfortunately, Sacramento had a terrible season. The team owners, the brothers Gavin and Joe Maloof, spent much of 2011 and 2012 trying to relocate the Kings to Anaheim, California. Because of a dispute between the players' union and the owners, the season didn't begin until Christmas Day, two months late, and Westphal barely lasted two weeks. The Maloofs fired him after the Kings lost five of their first seven games. A losing streak is not unusual in the NBA, but the Kings didn't simply lose. They were embarrassed. After winning their first game they lost four in a row, and the closest loss was by 10 points. The New York Knicks beat them 92–114 and the Portland Trail Blazers, 79–101.

Coach Westphal, who had a vision for Jimmer, was gone, and the new head coach Keith Smart didn't do much better. Because the season began late, the teams played sixty-six games rather than the normal eighty-two that 2011–12 season. Sacramento won only twenty-two. They ended the season tied for the twenty-fifth-best record in the thirty-team NBA.

Both Westphal and Smart gave Jimmer opportunities. Westphal made him the team's sixth man, the first player off the bench, playing half the game or so and coming in with a mandate to surprise the opposing team. Once Smart took over, he experimented with starting Jimmer and building his shooting into the team's regular offense. There were some bright spots. At the end of January he had a run of scoring, putting up twenty points against the Memphis Grizzlies and nineteen against the Denver Nuggets a few games later. But Jimmer couldn't quite get going. He had to work harder to get the open shots he was used to against NBA defenses. As predicted, he struggled to defend the quick and strong players he was matched against.

Devastatingly, his shot seemed to have deserted him as well. Even on those nights he scored well, his accuracy was never quite what it had been. The game of inches Uncle Lee taught him proved so much harder in the NBA. By the end of his first season he was making less than 40 percent of his shots and barely a third of his three-pointers. Those were bad numbers for any NBA player but particularly for a shooter who was supposed to be able to put the ball in the basket. That wasn't the Jimmer Fredette who ruled the Marriott Center. By the middle of the season, Smart was giving Jimmer's minutes to his fellow rookie Isaiah Thomas—a tiny guard four inches shorter than Jimmer who shared a name with the All-Star a generation older than him. As *The Sacramento Bee* wrote, "The Kings' shooting, scoring and assists all improved with Thomas in the lineup." The Denver Nuggets coach George Karl said the move was "common sense."[59]

Things didn't get much better. Jimmer spent another year and a half in Sacramento and managed to pull his three-point percentage past 40 percent, which is the mark of a quality shooter in the NBA. By the end of his time as a King, his percentage was closing in on 50 percent, which was elite. But his defense never really got there, and he was always outclassed athletically. Keith Smart said that Jimmer's constant worry that he wasn't as fast as whoever he was matched against made him "passive and ineffective."[60] Though his shooting percentages increased, his minutes dropped, and critics said that he was shooting better only because he was playing against the second or third string from other teams. He played less his second year than he had in his first, and less in his third than in his second.

After his second season the Kings declined to extend his contract, and at the end of February 2014, halfway through his third season, the team bought the contract out. Essentially, they paid Jimmer a lump sum to walk away from the team, bringing an end to a befuddling career in Sacramento. *The Sacramento Bee* noted, "No player generated as much discussion and passion among Kings fans." Even as his role on the team declined, the fan base continued to "argue for more minutes." Even as coaches questioned "his defense, ball handling, and the most suitable role for him," the media continued to wonder if the same Jimmer Fredette who dominated the NCAA was still there somewhere, if only a coach could put him in the right position or find the right plays to run.[61]

Over the next few years, some curious teams tried him out. He played eight games for the Chicago Bulls late in the 2014 season, and that summer the New Orleans Pelicans signed him. He was their backup point guard in the 2014–15 season, but early the next season the Pelicans traded him to the New York Knicks, who promptly bought out his contract. This time, nobody picked him up.

"We thought his momentum at BYU would just continue. And then year one didn't pan out, year two didn't pan out. Things slowly got worse," his wife, Whitney Wonnacott, told reporter Jesse Hyde.[62]

That was how Jimmer ended up in China. As Hyde observed, when Jimmer was at BYU, people "watched Jimmer." They didn't watch basketball, "They watched *Jimmer*, as if Jimmer was its own sport." Jimmer was not as well-rounded or physically gifted a player as Danny Ainge was. But his utter devotion to learning to score and the matchless skills that devotion had inch by inch cultivated outweighed those flaws in college. He developed these talents in the bosom of community, yet those same talents dragged him increasingly toward a new way of playing basketball: by himself, with his team merely his supporting cast. It was what some sportswriters called heliocentrism, emerging in the 2010s NBA with stars like James Harden of the Houston Rockets and Luka Dončić of the Dallas Mavericks. These teams orbited around a single star who dominated the ball and made all decisions. At BYU it created something we might call Jimmermania, and it left Jimmer alone, both on the court and in China.

Jimmer was in Shanghai because the Shanghai Sharks of the Chinese Basketball Association approached him after the New York Knicks cut him loose. They offered him a lot of money. The Chinese season wasn't very long, only four months, so Jimmer could be with his family in the United States as much as possible and cast about for opportunities. In the spring of 2019, he got a contract with the Phoenix Suns, but the team canceled it after only six games. A brief stint with a team in Greece ended similarly. It seemed that if Jimmer was going to have a real professional basketball career it would be in China.

While he was there, it was Jimmermania all over again. In his first game in China he scored forty-two points. The next he scored fifty. Once, he scored seventy-three. The crowds chanted his name. Fans followed him in the street.

Jimmer told Hyde he asked his translator why his nickname among Chinese fans was "the lonely master." He didn't like the moniker—it hit too close to home, with Whitney and their kids staying with her family in Denver. It's not like that, the translator told him. "You're so far ahead of everyone else in the league, you're lonely. Like a god."[63]

Mormon leaders had hoped for a long time that basketball would make its players more like Jesus Christ. But this was not what they had in mind.

The Persistent Challenge of Race

At the beginning of March 2011, two weeks before the NCAA selection committee announced that Jimmer's BYU team would be a third seed in that year's tournament, the team received a stunning blow. Brandon Davies, the team's starting center, third-leading scorer and leading rebounder, and defensive anchor, admitted to the university's Honor Code office that he had sex with his girlfriend. This was a violation of the Honor Code. Accordingly, the university dismissed him from the basketball team and announced that his status as a student was under review. The Associated Press had the team ranked third in the nation at the time of the announcement, but nonetheless, the Cougars reeled. On March 3 they played the University of New Mexico, the first game since Davies's dismissal, and lost badly, 64–82. It was only the third game they had lost that season.

Jimmer Fredette told the media that Davies "is like a brother to us, family. It is tough to lose a guy like that."[64] The team felt Davies's absence throughout the tournament. *Deseret News* columnist Dick Harmon marveled that the team was "without Brandon Davies for the final week of the conference season and still [made] it to the Sweet 16."[65] There was speculation that if Davies were in the lineup, BYU might have gone farther.

From the end of the twentieth century and into the twenty-first, BYU administrators were bolstering the authority of the Honor Code office Ernest Wilkinson had created several decades before. In 1987, the university began requiring students to receive endorsements from their bishops to remain enrolled at the university. Among other things, bishops would inquire whether or not students were abiding by the church's sexual ethic, which forbids premarital sex. Davies was a member of the church and had voluntarily confessed to his bishop and to the Honor Code office.

This Cougar team was the highest-ranked that BYU basketball had ever produced. Jimmer Fredette was a national phenomenon, and that had something to do with why Davies's dismissal became national news.

University spokeswoman Carri Jenkins said that "what matters is whether or not [students'] personal convictions match the principles of the Honor Code."[66] She argued that a stated purpose of education at BYU—sports included—was to inculcate moral discipline in students. In the university's view, then, Davies's suspension was merited. Coach Dave Rose said something similar. He argued that nobody had to agree with whether BYU's restrictions on students' sexual behavior was right or wrong. "It's not about right or wrong. It's about commitment," he said. Students, including Davies, had agreed to the code, and the school would hold them to it.[67]

This was the language of James Naismith and early-twentieth-century advocates of muscular Christianity, including Eugene Roberts and the other founders of BYU basketball. A good number of commentators, like the Gannett newspaper chain's Mike Lopresti, praised BYU in the same way. "There should be respect for a school that stands by its values," Lopresti wrote. "There's an example that should not be missed here."[68] John Jeansonne of *Newsday* agreed. There should be "no exception to a university rule just because Davies is a highly visible and productive athlete," he wrote. He praised BYU for holding its players to "accountability."[69]

This sort of moral language had deep roots in American sports. But commentators like Jeansonne and Lopresti avoided one factor that deeply complicated Davies's case. He was, to be sure, a member of the LDS Church who knew what the Honor Code required. He was also Black. A month after his dismissal, the sports journalism website *Deadspin* published a study coauthored by Darron Smith, a Black LDS academic in the health sciences. Smith was an alumnus of BYU and the University of Utah. He eventually expanded the *Deadspin* story into a book.[70]

From a series of interviews and research into media reports, Smith counted seventy athletes disciplined by BYU's Honor Code office and forced off of BYU sports teams since 1993. Only sixteen were white. Forty-one were Black. Many of the remainder were Polynesian or Latino. These numbers were far out of proportion with the racial makeup of BYU's student population.

Smith identified a genuine tension in BYU athletics, one that went back to early disputes over the purpose of sports on campus. Increasingly, as winning grew central to the school's athletics office, the university began recruiting non-LDS athletes to bolster its teams. And those athletes were, in comparison to the rest of BYU's student body, disproportionately Black. At the time of Davies's dismissal, *The Salt Lake Tribune* reported that 23 percent of BYU's athletes were not white. Most of that group were Black. But Black students made up only one half of one percent of the student body writ large, and many of them, especially athletes, were not members of the church.[71]

The state of affairs pointed to deep tensions in American culture: Black people performing for white people and old stereotypes about brutal, physical Black men. Amar'e Stoudemire, a Black All-Star forward for the New York Knicks, felt it immediately upon hearing about Brandon Davies's suspension. "Don't ever go to BYU," he wrote on social media. "They kick a Young Educated (Black) Brother OUT OF SCHOOL."[72] And bigotries were certainly present on campus. Only a few months after Davies's case was made public a BYU professor of religious education named Randy Bott, trying to explain why the church restricted membership on Black people until 1978, compared Black people to "a young child prematurely asking for the keys to her father's car." He told a *Washington Post* reporter that "the descendants of Cain, who killed his brother Abel, were black."[73]

The church's headquarters immediately disavowed Bott's statements and issued its own declaration—"We do not tolerate racism in any form."[74] But the disavowal did not mean that beliefs like Bott's were not present on BYU campus, and it did not prevent disparities in Honor Code enforcement.

Thomas Stancil, a former BYU football player who was not a member of the church, told Smith that "after [his] first meeting with the coaches" who recruited him "the honor code was never mentioned."[75] Stancil was one of a large number of Black, non-LDS players recruited by football coach Gary Crowton. Stancil said he told BYU recruiters that he was sexually active with his girlfriend and that the recruiters encouraged him to live with other non-LDS players and stay off the Honor Code office's radar. In 2004, Stancil was suspended and left BYU when caught having oral sex with a woman at a party—one of twelve dismissals of Black football players that year.[76]

Non-LDS players, who were disproportionately Black or Latino, were at a disadvantage. White players were far more likely to be LDS and thus far more likely to have a support system and the background necessary to navigate the Honor Code—even if they were caught violating it. "There's no way I would have signed those papers if the Honor Code had been fully explained," Stancil told a reporter. "When you invite non-LDS people onto your campus, you have to implement something different to help them succeed."[77]

Brandon Davies was exceptional in one way—he was both Black and a member of the LDS Church. But his story pointed to others. Davies affirmed to BYU officials his desire to repent, and with the guidance of his bishop, he was reinstated and played for the Cougars in the 2011–12 school year, after which he graduated. Rashaun Broadus did not have the same opportunity. He was not LDS, and when he was arrested on charges of driving under the influence of alcohol, he was simply dismissed from the basketball team. Broadus did not have access to the same support network that Davies did and simply finished his coursework and left the university.[78]

In 2022, Cougars coach Mark Pope made history. On November 16, in a game against Missouri State University at the Marriott Center, Pope sent out a lineup of Jaxson Robinson, Trey Stewart, Rudi Williams, Gideon George, and Fousseyni Traore. For the first time, five Black players represented BYU on a basketball court. George was Nigerian; Traori from Mali. More, neither were Latter-day Saints. Traore was Muslim. Over the next few years, more and more Black BYU athletes shared that faith. "We share a lot of similarities. Especially marriage-wise, the law of chastity is super-similar," said Traore about his experience among the Latter-day Saints at BYU.[79]

Yet the success of Black Muslim students like Traore did not obviate the challenges of recruitment and the Honor Code that had caused so many problems for students like Stancil and Broadus. That it took until 2022 for BYU to have an all-Black lineup on the floor was evidence that the problem of racism in the church's past still lingered.

5

KEVIN YOUNG PICKS BYU

In April 2024, Brigham Young University hired a new coach for its men's basketball team. The school's administration had an eye not only to winning at the college level but also finally earning the last piece of credibility for a university program—making a name for the school at the professional level. The number of BYU players with unqualified success in the NBA at that point could be counted on one hand—Mel Hutchins and Danny Ainge. By the time of Young's hire, Jimmer Fredette's NBA career was long past. The big center Shawn Bradley's career was generally considered respectable but disappointing given the expectations that accompanied him as the second overall draft pick in 1993. Fred Roberts and Greg Kite, old running mates to Danny Ainge, made the NBA but were professional backups. And that was about it for Cougars in the NBA.

Kevin Young was supposed to fix the issue. He possessed a sterling NBA coaching pedigree. And he arrived just in time. His first year coaching BYU was 2024–25, and it was a proving ground. AJ Dybantsa agreed to attend BYU in the middle of that season, in large part because of what he saw Young accomplishing.

In that time Young landed blue-chip recruits, dramatically vitalized the ethos of BYU basketball, and even enjoyed success in the 2025 NCAA tournament. And Young turned forty-three only a few weeks before Dybantsa committed.

Kevin Young inherited a program that had, for decades, sought a position not unlike that of the church that owned BYU. On the one hand, BYU basketball was a way for the university to prove it could compete in the world outside the church, attracting fans and players beyond its borders. But on the other hand, many leaders in BYU's history saw basketball as a way to preserve the sort of moral impulse that would set BYU and the church that owned it apart.

For Young, a Latter-day Saint who had built a career in the raucous world of professional basketball in the United States, this was a familiar struggle.

BYU in Trouble

Dave Rose retired in 2019. He had led the BYU Cougars for fourteen years and was indisputably the most successful BYU men's basketball coach in a generation. He won more than twice as many games as Frank Arnold, who had coached Danny Ainge, was the only coach since Arnold to make it past the first round of the NCAA tournament, and had a better winning percentage than Stan Watts did. He turned sixty-two the year he retired, claiming exhaustion. He had fought off cancer twice, after all.

But there were rumors. Under Rose the BYU program had been sanctioned by the NCAA. BYU agreed to vacate its program's forty-seven wins in the two seasons between 2015 and 2017 because Nick Emery, who played point guard for Rose in those years, was receiving money from fans of the program. They paid for a car and vacations and sometimes simply gave Emery cash—gifts of around $12,000, as the NCAA investigation claimed. When the sanctions were announced in November 2018, BYU officially protested and issued a statement declaring that "Coach Rose promotes an atmosphere of compliance and monitors the program," but the NCAA denied the school's appeal.[1] *The Salt Lake Tribune* reported that, by early 2019, Rose was meeting with BYU officials to discuss being bought out of his contract. The paper speculated he was gently being ushered out the door.[2]

Things weren't as dire as they seemed. First, BYU was hardly the only university to have suffered such sanctions from the NCAA in the twenty-first century. There were dozens. One 2012 study found that the NCAA's rules were so complex and sprawling that seven in ten student-athletes broke a rule while in college—most as minor as receiving small gifts or free dinners from fans.[3] From 2006 to 2015, the NCAA sanctioned more than a quarter of all NCAA Division I football teams.[4] BYU's penalties were embarrassing, but the school could pull itself up and keep going.

Second, Rose was replaced with Mark Pope. Pope had been a steady college player on the Kentucky Wildcats that won the national title in 1996, then played professionally in Europe and on the fringes of the NBA for ten years. After hanging up his jersey he went to medical school before the University of Georgia came to call. Pope dropped out of his program to join the school's men's basketball coaching staff. Two years later Dave Rose brought him to BYU as an assistant coach. He leaned on Pope for years before Utah Valley University, a sprawling public school the next town over from BYU, put Pope in charge of its team. UVU had been a community college not many years before, and Pope brought stability to its wildly gyrating program. Two years before his arrival UVU's team made the National Invitation Tournament; the next year it went 11–19. Pope spent the next few years balancing things and methodically building a team that was regularly winning twenty games every season. When Rose retired, BYU looked four miles up Interstate 15 to Pope's office. Pope couldn't say no.

Back at BYU, Pope picked up where Rose left off. By the end of his first year the Cougars were ranked eighteenth in the nation by the Associated Press. His team made the NCAA tournament twice over the next few years. And then on April 12, 2024, he announced he was signing a contract to become head coach of the Kentucky Wildcats, one of the most prestigious programs in college basketball, and his alma mater. Again, Pope couldn't say no.

Enter, Kevin Young.

The Rise of Kevin Young

It happened quickly. Pope left on April 12, 2024, and Tom Holmoe, BYU's athletics director, announced Young would be his replacement four days later. This was, in part, because Pope left the school in a bind. The NCAA's contact period, in which schools have numerous ways to reach out to potential recruits, usually ends in May. BYU's recruitment of new players took a gigantic hit when Pope left. Over the previous few decades players had grown accustomed to the idea that they committed to coaches as much as they did schools. By the 2010s they were not shy about seeking to transfer if the coach they had agreed to play for moved on. *Sports Illustrated* observed, "In this era of college athletics and the transfer portal, hiring a replacement [coach] quickly is extremely important to retain the existing roster." Three BYU players entered the transfer portal within days after Pope's departure.[5]

Deseret News sports columnist Jay Drew thought that the pressure to hire a new coach would be a major problem for BYU. "Could Pope's departure be a blessing in disguise for the Cougars? Yeah, probably not," he said.[6] Drew worried that BYU's religious and cultural commitments meant that the school would be facing an ever-growing disadvantage in college basketball. Between transfer portals and media scrutiny, the NCAA was becoming more and more like the NBA. And that meant a religious school like BYU faced unique challenges. Drew wrote, "That BYU has perhaps the most shallow coaching candidate pool in the country adds to the problem in Provo, especially if the school adheres to a long-standing practice that its head coaches be members of the faith that sponsors and supports the institution, The Church of Jesus Christ of Latter-day Saints."[7]

Drew pointed to a few potential replacements—all members of the church. He thought the best of the bunch would be Mark Madsen, a former member of the NBA's Los Angeles Lakers who had replaced Pope at Utah Valley University. But Madsen had just taken a new job himself as head coach for the University of California, Berkeley, and it was hard to imagine him leaving such a prominent and well-compensated position. Other than Madsen, Drew shrugged. He pointed to Pope's assistant coaches, including Nick Robinson and Chris Burgess (who had, apparently, forgiven BYU for Roger Reid's gaffe two decades before). But Drew thought neither were particularly exciting options. *The Salt Lake Tribune*'s Kevin Reynolds mentioned former BYU player Lee Cummard, who was coaching BYU's women's basketball team, and Alex Jensen, a former University of Utah player who was an assistant coach in the NBA. Jensen ended up taking over the men's basketball team at his own alma mater the next year.[8]

But then, BYU hired Kevin Young. It was a coup. Drew admitted he had been wrong. "Welcome to the big leagues, BYU," he wrote. For Drew this marked the point at which BYU athletics finally professionalized. "Remember the days when the knock on BYU athletics was that the department refused to pay market value for top-flight coaches, instead relying on their affinity for the place and willingness to work for less to be a part of the faith-based school?" Drew asked.[9] They were gone. BYU seemed willing to pay, and a coach like Young was willing to come. And that BYU was about to join the Big 12, one of the premiere conferences in college athletics, meant that his hiring came none too soon. BYU was pushing in the chips, to borrow a metaphor from poker. The school was doing what it took to compete in the modern world of college sports. BYU had become a typical university, at least when it came to sports.

For some this was a victory. Steve Young, the Pro Football Hall of Fame former NFL quarterback and BYU alum, cheered. "I'm not sure that we are related, but we are now," he said. (They are, distantly. Kevin Young is descended from Lorenzo Young, younger brother to Steve's far more famous ancestor, Brigham.) Steve added, "People worry about the Cougs being able to answer and build and rise up to the Big 12 challenge—this is our answer!"[10] Utah's governor, Spencer Cox, even weighed in on X (formerly Twitter) by writing, "Whoa! Huge get for BYU. Congratulations Cougars!"[11] Ryan Smith, owner of the Utah Jazz, wrote "Congrats KY! Those who know ... know. Big get for BYU. This is a real dude for a special place."[12] In short, various Utah sportswriters, analysts, and others connected to basketball thought Young was not the typical sort of BYU coach. He was different, even though Young had never coached a Division I college basketball game in his life.

Before April 2024, no one in the media seems to have taken Kevin Young seriously as a possibility for the BYU job. One reason was that BYU had a long tradition of hiring from within—among the ranks of its own assistants—or at the least from the Mormon corridor of Utah, Idaho, or Arizona. Mark Pope had been Dave Rose's assistant, Rose had been assistant to his own predecessor, Steve Cleveland. Cleveland's predecessor Roger Reid had been an assistant for ten years before getting a shot as head coach, and so on. Even Stan Watts paid his dues as coach of the freshman team. Some who were exceptions to the assistant rule, like Danny Ainge's coach Frank Arnold, shared something else in common with Rose, Pope, Reid, and Watts: all had roots in Utah. Arnold, Watts, and

Reid all grew up in small-town Utah or Idaho, playing and then coaching for local schools. Pope, who grew up in Washington state, put in his time at Utah Valley University, and Dave Rose, who grew up in Texas, played for what was then Dixie College in St. George, Utah, before joining the proud tradition of future BYU basketball coaches who ran teams at rural Utah high schools (in his case, Pine View High School in St. George). Steve Cleveland, who had lived in California his whole life and came to BYU after coaching at Fresno City College, was the only major exception to both rules.

And then Kevin Young came along. Like Cleveland, Young had virtually no personal connections to Utah. He was born in Salt Lake City, but before he could walk his family moved to Texas and then to Georgia. Young went to high school in Marietta, Georgia, a suburban town twenty miles north of Atlanta. There he became a basketball lifer. He played on the high school team, and his coach, Roger Kvam, made a large impression on him. Kvam was "the whole reason why I wanted to coach," Young told a reporter. "He had a great life. He had five kids and he coached basketball and taught P.E. every day, and I was like, 'That seems pretty cool.'"[13]

Young may have wanted a life built around sport and family—and eventually he would say this was a reason BYU appealed to him—but pretty soon he proved himself a basketball obsessive. Kvam could see it from the beginning. He told a reporter that when Young was a freshman he got into a "scrap" with a hulking senior on the team. "He was so little, but he was not afraid," Kvam said.[14] Despite a lack of outstanding natural gifts, Young was determined to play college basketball. He ended up at a junior college, Middle Georgia State, playing two years. Finally, he had his choice of scholarship offers from three local Georgia universities—among them Kennesaw State and Clayton State, all of which played in the NCAA's Division II, a league for smaller schools. Clayton State stuck with Young even after he announced he intended to take a leave from his studies to serve a two-year mission for the church, so he stuck with them. At every stop, Young was gritty and hard-working and, despite not having the natural physical gifts of an outstanding basketball player, made himself a starting point guard. His senior year, Clayton State was the runner-up in the Division II national championships. In one game against Kennesaw, a Kennesaw State student showed up in the stands with makeshift Clayton State jerseys that read "Kevin Sucks" on the back. Kevin Young loved it. He danced and shouted and pointed at the fan, who yelled right back, until Young's coach pulled him aside to whisper, "Don't rile up the fans."[15]

Playing for Division II championships brought little glory, but Kevin Young loved it anyway. He couldn't give it up. Immediately after graduating from Clayton State at age twenty-three, it was apparent he wasn't going to make a career playing professionally. So he landed a job coaching at Oxford College, a tiny undergraduate school in rural central Georgia affiliated with Emory University. For the next eight years he moved most summers—new teams, new cities. He coached for Division III schools even tinier than Kennesaw State or Clayton State like Oxford. He coached in Ireland for the Shamrock Rovers Hoops, a financially staggering team that folded three years after he left. He coached in the D-League, a scrappy minor league the NBA had started up less than a decade before Young landed there. D-League teams traveled by bus, often had to rent practice space, and sometimes had open tryouts for anybody who thought they could make it in the pros. In 2007, one local newspaper directed anyone interested in such a tryout to call Kevin Young personally, helpfully reprinting his phone number. That's how bootstraps the D-League was.[16] But he couldn't quit—didn't want to quit—even though he was making so little money that he was paying his rent by washing windows, driving for FedEx, and selling everything from software to tickets to the very games he was coaching in. Young told reporter Tad Walch that he knew "the locations of every CVS in Southern California, because one summer he joined a crew to replace the signs outside every pharmacy in the region."[17]

This sort of drive made him a good coach. While working in Ireland, Young wasn't just coaching the team; he was managing the roster, living with his players, and handling logistics like transportation and room and board.[18] Ben Bridges, the Shamrock Rovers Hoops' center, said of the living arrangements, "We had the starting four and the coach living in the same house. It was like college. We all got really close." Young, Bridges said, "is like a brother." The year before Young arrived in Ireland, the Hoops were the worst team in the league and in a tentative financial situation. Young at least turned their record around. The team started the next season winning eight games in a row, and Bridges gave all the credit to Young, who, it appeared, never slept. "The play calling. The sets. The scouting. Everything," Bridges said. "He was next level."[19] This experience taught Young how to connect with players on a personal level and gave him an early taste of the total responsibility that comes with leading a team. Perhaps most importantly, the experience taught Young that coaching his own team was not just a dream. It was something he could do and do well. That confidence carried him through pitfall after pitfall.

Kevin Young's basketball story shows both the strain and the energy that a basketball career can bring to life as a Latter-day Saint. Despite telling the universities that recruited him that he would be taking two years as a missionary for his church, Young, like Jimmer Fredette, never served, even though all four of his brothers did. A basketball player has only a scant handful of athletic years, and Young wanted to maximize everything. A few years later, in the spring of 2013, he was in his second year in a coaching job in the D-League, finally starting to relax, feeling that he was getting his legs under him as a professional who might be able to carve out a career, when he was suddenly fired. His wife was five months pregnant. The Youngs had to move back in with family and gather themselves as Kevin, humiliated, started looking for work again. Even when he got a new job that fall—as an assistant coach for the Delaware 87ers, yet another D-League team his family had never heard of—it was humbling. He was out of town on a road trip with the team when his wife, her mother, and their three-month-old son arrived at their new home in Bear, Delaware. The apartment was old and small and smelly and even though Kevin left some bath salts in the bathroom, it was grim.

"He wasn't there, and I'd never lived east of Nebraska and it was just in a bad part of town and my mom and I just held each other and cried," Melissa Young told Tad Walch.[20] Her mother was not happy. Kevin seemed like a husband with an unreliable career. That was a terrible thing in such a family-oriented faith, and everybody knew it.

But despite his struggles, Young got opportunities because the family the church built extended beyond the people to whom he was related by blood. For Mormons, basketball had long been about building teams, cooperation, and relationships, and Kevin Young was a part of that community from the beginning. He would eventually be able to give back, but, at least early in his career, he had to receive.

The head coach of Kennesaw State, the team that beat Kevin Young's Clayton State squad in the Division II championships, was named Tony Ingle. Ingle was also a Latter-day Saint. He had been a longtime assistant to Roger Reid, who coached BYU's men's basketball team throughout the 1990s, and his son Israel played for his father and against Kevin in that championship game. "We knew the whole Young family and they're awesome," Israel told a reporter. "Kevin is such a competitor. My dad hated coaching against him but loved him because he was so tough. He's an 'aw, shucks' kind of guy but when that ball goes up, he'll fight you to win. My dad really respected him."[21]

Tony Ingle believed in Kevin Young, and two years after that game he called up Dick Hunsaker, the head coach at Utah Valley State College (later Utah Valley University), and recommended Hunsaker take a look. So in August 2005, Kevin Young left Oxford College and moved back to Utah, where he hadn't lived since he was an infant. He met Melissa Bailey, his future wife. Then he got the year in Ireland because his old college teammate from Clayton State, Jonathan Reed, was playing in Europe. Reed both talked Young up to the Shamrock Rovers Hoops and talked Young into taking the job. Reed told Young, "If you want to be a head coach, you've got to *be* a head coach. Not an assistant. Come out to Ireland and take the lead seat."[22] Young thought Reed was right. So he decided to be bold, walk away from UVSC, and try it.

And after his year in Ireland, Young was called back to Utah. Brandt Andersen, a Utah businessman, had entered into negotiations with the NBA to put a D-League team in Utah. It would be called the Utah Flash, and it would play at a public arena in Orem, only a few minutes from both UVSC and BYU campus. Andersen would own the team, but the Utah Jazz agreed to affiliate with the Flash organization. The pro team would use the Flash as a spot to work out their players, and Jazz coaches would regularly counsel with the Flash staff. Andersen and his team remembered Young from his time with UVSC. His do-everything experience with the Shamrock Rovers Hoops was also a plus.[23] He filled a similar role with the Flash, working both as a team administrator and sometime coach. He did everything from video analysis to airport pickups. Brad Jones, the Flash's first head coach, said that Young "was willing to do anything to learn, get experience."[24] During the summers he didn't quit, either. He took American professional basketball players on tours of the European leagues he had grown familiar with. And sometimes while in Utah, he went to the Marriott Center to watch Jimmer Fredette play and thought about basketball glory.

Gradually, Young developed a basketball philosophy. After three seasons, the Flash owners let original head coach Brad Jones go and handed the keys to Young. Lance Allred, a player who had bounced around the NBA, the European leagues, and the D-League, played for the Flash and praised Young for developing a smart, low-key offense. "A lot of guys get cute," he explained. In Allred's experience new coaches tended to want to put their own plans front and center, designing elaborate, complicated schemes for their players to struggle through. On the other hand, Allred said Kevin Young designed "a very simple, quick-hit offense.... He is good enough to have a quick counter to whatever the defense gives." Allred thought Young trusted his players and emphasized flexibility over pre-arranged schemes.[25] That went hand in hand with the culture Young built in Ireland: For him, coaching was mainly about building relationships with his players, showing them he relied on them as much as they were responsible to him, getting everybody to trust each other, and having faith that the wins would come. As he said later, "I've learned that there are many, many different ways to do things. I think the key things I've learned are to find what you believe in as a coach and run with that, don't overcomplicate things, and learn how to communicate with players.[26]

In 2011, Young hit the national media for the first time. A few newspapers picked up the story, but it caught fire on the internet. As the popular NBA blog *Ridiculous Upside* described it, "Eric Musselman and Kevin Young got into a bit of a confrontation on Saturday night prior to halftime of the Utah Flash game versus the Reno Bighorns."[27] The Flash were in Reno, Nevada, to play the Bighorns.

Musselman was the Reno head coach, and one might assume he would have intimidated Kevin Young. He was the son of a longtime NBA coach and had been walking the sidelines for nearly as long as Kevin Young had been alive. The job in Reno was a career reset for Musselman after multimillion-dollar jobs coaching the NBA's Sacramento Kings and Golden State Warriors went sideways. Musselman told a reporter, "I'm not doing this for the money. I'm doing it because I love the game."[28]

He had a legendary intensity. A few years before he began coaching in Reno, a journalist accompanied Eric to his twelve-year-old son's basketball camp and watched as Musselman got twitchy. He simply couldn't bear the sloppy play. Musselman started "shaking his hand frantically in a sixth grader's face. 'This is how you defend,' said Musselman, his eyes glaring and voice rising with each wag of the hand."[29]

But in Kevin Young, Eric Musselman met his match. Never mind that Musselman was twenty years older and had a much more distinguished resume. Young, who had walked away from a job and a comfortable home in Utah because he was ambitious and gritty enough to want a step up even if that step up was thousands of miles away, was not going to back down. At halftime of the March 2011 game, the Flash led the Bighorns, but Musselman was convinced the first-year head coach was abusing the rules about substituting his players in and out. When the buzzer sounded to put the game into halftime break, he stalked toward Young and did not stop until he bumped the younger man's chest with his own. Things escalated quickly. Musselman cursed at Young, and Young cursed right back. A journalist in the arena wrote, "Both coaches screamed obscenities at each other before cooler heads prevailed." The players, of all people, separated the two, and the referees threw Musselman out of the game. Young composed himself, turned back to the court, and the Flash left Reno with a 100–90 victory.[30]

The whole thing turned out to be a test, one Kevin Young did not see coming. But he passed. He won the game. He also didn't give an inch to Musselman, and other people in basketball noticed.

At the end of the 2010–11 season, the Utah Flash abruptly shut down. Brandt Andersen, the owner of the team, had moved to California. He had been right that Utah was a basketball-hungry market;

the Flash's home games in Orem had consistently packed the house. But the Jazz sucked up most of the sponsorship and business partnership opportunities in the state, and the D-League team never turned a profit. Young was caught off guard. "It's unfortunate," he told *The Salt Lake Tribune*. "We had a good thing going."[31]

Suddenly he had to find a new job, and luckily for him, Jerry Crawford remembered him. Crawford was a managing partner for another D-League team, the Iowa Energy, which happened to be looking for a new head coach. Jerry Crawford showed his colleagues the video of Young's run-in with Musselman and told them, "That guy has the DNA of a winner."[32] The Energy was in a good place since it had won the D-League championship in the spring of 2011. The team's head coach, Nick Nurse, had spent most of his career coaching in Europe before jumping to the D-League. His win with the Energy earned him an offer to coach in college, and he was hoping that offer would eventually lead to the NBA. (It did—in 2019 Nick Nurse won the NBA championship as head coach of the Toronto Raptors.) Kevin Young saw himself on a similar path. He took the job.

Unfortunately, it didn't work out. The Energy was wracked with injuries in Young's year and a half tenure, and he was fired in his second season as the team collapsed into a morass of mediocrity. Young felt lucky when the Delaware 87ers offered him an assistant coaching position a few months later even though the change meant moving his family to that aging apartment in Bear. Ironically, the 87ers were in fact the Utah Flash—the NBA's Philadelphia 76ers organization bought the moribund Flash from Brandt Andersen, renamed the team the 87ers (a reference to the year 1787, the year Delaware became the first state to vote to adopt the United States Constitution), and moved it to Delaware in April 2013. Young was grateful the team suddenly needed to hire an entire staff, but he was now an assistant in the same program he had been running only two years before.

No wonder his wife felt so stricken when she arrived in that small, smelly Delaware apartment.

But finally, finally, Kevin Young had a place where he could plant his feet, look around, and consider the forces that were tugging on his life. He recalled long conversations with John Bryant, another coach with the 87ers. Bryant said they were "questioning whether our profession could allow us to be the fathers, the husbands that we strive to be."[33] The chaotic, itinerant coach's life Young had experienced was hardly a unique experience. Bryant had moved from California to the East and eventually to Chicago to pursue the same career.

But Young thought he knew how to make this work. "A lot of things lined up for us" after they arrived on the East Coast, he would later tell the *Deseret News*.[34] Once again, he was where he had been in Ireland and at UVSC. He was doing everything, all the little things: preparing video of past games for the team to watch, making airport runs, and helping to organize workouts for the dozens of college players the Philadelphia 76ers might draft every May and June, because some of them might land with the 87ers. Young knew how to get into the grit of things. And this time, the fact that the 87ers were owned by the Sixers meant that this team wasn't teetering on the edge of financial collapse like the Flash or the Shamrock Rovers Hoops.

This was his opportunity. In organizing the draft workouts, Young got to work closely with coaches who worked for the Sixers organization. Sixers assistant coach Billy Lange, only a rung below the organization's head coach, Brett Brown, was impressed. Lange showed up for an early meal with Young to discuss the Sixers' summer doings, and "breakfast would be served and as soon as we sat down it was like we were already talking about how we were going to help Brett with the practice meeting or the next game or training camp."[35] Young, Bryant, and Lange organized the workouts, and then they would get on the court. The ex-college guard Young would play defense while prospects tried to score. It was exhausting work, but Young made himself essential. By 2014, Kevin Young was the head coach of the 87ers. By 2016, Brett Brown was impressed, and he added Kevin Young to the staff of the 76ers. He was on his way.

In his time working in Philadelphia, Young refined a specialty. In basketball terms it was called "development." In the D-League he worked with young players—those college kids who hoped that the Sixers organization might draft them and the young professionals who played for the Flash, the Energy, and the 87ers, hoping that an NBA team might notice them. When Young joined Brett Brown's staff, Brown noticed his talents and put him in charge of the Sixers' summer league team. Every NBA team recruits a squad to play in one of the brief tournaments held in July and August after the professional season is over, but most of the top players don't participate. Instead, summer league teams are made up of a mixture of young NBA players who need some additional work, newly drafted recruits who want to prove they deserve time on the NBA court, and longtime professionals who may be playing in Europe or the D-League hoping to latch on to an NBA franchise. All these competing agendas made for a tricky assignment. But from his time in the Flash, Kevin Young had figured out how to balance his competitive fire with an ability to listen to and work with his players. His shoving match with Eric Musselman sat in the same history as the ecumenical offense that Lance Allred had praised.

Billy Lange saw it. He told *The New York Times* this balance was why Young was promoted. Lange called it Young's "appropriate edge." Young dealt with players "with humility. But he is not afraid of the confrontation or the moment or the conversation." Similarly, "he understands the NBA's a player's league," Lange said. "His philosophy will be built around their skill sets, not the other way around."[36] This was precisely what Young's players had praised him for, and it made him an ideal developmental coach. He could see how each player would flourish and thrive based on their own strengths rather than on his system. But he could also gently, firmly, push them to get there.

He had lost none of his confidence. Brown said that from the moment Young arrived he was "a cocky white kid with wiggle and bounce" who would challenge members of the staff to three-point shooting contests. But he also could be thoughtful, which made his cockiness a reason for players to take him seriously, because they saw he had confidence in himself. Bryant described one incident with Christian Wood, a talented but moody big man with a real gift for scoring. During one practice Wood "got a little mouthy," turned, and walked away from the coaches. According to Bryant, Young simply walked right after Wood and talked back to him "in front of the entire team and kind of let him know where he stood, and that was that. He wasn't afraid to take it there with guys, because, ultimately, he knew that would gain their respect."[37]

Success, All at Once

In August 2020, Brett Brown was fired. The head coaching job of the Philadelphia 76ers stood open for the first time in seven years. Suddenly, Kevin Young was a hot commodity. He had mixed feelings about it. He liked Brown and was well aware of what he owed the older coach. Brown was "by far the most influential coach I've worked with and for," Young said. "It was the most important time of my life as a young coach."[38] He certainly picked up some tips and tricks from Brown—plays to run, game management, and the rest. But he also learned from Brown what it looked like to manage a massive basketball organization. Brown had a roster of assistant coaches, and he kept an eye on what the staff of the 87ers were up to. He dealt with the ownership of the 76ers, the business side of the franchise, and, of course, the players. Young's time with the 76ers was the first time that he saw such a massive basketball operation up close, a long way from the shoestring of the Shamrock Rovers Hoops. He filed it all away.

Brown had seen Young's potential and moved him to what NBA people call the front of the bench in 2018. He was Brown's lead assistant, and that made him a leading candidate to replace Brown. In summer 2020, for the first time in his life, Young was interviewing for an NBA head coaching job. He was thirty-eight years old. It was only seven years since that rainy move to Delaware that had felt like such a step backward that his wife had cried when she arrived. The experience must have been surreal.

He didn't get the job. In part the problem was that he and the rest of Brett Brown's coaching staff had been too successful. Brown had been hired in 2013 and knew that the team was beginning a long rebuilding process. Sixers management was starting over, they told Brown, and they wanted him to focus on teaching young players and slowly building up a winning franchise. It took five years, but the Sixers finally made the playoffs in 2018. In 2019 and 2020, their center Joel Embiid and versatile young forward Ben Simmons were both named NBA All-Stars. Management was ready to win. But both years the team lost in the playoffs earlier than expected and finally Brown was cut loose. Management was not in the mood to hire an unproven, young coach with a reputation for development rather than taking teams to the promised land.

Doc Rivers, a long-time NBA head coach who had won a championship coaching the Celtics, fell in the Sixers' laps instead. He'd spent seven years leading the Los Angeles Clippers, a long tenure in NBA coaching terms, and stepped down in September 2020. The Sixers had been waiting for something like this, and they snapped Rivers up. He agreed to coach the team five days after he left the Clippers. An established coach like Rivers would want to put together his own team of assistants. That meant that Kevin Young again found himself out of a job.

But this time he was ready. Young had built connections and community, and so he found a home. Monty Williams, another of Brown's assistants, had become head coach of the Phoenix Suns the year before. In mid-October 2020, Williams brought Young to Arizona. Duane Rankin of the *Arizona Republic* reported that "the familiarity is there, but that's not the only reason the Suns hired him." Asking around the Suns organization, Rankin heard two things. First, the by-now-familiar story of Young's confrontation with Eric Musselman was circling. Young was "battle tested," Suns sources told the reporter. Second, Young was a teacher, and that's what Williams needed. The Suns were a green team, led by twenty-three-year-old first-time All-Star Devin Booker, a wily shooting guard who could score. But other than Booker, the team relied on a crowd of promising first- or second-year players, such as big center Deandre Ayton and versatile swingman Mikal Bridges. Williams wanted to create exactly the sort of offense Young had been building in the D-League. It was one that "emphasizes ball movement and player movement," and Williams needed an assistant who could teach Booker that he would have more success if he relied on his teammates, and one who could show those teammates how to work with Booker's talent.[39] Kevin Young was delighted to sign up.

None too soon, because a month after Young was hired, the Suns management pulled off a coup. They traded a draft pick and four players to the Oklahoma City Thunder for point guard Chris Paul. With that, Kevin Young's mandate, and that of the entire coaching staff, suddenly changed.

In 2021, to commemorate its seventy-fifth anniversary, the NBA released a list it called "the NBA 75." Voted on by a panel of journalists, players, coaches, and team officials, the list was trumpeted as definitive: These were the seventy-five greatest players in NBA history. Chris Paul was one of the eleven on the list still playing in the NBA. His name always came up in conversations about the best point guards of all time. But he was 35 years old when Phoenix traded for him, an age when many NBA players retire, and reporters generally considered him on the downward slope of his career. "Not many NBA teams improve long term by trading for a 35-year-old point guard," worried *Arizona Republic* columnist Kent Somers. But, Somers said, if there was an exception, Paul might be it.[40] The Suns, though young and not particularly experienced, had finished the previous season strong, winning their last eight games in a row and making a surprise push for the playoffs even though they eventually fell short. Paul had that very same season taken control of another young team in Oklahoma City, leading them to a record miles better than anybody had guessed them capable of. James Jones, the Suns executive who orchestrated the trade, praised Paul's "leadership and competitive approach." Paul had been in the NBA for fifteen years and understood every aspect of the game. Monty Williams said the Point God (as Paul was called) would be a "coach on the floor."[41]

The Suns, it seemed, were accelerating their timeline. This was not going to be a gradual build like the seven years Philadelphia had given Brett Brown. Trading for Chris Paul meant the team had to win right now.

And Paul, renowned for his assertive personality, was not the type to bend to assistant coaches barely older than he was. But by the very next year, Paul was telling reporters that Young was "an unbelievable coach, a great coach."[42] And in the spring of 2021, the Phoenix Suns were in the NBA Finals, playing for the league championship.

It all came together, and Kevin Young was at the heart of it. Another assistant handled the defense, and Young took charge of the team's offense, a "point-5" offense in which every player was moving around the outside of the court. It had roots in Young's work in the D-League and his time in Philadelphia.[43] Phoenix's 2020–21 season was a stunning turnaround from the previous season. The team hadn't made the playoffs the year before, but in 2021 they entered the eight-team Western Conference playoffs as a second seed. They beat the defending champion Los Angeles Lakers in the first round and then plowed through the Denver Nuggets and the Los Angeles Clippers. By June they were playing the Milwaukee Bucks for the NBA championship. They lost the seven-game series four games to two, which was bitter. But both Chris Paul and Devin Booker were All-Stars, and around the NBA observers thought that the Suns would be a force the next year too. "There is always next year," wrote Kent Somers. "We will praise the Suns for all they accomplished in the 2020–2021 season instead of lamenting what they didn't."[44]

The Suns didn't make it back to the finals the next year or the year after that, but they were consistently one of the best teams in the NBA in the early 2020s. Williams was a grinder and a night owl, sometimes texting his assistants at four in the morning. And Kevin Young loved it. He was on top of each text, and in the summer of 2021 he became Phoenix's lead assistant coach, just as he had been in Philadelphia. He got the job for two reasons. First, Williams's chief assistant was made the head coach of the New Orleans Pelicans, which will happen to assistants on coaching staffs that make it to the NBA Finals. The second reason was more prosaic. "Kevin Young did a really good job," Monty Williams told the media. The organization gave Young a topper: the title of "associate head coach."[45]

Over the New Year holiday the next season, Kevin Young took over the Suns for four games while Monty Williams struggled with COVID-19. "Holy toast, this thing has really hit me in the head," Williams confessed. It frustrated him deeply. "My wife bought half of Whole Foods and put it in the bedroom," he said. He sat and ate and stewed as he watched games, texting and calling his team and coaching staff, sometimes even while players were on the court.[46]

Williams wasn't the only one; four players with significant roles on the team also caught the virus. Kevin Young was working with a skeleton crew. "This thing has really derailed a lot of routines," he observed. It was the complaint of a perfectionist, a coach who, like Williams, wanted all the planning and preparation he could get. But in his characteristically generous way, Young praised his players. "Give them credit for being able to adjust on the fly," Young said.[47] In that line, we see the two sides of Kevin Young the coach: demanding, precise, and well-prepared but also flexible, a coach who understands his preparation is not more important than the relationships he builds with his players. His best players saw this. Booker said that he spent a lot of time with Young and would "pick his brain. We'd talk about a game that was on TV last night and what we would've done differently. Usually, we'd end our conversations on the same exact page."[48] Chris Paul agreed. "He did a great job," Paul said. "KY will be a head coach very soon in this league."[49] He was right about one thing. Young and his tattered band of COVID survivors did a fine job. They won two games and lost two during the week and a half Monty Williams was stuck in his bedroom.

But Chris Paul was wrong about the other thing. Kevin Young took a job in college basketball.

A Courtship

It was inevitable because firings are always inevitable in the NBA's coaching ranks. The Phoenix Suns fired Monty Williams in May 2023, almost immediately after the Suns lost in the second round of the playoffs for the second year in a row. The Suns management was still in a hurry. A new owner had purchased the team a few months earlier, and he was frustrated the team had not made it back to the NBA Finals after two years of trying. In the first six months of 2023 he traded nearly all the cornerstone players the coaching staff had been working with for years. Mikal Bridges and Deandre Ayton were out, and in came Kevin Durant. By acclamation Durant was one of the greatest players in NBA history, another member of the NBA 75, a seven-foot lanky forward who could score from anywhere on the court without breaking a sweat. Chris Paul was traded too. Paul was by then thirty-eight and the team's new owner appeared to believe Paul had finally reached the end of his basketball road. Paul went to the Washington Wizards in exchange for the scoring guard Bradley Beal. Both Beal and Durant were talented, but both had reserved personalities and neither was the caliber of leader Paul was. As management began looking for a new coach, it became clear that the joyful Williams days were over.

There was a lot of speculation that Young would get the promotion. Devin Booker, the Suns' one remaining star with tenure, praised Young to whoever bothered to ask. He "has been a big boost to my career," Booker told a reporter asking whether Young would be a good candidate for the top job.[50] Greg Moore, a sports columnist for the *Arizona Republic*, said that "Young will make a great coach one day."[51]

Young didn't get the job. He was one of three finalists, but the Suns hired Frank Vogel, who had won a championship coaching the Lakers three years earlier. As with Philadelphia, Suns management wanted a proven head coach. But the *Arizona Republic* confirmed that the organization felt strongly enough about Young that they offered him $2 million a year to stay in his position as associate head coach. Vogel was simply informed that this would be the case. "New head coaches typically pick their own staff," reporter Duane Rankin wrote. "But retaining Young is a way for Phoenix to continue the continuity and connection he has with Booker."[52]

That was some security, but it was not clear that the chaos engulfing the Suns would end anytime soon. So Young was looking around. Rankin reported that three other NBA franchises reached out to him asking for interviews while the coaching carousel that followed the end of the 2023 NBA season whirled. Young might have thought he wouldn't be long for Phoenix, but it turned out he wasn't long for the NBA.

Mark Pope's departure did not take BYU wholly by surprise, so the school was prepared to move quickly. On Thursday, April 11, 2024, a staffer at the University of Kentucky called Tom Holmoe, BYU's athletic director, to formally ask for permission to interview Mark Pope. Holmoe granted permission, Kentucky called Pope, skipped the interview and offered him the job of head coach, and Pope accepted right away. That evening, Kevin Young landed in Sacramento. Earlier that day he had met with the management of the Brooklyn Nets to discuss their open head coaching position before hopping on a plane to catch up with his team, who were playing the Sacramento Kings on Friday. Shortly after his flight touched down he received a text message: Pope was gone. Later that night he received a phone call from Holmoe's assistant, who told Young that if he was interested in Pope's old job, BYU would be interested in talking with him.

Young pondered the offer. He had been invited to interview for the job in 2019, when Pope was hired. But now the Brooklyn job was still out there, and he was in Sacramento in the first place to help Frank Vogel run a game against the Sacramento Kings the next day. His head was spinning.

He called his wife, Melissa. They talked about it. The Suns beat the Kings Friday night. The next day, Saturday, April 13, Young and the Suns boarded a plane to Minneapolis to play the final game of their season against the Minnesota Timberwolves. When the plane landed, Young powered up his phone and saw a tremendously long text message from Melissa.[53]

She told Kevin she hoped BYU could be a refuge from the strain that the business of the NBA was putting on their family. She had followed Kevin for the thirteen years of their marriage—that small, smelly apartment in Delaware, the sudden and abrupt moves from Utah to Iowa to Philadelphia to Phoenix. The NBA regular season was eighty-two games long. Kevin was gone sometimes half the year, in airports and places like Sacramento and Minneapolis.

"We can give the NBA up. We can. We can give up the fun, the cool—it is cool, it's fun, it's exciting—but we can give it up for our family," Melissa wrote.[54]

She had put her finger on the powerful tensions moving within modern basketball. By 2024, the NBA was big business—hundreds of millions of dollars, television contracts, and media. That business was often destructive to the unselfish impulses that James Naismith had wanted basketball to promote. It could also be destructive to families, friendships, and community. Kevin Young was trying hard to keep success at his job and at home in balance.

This was the NBA's version of amateurism. Every coach Kevin Young spent time with believed that basketball should bring people together. Monty Williams's grandfather was a Disciples of Christ minister who made sure that Williams grew up attending church. As an adult, Williams led his teams in the Lord's Prayer before every game and often spoke with other players and coaches about "Christ, and how he gets us through difficult times," as one of Williams's friends put it.[55] Williams told a journalist that part of his business was teaching each player that "winning or losing or getting a contract or not getting signed by a team" wasn't the real purpose of the game, that they couldn't "change consequences with lifting more weights or getting more shots." Instead, he said, "you need a relationship." Williams thought basketball should teach players to depend on each other and on God. When his players or colleagues were suffering, he always showed up with gifts and time and prayers, if people wanted them. And that's why Melissa and Kevin Young clicked with him.[56]

Monty Williams was beloved by his players and his staff for this. But Williams also got fired when his teams stopped winning as much as the owner thought they should. Even players as admired as Chris Paul got traded. He was sent from Oklahoma City to Phoenix, where he was welcomed with open arms, celebrated, and then three years later, once the team disappointed, was shipped off to Washington, DC, for a younger player the team thought would help them win more than Chris Paul could. Paul found out that the Suns traded him to Washington from text messages from his son, who saw news reports about it while Paul was on a plane flight. The trade happened only a week after Paul told Duane Rankin he "wanted to stay in Phoenix." Paul was on that plane to New York to appear on a talk show to talk about a book he had written about his father. When a reporter on the show asked Paul how he felt about the trade, a friend of his also on the show interjected before Paul could answer: "He's trying to be nice about it." Paul simply said that the Suns ownership, "I guess, just wanted to go in a different direction."[57]

That was what Melissa Young worried about. The NBA was the place where Kevin could reach the heights of his profession, but more and more it felt as though basketball was pulling him away from his family. Melissa told Kevin that if he coached BYU, he would travel less, his season would be shorter, and he would have at least one day a week—Sunday—always off. So Young told Tom Holmoe at BYU he'd be willing to talk.

BYU moved as quickly as any other major collegiate basketball power did. Young was meeting with the president of BYU by Monday, April 15. But by the mid-2020s, Clark Gilbert, the church's new commissioner of education, was prodding BYU to emphasize its religious character in new ways. Religious universities might express their identities differently. Some promote the study of theology, others encourage service, and still others require statements of faith. By the 2020s BYU administration was hearkening back to Ernest

Wilkinson's conviction that the best way to maintain a distinctive identity was through enforcement of the norms of The Church of Jesus Christ of Latter-day Saints on campus. This meant that Young, like other staff members, would sit for an interview with a high-ranking leader of the church after his interview with the president, and that Melissa Young would be expected to join.[58] The interview happened April 15. Both Youngs were happy with it, and the next day, April 16, they agreed that Kevin should take the job. He called Tom Holmoe, and informed Brooklyn and Phoenix shortly afterward.

These twin imperatives—toward making BYU basketball competitive in the modern, professionalized, lucrative world of the sport on the one hand and emphasizing BYU's religious identity and mission on the other—became visible almost immediately. Matt Norlander, a reporter for CBS, got wind of the hire the afternoon of April 16 and reported, citing an unnamed source, that the deal was for seven years and "in the neighborhood of $30 million."[59]

The number startled Jay Drew, a sports columnist for the LDS Church-owned *Deseret News*. "If true, that financial figure, which will never be acknowledged by BYU as the school is private and not subject to open records requests, is as surprising as the hiring itself," he wrote.[60] Norlander also reported that Ryan Smith, alumnus of BYU and billionaire software entrepreneur, had been instrumental in the hire. Smith was also the owner of the Utah Jazz and an evident basketball fan. According to Norlander, Smith had committed to major financial support for BYU's basketball program in order to make Young's hiring possible.

Funding from outside sources is hardly unusual in the world of college sports. Boosters, as wealthy fans willing to donate to a university's sports programs are often called, have become more powerful and important to those universities as collegiate sports has professionalized, and coaches' compensation packages are no exception. If Norlander was right about the deal, Young would be making roughly the same as Mark Madsen, the head coach at the University of California–Berkeley, but not as much as what the highest-paid college coaches in the country were getting. Coaches like Bill Self, Dan Hurley, and John Calipari—all of whom were considered the best of the best in the 2023–24 school year—made in the range of $8 million that year alone.[61] In 2012, one scholar estimated that wealthy boosters cover anywhere from 50 percent to 75 percent of many college coaches' compensation packages, sometimes funneled through perks like free automobiles, housing, or large fees for speaking engagements.[62]

Sociologist Howard Nixon credits these patterns to what he calls a sports "arms race," in which programs compete with each other for the best players and the most famous coaches in the hopes of attracting more and more money. That revenue came not simply from ticket prices and selling T-shirts with logos, but from broadcast deals with television networks and, most of all, from pleased boosters. "Campus leaders believe that winning translates into money, status, and power for the institution," Nixon says, and they are "driven by the assumption that outspending your competitors leads to more wins."[63]

In 2023, BYU joined the Big 12, an athletic conference that included the University of Arizona, Arizona State University, the University of Utah, Baylor University, and a number of other schools in Texas. (Despite the name, as of 2025 the conference had sixteen members.) In 2023, Big 12 schools averaged $129 million in athletic revenue—from boosters, tickets, and media rights, among other things. *Sports Illustrated* wrote that in 2021, that BYU reported far less than the average—$106 million in athletic revenue to the Department of Education.[64] That difference, perhaps, is why the media reacted as it did to Kevin Young's hire. "The Cougars are investing like a program that wants to compete for Big 12 championships," wrote *Sports Illustrated*'s Casey Lundquist.[65] And Gordon Monson, one of the leading sports columnists in Utah, marveled at the "improbable and downright wild hire." Monson believed that while BYU had often underpaid its coaches, boosters Ryan Smith and Danny Ainge had forced "a new level of commitment to sports at the school."[66]

To the media, the Cougars seemed to have finally committed to the world of sports as business, sports as media, and sports as fundraising.

But the school also seemed uncomfortable with that assumption, whatever level of truth it might have held. BYU administrators hoped instead to emphasize the appeal of working in the religious atmosphere of the school. They pushed back hard against CBS's report of Young's salary in the LDS Church-owned *Deseret News*. Matt

Norlander's report "about Young's contract was inaccurate and overstated. It is not worth 'in the neighborhood of $30 million' and is not being financed by outside donors," wrote reporter Tad Walch, referring to "multiple BYU sources." Walch did not share alternative numbers. But Keith Vorkink, BYU's vice president for advancement, did tell the reporter that "donor funds are vital to supporting Cougar sports, but the department pays the contracts of its employees and coaches." Of course, Vorkink's wording does not preclude CBS's report that Smith has committed to make financial gifts to the BYU basketball program in the wake of the Young hiring; it also does not preclude multiple sources of compensation aside from direct salary. The university wanted to emphasize that BYU did not understand Young's hire as a commitment to upping the ante in an ongoing game of financial, media, and sports success. Instead, Vorkink told Walch that "BYU is also different than many schools . . . We ask that of many of our coaches, several of whom face more lucrative options but choose to stay at BYU to contribute to the university's distinctive mission in a spiritually supportive and family friendly environment."[67] Vorkink wanted to frame Kevin Young's hire as a moral choice on the part of a coach who was choosing a community, not a salary.

That language echoes the old debates on BYU campus—debates about what basketball is for. Winning or character? Money or community? It was the age-old debate between Ernest Wilkinson and Stan Watts. This tension was one Krešimir Ćosić, Jimmer Fredette, and Danny Ainge all felt, and it left a mark on Kevin Young's decision.

The Ground, Running

BYU held a press conference to announce Kevin Young's hire on April 17. According to the *Deseret News*, Ryan Smith picked Young and his family up in the official Utah Jazz plane and flew them from Phoenix to Utah.[68] Young had only a few hours to enjoy the announcement because the Suns had a seven-game playoff series against the Minnesota Timberwolves beginning April 20, and Young insisted that he wanted to finish out his commitment to the team. The two teams played a series of games in Minneapolis and then Phoenix. But the new Suns, Kevin Durant and all, were swept by that pesky young Timberwolves team, four games to nothing.

Kevin Young and his wife, Melissa, aboard a flight to Provo in April 2024, where Young shocked the basketball world by announcing he was leaving a promising coaching career in the NBA to become head coach at BYU. *Courtesy BYU Photo/Nate Edwards*

They were out of the playoffs in barely more than a week's worth of games. It was an underwhelming end to a rapid rise through the NBA, but Young was ready to focus on the Cougars.

That he was juggling his obligations in the NBA and the NCAA for a couple of weeks was emblematic of the tensions that dogged his career. Even as he was helping Frank Vogel make a plan to handle the Timberwolves, he was also beginning some of the most important work of a college coach: recruiting.

A few months before BYU hired Young, the school's football coach, Kalani Sitake, spoke to the media to announce his crop of recruits for the 2024–25 school year. Sitake said out loud what Utah journalists had often concluded: BYU faced both unique opportunities and unique challenges in its recruiting, just as it did in its coach hiring. The football team had just endured a middling season, and it was getting harder and harder to recruit good players. Both Sitake and Mark Pope, before he left, said that their programs lacked the financial "war chests" to compete with many other schools in attracting students. Journalist Gordon Monson said that BYU administration was "uncomfortable" talking about money and athletics and always had been. Though BYU's fan base was rabid and its pockets deep, the school's leadership, including the church leaders who ultimately were in charge, found thinking about the overlap of sports, business, and education awkward.[69]

Sitake, Pope, and others instead pointed to distinctions they believed would attract players to BYU, whether those players were LDS or not. "We are never going to be a program focused on the money as the attraction," said Sitake. "The value of mentoring. The value of leadership and camaraderie, fellowship. To build yourself spiritually, physically and mentally. We have all those things."[70] Sitake was careful—as James Naismith had been careful—not to emphasize virtues exclusive to a particular religious denomination as the number of non-LDS athletes at BYU grew throughout the early 2000s. Many of those athletes were religious, though not Latter-day Saints. A rising number were members of other religious traditions that embraced behavioral expectations like those of the LDS Church. Muslim players like Fousseyni Traore praised the lack of alcohol and the devotion to prayer on campus to the *Daily Universe*.[71] As BYU's leadership was emphasizing adherence to the church's expectations for LDS members of the university community, reaching out to athletes from similar religious groups was a way to broaden the pool of potential recruits in an increasingly competitive athletic landscape.

Kevin Young brought yet another recruiting advantage to BYU. He said at his introductory press conference that it was his aim to "make this place the best place in college basketball to prepare young men to play in the NBA, and with my background, I think we're going to get that done."[72] He said he would run a version of the point-5 offense he had developed with Phoenix so his players would get a sense for how the NBA game worked. He promised to be a bridge between the Marriott Center and the NBA game. His players might meet NBA players. They might learn from NBA coaches. Most of all, they would know they would have a name trusted in the NBA advocating for them.

That a coach in the NBA, a young assistant with a good shot at getting a head coaching job, would walk away from the league in favor of a college program with a solid but unspectacular track record was baffling to many. But the move also carried with it a certain mystique. Young players, their families, and the media seemed to believe that Kevin Young brought with him secrets that most college coaches didn't have. This belief meant that Young could pitch his recruitment of players in ways that someone like Sitake could not. Young could promise all that Sitake could: BYU could offer a moral and mature program, one that would develop athletes as men as well as players. But he could also promise professional and financial opportunities that few other college coaches could. Kevin Young was the best of both worlds.

Devin Booker, the All-Star for the Phoenix Suns whom Young coached for years, said everything BYU might have hoped for. "I'm excited for him and his family, man. He's somebody that I developed a great relationship with, somebody that, you know, I wish I could have played college basketball for or have somebody like him recruit me. So I'm keeping a close eye on that program and everything that he's doing. I know they're in really good hands."[73] A high school player hearing that was worth its weight in gold to recruiters.

April is a late date for recruiting to college programs, particularly when a coach is juggling the NBA playoffs. But Young got started immediately. A month after he signed his contract with BYU, word leaked that Egor Demin, an eighteen-year-old Russian who had been playing professionally in the European leagues, would play at BYU in the 2024–25 school year. The *Deseret News* claimed Demin was the first consensus top-tier basketball player to ever commit to BYU.[74] But he was not a Latter-day Saint. It was also clear that Demin would probably play for only a year in the American college system, enough to get his feet wet, learn about life in the United States, and get a feel for American basketball. As expected, after his year at BYU Demin entered the June 2025 NBA draft. Brooklyn selected him with the eighth pick.

This sort of one-and-done commitment had been common in many of the top basketball programs in the United States for years. Players like Syracuse's Carmelo Anthony wanted to get their feet under them before jumping directly into the pros, but also didn't want to spend four years of their youth toiling at a university while the money and fame of the NBA beckoned. In 2006, the NBA formalized the impulse into policy. But such a thing had never happened at BYU before, with the exception of Shawn Bradley foregoing the final years of college after he returned from his mission for the church. Demin's commitment was a further signal that Young was professionalizing the school's program. The *Daily Universe* noticed. A "new standard in 'Pro-vo' is being set," cracked a columnist.[75]

Demin himself certainly agreed. In a press conference at BYU he said precisely what Young and BYU officials hoped he would, that he picked the school for Young's expertise and potential for career development, but also because of BYU's unique community. Demin's connection to BYU began with Travis Hansen, a former BYU basketball player who had a long career in the Russian basketball leagues. Hansen knew the Demin family, put them in touch with Young, and, once Egor arrived in Provo, Hansen's family fed him dinner every Sunday night. Travis walked Egor through getting a driver's license, getting through the college basketball season, and preparing for the NBA. "This place is amazing for development," Demin said. "And to the young guys who are [considering] BYU, this place is full of smart people and dedicated people who are putting in the work into the process for you and trying to make you better, not just on the court, but off the court." Demin also found BYU congenial because its atmosphere was congruent with his religious beliefs. He is a practicing Russian Orthodox Christian. "I was coming here with faith, and I am leaving here with a bigger faith," he said.[76]

That attitude was a particular cocktail of professional competence and distinctive religious commitments. It was a resolution of the tensions that have dogged BYU basketball for decades, an assertion that BYU can, indeed, have both. And in Kevin Young BYU landed a coach who seems to have figured out the recipe.

6

AJ DYBANTSA AND THE CHANGING OF THE GAME

The ball skipped into the corner, bouncing into AJ Dybantsa's hands where he stood six feet from the baseline. Without hesitation, he jab-stepped right, then drove left—fast, low, hungry. A French defender slid into his path. Too late. In just three long strides, Dybantsa was at the rim, twisting midair to shield the ball with his body. The defender stumbled and fell, crashing to the hardwood. Dybantsa laid it in off the glass—clean, smooth, inevitable. It was the opening play of Team USA's game against France in the 2024 World Cup's seventeen and under bracket. It was late June in Turkey, and it was clear from that first move: AJ Dybantsa wasn't just here to compete. He was here to dominate.

He had turned seventeen that January. He was six-foot-eight and a lanky 210 pounds. He looked like a man playing against boys. The tournament, of course, was for boys. But these were the best boys, the top young talent from around the globe. He didn't score the most among the Americans, but he scored the second most (twenty-five points), and in every way—pull-up midrange jumpers, Euro-step floaters, thunderous dunks. He didn't have the most assists, but he had the second most (five). He didn't have the most rebounds, but he had the third most (five again). He also had five steals. He snagged rebounds, smoothly guided the ball up the court, and made precisely the right pass to teammates sneaking behind defenders fixated on Dybantsa himself.

In short, AJ Dybantsa did everything, and he did everything well. On a team loaded with future collegiate and NBA talent, Dybantsa was the compass. The Americans won by twenty-three points. Later in the tournament, the Americans were thumping the Filipino team

AJ Dybantsa led Team USA to the 2024 World Cup under-seventeen championship. *Courtesy Altan Gocher, Getty Images*

by nearly one hundred points when Dybantsa dove onto the floor to grab a loose ball, giving himself a nice skin burn. Then he stood up and sprinted back to be in position on defense. He didn't showboat. He didn't take possessions off. He was calm yet relentless. He passed up shots to set up his teammates.

Team USA easily won the 2024 World Cup under-seventeen championship. They beat their opponents, on average, by sixty-four points. AJ Dybantsa was named as one of five tournament-wide All-Stars. He helped lead Team USA to the gold medal, so mission accomplished. But his real victory was in the message he sent to the basketball world: Dybantsa was coming.

Say you'd never heard of Dybantsa, never seen him play. Say you went to the internet to find out about him what you could. One of the videos that would likely be at top of your search results is from the YouTube channel *Ball Game*, and it is called "AJ Dybantsa Senior Season Highlights! Craziest Posters, Crossovers & More!" It's from January 2025. Dybantsa has just turned eighteen. Watching Dybantsa play against high school competition in these highlights is, at times, like watching Beethoven give a master class in composition to elementary school students. The video is twelve minutes long and amateurish, shot from an awkward angle. The squeaks from the players' shoes are audible, and so are the ragged shouts from fans. The video is charming, but the key is this: Dybantsa scores, sure. But what he doesn't do might be as important.

The first highlight shows an inbound play on the baseline. One of Dybantsa's teammates is tossing the ball into play. Before the play begins, Dybantsa drifts over to the sideline, almost casually. When the whistle blows, he immediately darts toward the basket so quickly his defender is lost. Dybantsa floats toward the basket, catches the ball in midflight, and easily dunks it. And then he seems almost puzzled. He pauses and glances to the side as though he's thinking about staring down the poor guy he just dunked on. But he doesn't. It's as though he changes his mind and runs back up court.

He shows this respect every time. He makes his defender stumble with a crossover dribble and lobs a pass toward the rim for a teammate to dunk. He shakes off a defender, bounces the ball off the floor, leaps into the air, catches and dunks. And every time, he immediately turns and rushes back to pick up the person he's supposed to be defending.

Basketball knowers have caught on to this. Krysten Peek of *Yahoo! Sports* wrote that one of Dybantsa's great gifts is a willingness to do the unglamorous work on the court with a lack of interest in celebration. He's an "elite defender, sitting down and guarding the switch off the perimeter," she wrote. The journalist Erikas Polockas talked to one of Dybantsa's old high school coaches. "He is extremely respectful," said Ryan Bernardi, who praised Dybantsa's "maturity and personality." [1]

But Dave McCann of Salt Lake City's *Deseret News* noticed something else. "There are two AJ Dybantsas," he said. One certainly was "a quiet, humble, genuine young man from Brockton, Massachusetts." But the other—well, Dybantsa himself told McCann: "I am mad on the court. I play angry. I'm very passionate." The first Dybantsa is the one that's thrilled people at BYU. He's the one who talks about family and is the rare American teenager who says he's grateful for "unconditional love" with a straight face. [2]

The other Dybantsa is a fiery competitor who wants to win and be famous. That Dybantsa showed up on ESPN's morning talk show *First Take* in December 2024. The show is hosted by Stephen A. Smith, whom the *Dayton Daily News* called America's premiere "sports yeller."[3] *First Take* is not a place to modestly contemplate how unconditional love has built one's character. The veteran sports journalist Scoop Jackson called Smith's reign on *First Take* "Dramatic, yes. Over-the-top and loud, always," and "sports-journalism-shared-performance art."[4] But make no mistake—Smith is a consummate professional and knows exactly what he's doing. Few people are harder workers than a journalist who is either hosting his own show or appearing on somebody else's upward of six hours a day, every day. Smith knows better than most that sports in the United States today is a business, and that business is driven by ratings, and those ratings are won by exactly the sort of thing that Dybantsa generally does not do on a basketball court: yelling, controversy, and swagger. This might seem cynical, but it's not wrong.

When he appeared on *First Take*, Dybantsa seemed to know exactly what he was doing, too. He was there to announce which college basketball program he was going to play for in the fall of 2025. He had been recruited by virtually all of them, including longtime titans Kansas, North Carolina, Auburn, and Baylor. The episode began with a scripted video introduction in which a skydiver wearing a helmet advertising the energy drink Red Bull leapt out of a plane to bring Dybantsa the gear that he would wear to make his appearance on the show.

This was, of course, ridiculous. But it happened because Dybantsa has an endorsement deal with Red Bull. Then, while seated in the studio across from Stephen A. (as he is known), Dybantsa unzipped his jacket to reveal a BYU T-shirt. Stephen A. and his co-host Molly Qerim looked baffled. Smith said, "I'm shocked, I ain't gonna lie, that it's BYU.... I thought you were going to pick North Carolina because of the ACC [Atlantic Coast Conference] and the Duke-North Carolina rivalry." But Dybantsa explained, "My ultimate goal is to get to the NBA, and he coached one of my favorite players of all time, Kevin Durant." The "he" Dybantsa was referring to was Kevin Young. More important than Young himself was what Young represented: the NBA.[5]

That is the *First Take* Dybantsa, the Dybantsa who sometimes bounces the ball off the floor to himself as he's dunking, a moment of showboating nobody would call humble. But there is also the Dybantsa who dazzled the Latter-day Saints at BYU by saying, earnestly, "I'm a big family guy. I do everything for my family and with my family. It's good to have my family around." This is the Dybantsa who brushes off the dunks, doesn't stare down opponents, and seemed to one reporter vaguely embarrassed by antics like those highlighted on *First Take.* "If you see me on the court, it's like a horrible representation of who I really am," he told Dave McCann. "Off the court, I'm just chill."[6] Dybantsa said, with all sincerity, that he'd have been happy clapping at the end of the bench for Team USA at the World Cup, and credited his parents for instilling an ethic of "hard work" that has taught him to enjoy the game more than the praise. Dybantsa is an American teenager who doesn't seem like an American teenager. "I really don't have hobbies," he said. "I don't play video games. If I'm not playing basketball, I'm watching basketball. If I watch a [Netflix show] now, I'm sleeping through it. I can't watch anything else."[11]

It is possible that this Dybantsa is a shrewd media creation. Both AJ and his father, Ace, who has retired from his earlier life as a law enforcement officer to manage his son's career, have been around the media for years now and know how it works. But that possibility seems unlikely. AJ was raised the way he was raised long before the NBA became a serious option. The two AJs might be an exaggeration, but there is truth in each of them.

What BYU managed to pull off is this: getting both Dybantsas to sign. And that's because both BYU and AJ Dybantsa know better than most that the two Dybantsas reflect two impulses—sometimes competing, sometimes harmonious—within basketball itself. AJ grew up understanding what it means to bring these impulses into alignment. And BYU has been working for decades to figure it out, too.

Genealogy

Brazzaville, the capital of the Republic of the Congo, is a sprawling city of two million on the western bank of the Congo River, three hundred miles south of the equator in Central Africa. The French explorer Pierre de Brazza planted a small military outpost on the site in 1880. At the time, European states were busy subjugating the indigenous nations of sub-Saharan Africa. The site that would become the city called Brazzaville was right across the river from territory King Leopold II of Belgium was ruthlessly exploiting. That territory has become the Democratic Republic of the Congo, the Republic's much larger, though similarly named, neighbor. On their side of the river, the French strongarmed King Makoko VIII, ruler of the Teke people, into becoming more or less a vassal. When the Belgians began to construct a major city called Leopoldville on their bank, the French turned Brazzaville into a major hub in order to counter Belgian attempts to control trade in the area. In 1910 Brazzaville became the capital of French Equatorial Africa, a large chunk of territory sprawling across what today belongs to four independent nations.

During the Second World War, the Black French military leader Félix Éboué rallied French Equatorial Africa against Germany. After the Nazis conquered France proper, a good chunk of the French Resistance fled to Brazzaville. In 1958, the regions within French Equatorial Africa voted for independence, and the next year the Republic of the Congo held its first-ever elections. But the country almost immediately fell into factional struggles among various ethnic groups, and by the mid-1960s a series of military leaders seized control of the nation. An officer named Denis Sassou Nguesso was assigned control of Brazzaville itself. He slowly, steadily ascended through the chaos of the 1960s and 1970s, and he asserted power over the entire nation in 1979. Except for a brief period in the mid-1990s, he has held the presidency, and authoritarian control, of the Republic of the Congo ever since.

The Congo is relatively small, with only six million inhabitants as of 2020. A third of those live in Brazzaville proper. The city is a major port on the Congo River. Oil and other natural resources extracted from the heartlands of the Congo and other central African nations move through Brazzaville, and as trade rises so does the city's population—it has quadrupled since the 1990s. The Livingstone Falls, a stretch of massive churning rapids in the Congo River, sit right outside the city. Brazzaville's residents do good business hauling cargo out of the river and moving it past the rapids on railroads.

In the late 1960s, long before the city's population passed one million, and just as the new independent Congolese government was dismantling the infrastructure that had divided the city into European and African sections, a boy named Anicet Dybantsa was born there. His parents had moved to the city hoping for work and better opportunities as other of their relatives had done in the past. Like many inhabitants of Brazzaville, Anicet had family throughout Congo and in France. He grew up speaking French, as do most people in Brazzaville, but he also learned the Kilari and Kikongo dialects to talk with his grandparents. In 1980 his parents sent him to live with an older brother in France to get an education, and nine years later he followed family networks again and moved in with a cousin in Boston. There he began going by Ace.[7]

The Dybantsa family in the United States is an immigrant family. Ace calls them "Jafrican," because he is Congolese and his wife, Chelsea, is Jamaican.[8] As such, they fit archetypes scholars have observed in immigrants to the United States. The economists Ran Abramitzky and Leah Boustan, blending together historical and social scientific research, debunk some myths about American immigration and offer conclusions that affirm others. Their work helps to describe the Dybantsa family's experience. Immigrants to the United States tend to rely on family and community networks, as Anicet did. They tend to settle in places that offer both proximity to family and economic opportunities, education, and a variety of jobs.

The Boston area provided all these things for Anicet. Like many other immigrants, when he arrived in the United States he took a series of jobs that didn't require English language skills—janitorial work and cooking at fast food restaurants. He learned English by watching television and talking to people in stores and on the streets. He put himself through a local community college, found better jobs in retail and security and, at long last, landed stable employment as part of the police force at Boston University. Ace told a reporter that he hunted down this job in particular so his children "could get free tuition" at the university. Children he didn't have yet. But he was planning ahead.[9]

Ace's strategy is consistent with Abramitzky and Boustan's findings. A first generation of immigrants might not achieve great economic success—indeed, the scholars argue that while modern immigrants to the United States tend to achieve the same degree of economic success as those in the great wave of migration to the United States just over a century ago, that success tends to be moderate. But those immigrants tend to embrace the sort of lifeways—learning English; marrying people they would not have met had they stayed at home; taking on English-sounding names like "Ace"; and joining institutions like churches, community groups, and sports teams that foster both assimilation and a better life for their children. Ace met Chelsea Hudson in 2005 in a gym parking lot in the Boston suburb of Brockton when he was headed to his car and she was looking for a space to leave hers. He had just landed the Boston University job. She was born in Hanover, Jamaica, in the early 1970s and had moved to Boston in 1985 with her mother, following other family members as Ace had. She had earned a college degree and was working as a health-care consultant. The two soon married and had their family—two daughters, Jasmyn and Samarra, and a son, Anicet Jr., born in January 2007. The Dybantsas called him "AJ," for short.

Ace hung a plastic Spider-Man basketball hoop on his son's bedroom door when AJ was five years old. Ace built a half-court with a basketball hoop in the backyard a few years later.

He did these things quite consciously. Ace told reporters later that he hoped AJ would enjoy the sport because he understood that while professional basketball might be a long shot, it could become an incredible financial boon for his family if it worked out. Ace always said that he liked the character development sports offered, but in the back of his mind he also knew it might be a way to ensure the Dybantsas' financial security. His instincts were right. AJ started to sleep with a basketball under his arm. Chelsea once showed a reporter a "dream book" that he and the other seven-year-olds in his

Four-year-old AJ Dybantsa visits the White House, wearing the jersey number of Boston Celtics great Kevin Garnett. Dybantsa is still a Celtics fan. *Courtesy Dybantsa family*

elementary school class made. AJ's opens with four sentences written in the careful, neat penmanship of a child. "My name is Anicet Dybantsa. I am seven years old. My favorite thing about first grade is gym class. When I grow up, I'd like to be a basketball player."[10]

A few years later, young AJ told his father, in all seriousness, "Dad, I'm not going to BU." His basketball ambitions were rising higher than the prospect of joining Boston University's Terriers, whose basketball program had last won a game in the NCAA tournament in 1959 and might be most generously assessed as fine. Ace told a reporter that he did a doubletake, considered the reasons for choosing to work at BU, and started laughing.[11]

By seventh grade, AJ was getting tall. And he was getting good. Ace put AJ into a developmental class run by private coach Brandon Ball. AJ showed up four times a day for workouts and training—skills at six a.m.; weights at nine; shooting at noon; and a wrap-up workout late in the evening, even on nights Ball's students played intermural games. Ball's other students were older than AJ and the boy got knocked around some. "He'd come home crying because the bigger kids were beating him up," Ace told a reporter. AJ's father told him, "If you don't want to do it, you don't have to." But AJ said, "I am not quitting."[12] Before long he was one of the bigger kids. By the time he was in eighth grade he was six-feet, six-inches. In ninth grade he was named the Massachusetts Gatorade Player of the Year. In tenth grade, he played for the US National under-sixteen team and won the gold medal at the Tournament of the Americas. By then a lot of people were wondering which college program he would end up in.

Abramitzky and Boustan argue that the children of immigrant parents tend to be more upwardly mobile than either their parents or the children of US-born parents in comparable situations. The reasons why are varied, and the authors think it has a lot to do with the parents' willingness to take risks and dislocate themselves geographically. These families have already done it, so they are not always reluctant to move homes in pursuit of better schools, more economic opportunities, and new communities. Ace and Chelsea picked where they lived and even, in Ace's case, the job he took at BU with an eye to his children's success. And when AJ proved gifted, they did not hesitate to move him around the country. Abramitzky and Boustan also offer qualified support to another common belief about immigrant families: parents work hard to "transmit education and skills."[13] What parents learn in their own journeys, they pass on to children.

And so AJ Dybantsa's parents constantly reminded him where he came from and how he might progress. When he was four years old, for the first time but not the last, his parents took him to Brazzaville. When he was a teenager, they took him to Jamaica. They wanted him to feel rooted in a history that went beyond Brockton, Massachusetts, and in a vast extended family that lived very differently than he did. AJ met his extended family in Jamaica and Congo, and he remembered. He later told a reporter that he had a vivid memory that whenever they were in the Congo his father would carry pens and pencils that he would give children they met along the way. Ace said that when his son asked him why he did that, he told him "because they . . . need help."

When AJ got a check for $1,000 from PepsiCo, makers of Gatorade, upon being named the Massachusetts Player of the Year, he decided to donate the money to the Boys and Girls Club in

Brockton. "People are less fortunate and don't have what we have," AJ told the press. "So I might as well just donate back to the community."[14] After he committed to BYU, he went to Jamaica to work with the Bob & Rita Marley Foundation, named for the singer (and perhaps Jamaica's most famous son) and his wife. Dybantsa appeared at foundation events to raise money to support childhood education and sports programs. "I was taught by my parents to give back, and what better way to do that than the place where my mother was born," Dybantsa told a Jamaican reporter.[15]

These sorts of public appearances are, of course, expected of any major athlete in the United States. And to a certain extent, the fact that the media knows what AJ Dybantsa did with the Gatorade money reflects Ace and Chelsea's careful management of their son's public image. They are savvy enough to understand that widespread knowledge about their son's charitable giving is worth more than a thousand dollars. But Dybantsa's parents ensured that these lessons were present in his private life, too. Ace Dybantsa maintains that "Jafrican" is a parenting style as much as a legacy. AJ agrees. "I think I can speak for 90 percent of kids of African descent when I say African parents are very strict. So, I just see the world really differently," he told a Utah-based reporter.[16]

Ace required AJ and his two sisters to do pushups every morning, with a few extra for AJ in the evening. He also installed a video camera in their home's common area so he could make sure they wouldn't skip the workout. "My wife wasn't happy, but I told her I knew what I was doing," he explained. When the kids went to visit Ace's brother in France, he told Ace he was puzzled when he found them doing pushups every morning. They told him that they were sure their father would somehow figure it out if they didn't. "I'm big in accountability," Ace told a reporter. "If you don't do this, this is going to happen to you. Ask AJ how many times I took his phone for not doing what I told him to do."[17]

In the sixth grade, AJ had not made the honor roll, which the Dybantsas expected of all of their children. Ace found out about this just before his son was to play in a tournament in New Jersey. Ace called AJ's coach and told him that while the Dybantsas would be making the drive to the event, AJ should not be allowed to

AJ Dybantsa in his Brockton community team jersey, 2017. *Courtesy Dybantsa family*

play. AJ warmed up, shot around with his teammates, and spent the first game of the tournament on the bench. In the second game, the coach put AJ in. Ace told a reporter that he wasn't happy with that. Back in the car on the way home he told AJ, "Next time, I won't even bother bringing you to the tournament." He grinned at the reporter. "Ever since then, honor roll."[18]

Ace and Chelsea did not let up. When AJ came home from the basketball-focused prep schools he began attending at age sixteen, no matter how long he was in Brockton—for a weekend or the whole summer—his name went back up on the chore chart on the fridge. He'd stoop to load the dishwasher and be told to clean his room.

"Basketball was funner when there was nothing going on when we were all 10 years old," AJ told a reporter, almost wistfully. "Nobody got skill, everybody's the same. It was way more fun." And yet, Dybantsa internalized what his father taught him. "If you get sugarcoated your whole life, you ain't ever gonna get better," he said. "People always ask me if I have a Plan B. Nah, I don't."[19]

Basketball Factories

Ace Dybantsa wanted his son to cultivate relentlessness and hard work. By the time of AJ's youth, stories about the legendary focus of players like Michael Jordan and Kobe Bryant were well known. The journalist David Halberstam made famous the discipline that Michael Jordan's parents instilled in him. One day, when Michael's mother, Deloris, caught him skipping classes, she took him with her to her job at the local bank. Deloris took a position near a window overlooking the bank's parking lot where her car sat, locked tight with Michael inside with nothing but his schoolbooks. Jordan said it taught him focus. Danny Ainge, who had to guard Jordan occasionally, later said that such lessons turned Jordan into "an assassin who comes to kill you and then cut your heart out."[20]

Kobe Bryant grew up idolizing Jordan and famously tried to emulate him, all the way down to Jordan's habit of sticking his tongue out while driving to the basket. But Bryant also wanted to replicate the intensity and concentration of his icon. Bryant broke his wrist in a preseason game in 1999. A few days later, the legendary, long-retired Laker Jerry West called Kobe's coach, Phil Jackson, to report on a conversation he'd had with the young man. West explained that because of the injury and the sort of offense Jackson was beginning to implement, Kobe, only three years into his pro career, was already fretting that "he wasn't going to score enough points to become one of the greatest players of all time."[21]

Bryant retired when Dybantsa was nine, and Jordan was out of the league years before that. But Jordan and Bryant were players that Dybantsa's idols grew up watching—All-Stars and MVPs like LeBron James, Paul George, and, more than anybody else, Kevin Durant. James and George and Durant learned from Bryant and Jordan and those before them that they were expected to at least pay lip service to Jordan's brand of unflinching intensity and ambition.

Dybantsa, two generations of players removed from Michael Jordan, learned this too. While in high school he appeared on a podcast hosted by Paul George, a lanky All-Star who was then on the downward slope of a distinguished career playing for the Indiana Pacers, Oklahoma City Thunder, and, at that point, the Los Angeles Clippers. They chatted about Dybantsa's international play, and AJ told George that he "was trying to be a three-time gold medalist before I even start college." George asked Dybantsa whether he had any ambition to play for Team USA in the 2028 Olympics. Dybantsa said, "Yes," and mused that he'd be "two years in the league" (the NBA) at that point.[53]

Dybantsa's ambition also spoke to how his basketball world was also quite different from that of the players two or three generations removed from him. Michael Jordan left the University of North Carolina after his junior season to enter the 1984 NBA draft. Leaving school early for the pros raised eyebrows in those years, and Jordan's college coach, Dean Smith, had to pressure him to do it. Jordan wanted the full college experience. Smith told his star that he had little left to learn in the college game. When Kobe Bryant skipped college entirely to enter the 1996 draft directly out of high school, the move was almost unheard of. But a generation later, college basketball had little mystique left. Players like Dybantsa began preparing for the pros when they were teenagers.

In some ways, that transformation began in rural Virginia.

Mouth of Wilson is a tiny town in southwestern Virginia, half an hour from the closest interstate highway and barely three miles from the North Carolina border. In the 1970s it had a population of one hundred and was best known for Oak Hill Academy, a small Baptist school that had been around since the 1870s. A hundred years later the academy had become a boarding school specializing in what they then called "troubled teenagers." The school was having difficulty keeping the lights on. One day in 1976, the school's athletics director, Chuck Isner, had a brainstorm. He persuaded his father, Robert, the school's president, to give him four scholarships he could distribute to basketball players. The plan was to attract some attention to the school. Chuck went on a recruiting trip.[22]

It worked. Oak Hill Academy, which now functions as a private high school, boasts that since that recruiting trip, its basketball team has won 94 percent of its games. The school's record for the ten years after the famous trip was 271–35. It has won nine national championships and has had some three-dozen players drafted into the NBA, including All-Stars Carmelo Anthony, Rajon Rondo, Jerry Stackhouse—and Kevin Durant.[23]

Oak Hill Academy became if not the first then certainly the most prominent of what some journalists have come to call "basketball factories," along with Montverde Academy in Florida, Mater Dei High School in California, St. Anthony High School in New Jersey, and a dozen others. These schools take on basketball stars who might wrestle with coursework or might prefer to work on their game first and mathematics second. Carmelo Anthony, who would later shine at Syracuse University and end up in the Naismith Memorial Basketball Hall of Fame, landed at Oak Hill after struggling academically but flourishing on the court in Baltimore schools. He thrived on the competition he found there. "We could all play. So I had to walk into that situation wanting to be better," he wrote in his memoir. But he bristled at the strict discipline and didn't mention anything about the academics.[24]

And yet Oak Hill, like other such schools, offers a teacher-to-student ratio of 9–1. Students are required to abide by rigorous curfews, academic standards, and lifestyle codes and to bus their own tables at meals. At Oak Hill, coaches help enforce academic requirements. And students cultivate close relationships with faculty and administrators. Carmelo Anthony told a reporter that Steve Smith, the coach at Oak Hill, "stepped up and became a major part of my life. I remember crying in his arms."[25] Anthony and Smith regularly talked about life, dating, graduating, college, and careers. Anthony's experience was hardly his alone. Kevin Durant told a reporter that Oak Hill "was my first time out there on the national stage, being exposed to the highest level of talent. That experience catapulted me."[26] At Oak Hill, the student body was required to attend all home basketball games, but this was less onerous than it might seem. Most of the school's games were on the road because road games increased the team's profile, attracted attention, and earned money.

Several times in the early twenty-first century, the NCAA initiated investigations of schools like Oak Hill, suspicious of the transcripts that universities were getting from high-end basketball talent. According to one reporter, the NCAA was looking for "one-year students, dramatic academic improvements or uncharacteristic classwork patterns."[27] Oak Hill's coach Steve Smith was indignant. "Oak Hill," he said, was one "of the most respected schools in Virginia," and yet "we're on a watch list with a bunch of basketball factories."[28] But even as he defended his school—it was true Oak Hill's academics held up better than most—Smith acknowledged that there was a problem. Over the past two or three decades, many young players had come to treat college basketball as a one- or two-year pit stop designed simply to showcase their skills and maximize their professional opportunities. Now, it seemed, high school was becoming the same thing.

Money was key. Oak Hill, along with many less prestigious schools, acknowledged that much of the funding for their basketball programs came from donations, fees, and especially sponsorships. Other schools paid Oak Hill to come to their campuses for a game or two. Tournament promoters paid Oak Hill to participate. And, like many such schools, Oak Hill cultivated a relationship with corporate sponsors, particularly Nike. Ever since the tremendous success of the Air Jordan line in the 1980s, the company had become both a beneficiary of and engine for a wave of endorsements and sponsorships that flooded basketball—even high school basketball—with money. At Oak Hill, the shoe company provided uniforms, funding for travel and publicity, and of course, shoes. In exchange, the familiar Nike logo—the swish—appeared on the school's uniforms and promotional materials. And Nike got an early shot at signing some of Oak Hill's more prominent alums to endorsement and sponsorship contracts.[29]

Ace and Chelsea Dybantsa had their eye on the basketball factories from the time AJ was a teenager. They had him repeat eighth grade even though his grades were solid. This is a common move for promising young basketball players because it gives them a year to build up additional bulk and height. AJ was then at St. Sebastian's, a Catholic secondary school. Despite his age, he was on the varsity team and scoring seemingly at will. His parents also entered him into what is sometimes called the AAU circuit.

Short for Amateur Athletic Union, "AAU" has become shorthand for a series of intramural tournaments and leagues where young basketball players hoping to gain attention from college recruiters and professional scouts and agents play. They are, for the most part, sponsored by shoe companies, McDonald's, and other corporations that see the students as an access point to the lucrative world of professional basketball. The AAU circuit has been roundly criticized. Kobe Bryant, four-time NBA champion, former NBA Most Valuable Player, and highest-scoring player in the history of the Los Angeles Lakers franchise, grew up in Europe, where his father was playing the sport professionally. Because of that background Bryant despised the youth basketball system in the United States. "Horrible, terrible AAU basketball. It's stupid. It doesn't teach our kids how to play the game at all," he once told a reporter for ESPN, and he wasn't shy about repeating that opinion elsewhere.[30]

Bryant of course preferred the European system he grew up in, where young basketball players could become professionals as teenagers. But he also put his finger on something genuine. The AAU leagues and tournaments are fluid—young players rarely play with the same teammates or coaches for more than a few games at a time and thus don't really learn to play as part of a team. The incentives are more to be noticed than to win. Wanting to catch the eyes of agents and recruiters, players thus feel little reason to sacrifice their own scoring opportunities even if it would be better for the team. In short, for critics like Bryant, the AAU doesn't actually teach young players how to play basketball. Even Adam Silver, commissioner of the NBA, showed some worry. NBA doctors were "seeing wear-and-tear issues in young players that they didn't used to see until players were much older," he said in 2017, and he blamed the relentless pressure young players feel to play the AAU circuit.[31]

The NBA has attempted to address the problem, but ironically in some ways simply exacerbated it. In 2006 it implemented the one-and-done rule, blocking players from leaping directly to the NBA from high school. The aim, said then-NBA commissioner David Stern, was to guide players into college programs for at least a year. Stern thought this would have many salutary results. For one thing, it was good for the business of the NBA, ensuring rookies would have at least some polish. "We would like a year to look at them,"

Stern said about prospective players. "It's been interesting to see how the players do against first-class competition in the NCAA." But Stern also hoped the requirement would prevent players from fixating on the NBA too quickly, to work to develop good fundamental skills, and to resist the centrifugal force not only of AAU basketball but also of the marketized, commercial forces surrounding it. The NBA had "scouts all over the high school gymnasium," Stern said. "We're very happy to have improved" young players' skills.[32] But at the same time, the heady anticipation of the NBA had driven players to calculate not only their colleges but also high school programs. Basketball had become marketing all the way down.

The Dybantsas, for their part, were torn about AAU culture. Ace and Chelsea tried to shield AJ from the worst of it. "I handle everything," Ace told a reporter for *The Salt Lake Tribune*. AJ did not get involved in negotiations, he did not talk to recruiters, he did not deliberate endorsement contracts, he did not take phone calls from shoe companies. Ace explained, "He just focuses on two B's: basketball and books. Coaches don't talk to him. Agents don't talk to him. A coach calls me. If they by chance get his number, he won't answer."[33] Ace eventually quit his job to take on the full-time role of manager and agent for his son. AJ got a modest allowance, but his parents were determined to not let the money go to his head.

Nonetheless, starting in grade school, AJ spent most summers playing in tournaments and attending basketball camps across the country. He got what he and his parents wanted—attention. The Dybantsas started to hear from professional sports agents and university recruiters. LeBron James's agent, Rich Paul, called the family home. And AJ got invitations to basketball camps run by the agents and trainers for stars like Steph Curry.

Ace and Chelsea decided the time had come. AJ transferred from St. Sebastian's to Prolific Prep School in Napa, California—a basketball factory, but a good one. The Dybantsas made the move for two reasons. It was becoming clear that AJ was going to have a shot at a lucrative professional career, and he wanted to get better. But also, a basketball factory could pay AJ to attend.

The revolution in court cases and NCAA policy that changed the place of money in college sports hit just as AJ entered high school.

The phrase "NIL" became common. Even high school and college athletes began signing endorsement deals.

AJ benefited. When Ace told AJ's coach at St. Sebastian's that they were leaving, the coach said he was puzzled—AJ was receiving the school's most generous scholarship package. "Coach, you don't understand," Ace said. "If he goes to another school, they will actually pay him."[34]

The coach at Prolific Prep, Ryan Bernardi, was from suburban Boston himself and had been in contact with the Dybantsas for months before AJ decided to transfer. He offered the family a plan: AJ would be put on track to graduate in 2025 and would get an NIL package. The school would pay him to use his image. He would be able to sign endorsement deals. He would also play the basketball factory circuit—traveling all over the country to play top teams. And, important to the Dybantsas, he would live with a host family instead of in a dorm.

The Bettinellis were wine farmers and supporters of Prolific Prep. They agreed to put AJ up in the guest house on their Napa farm. He ate meals with them. Giancarlo Bettinelli taught AJ how to drive. With the blessing of Ace and Chelsea, the Bettinellis also put AJ on the chore list with their own four sons. AJ was cleaning bathrooms and setting tables for the months he lived there. Ace flew back and forth across the country regularly that school year. Chelsea missed AJ so much that she couldn't bear to set foot in his room while he was gone.

But AJ left Prolific after a year because Ace brokered a shoe endorsement deal with Nike, and Prolific had a pre-existing deal with rival shoe company Adidas, who provided the school with uniforms and shoes. Dybantsa's deal had been carefully negotiated; it lasted only until he entered college so as not to interfere with the situation at whatever university he might play at. But for the time being it made his relationship with Prolific awkward. Bernardi was bemused but resigned himself to losing AJ. In this new world, coaches had to consider which companies their athletes were dealing with. "We are all trying to figure it out as it goes. I think the mindset of 'What's your offer' has been the biggest change and you have to make quicker decisions," Bernardi told a reporter.[35] Other schools, like Montverde Academy in Florida, smelled opportunity as soon as the Nike deal became public and offered deals to AJ to transfer to their programs for his junior and senior years.[36] But AJ turned them down. He and his family had decided he would move to Utah.

Utah Prep

Utah Prep Academy did not exist in early 2024, when the Dybantsas began looking around for a possible alternative to Prolific Prep. The campus sits off a highway that winds between parched, red sand bluffs to connect St. George and Hurricane (the last syllable pronounced to rhyme not with "Spain," but with "spun."), two towns tucked into the southwestern corner of Utah. They are desert communities a half-hour drive from the Arizona and Nevada borders, settled by Mormons in the late-nineteenth and early twentieth centuries. The towns are growing fast, having been discovered by migrants from California and northern Utah who come for the relatively low property prices and warm, sunny weather, respectively.

In the spring of 2024, Ace and AJ Dybantsa arrived in Hurricane. They were shown around a campus that until August 2023 had been Diamond Ranch Academy, a residential treatment center and boarding school for teenagers with psychiatric disorders. In December 2022, Taylor Goodridge, a seventeen-year-old student, died of peritonitis—inflammation of the stomach lining—on campus. Goodridge's mourning family sued, pointing out that academy staff had dismissed her complaints of pain and vomiting for weeks. The Utah Department of Health and Human Services launched an investigation, and in the summer of 2023 the state shut down the facility. A real estate developer purchased the property, which included a football field, dormitories, and classroom buildings, and he leased the place to Brent Woodson, a Salt Lake City businessman. Woodson had worked with the Real Salt Lake Basketball Academy, a small-scale organization that shuttered in 2022 when its chief investor, Ryan Smith, the BYU alum and software billionaire, traded up and bought the Utah Jazz NBA team. Woodson also had grand ambitions. He looked at academies like Oak Hill and dreamed of something bigger—a school that would produce not merely basketball stars but also tennis stars, football stars, and baseball stars. "I think we can do better, frankly," he told a reporter who compared his project to basketball factories.[37]

Woodson renamed the school Utah Prep Academy, then went recruiting. In March 2024, he met the Dybantsas at a Las Vegas AAU tournament, and in April and in June he finally got them to visit the campus outside Hurricane. He walked them through the original Diamond Ranch gymnasium and explained that he was expanding and renovating its locker rooms. He showed them around a half-built, world-class new gymnasium and a storage facility being transformed into a hotel. He told them he was going to build an arena three hundred miles north in Salt Lake City, where Utah Prep could conveniently play rival teams traveling through the airport. He dropped names, claiming the former Major League Baseball pitching star Pedro Martinez and the tennis pro Novak Djokovic had both expressed interest in the school. And then Woodson pitched the Dybantsas on a radical possibility. He could not give them as much NIL money as Montverde Academy had offered, but he promised them an ownership stake in the campus. He had a dream that the Dybantsas could become involved in recruiting and would then receive a cut of the profits. "AJ will keep buying us students," Woodson said, according to reporter Kevin Reynolds. "That is our business plan … I told Ace, we want to partner with you long-term. Your kid is in college or the NBA, and he calls up a kid for us." AJ would recruit, and Ace would help run the school. Woodson told Ace that too many people in the basketball factory business "were basketball people doing business. We're businesspeople doing basketball." [38]

Ace and AJ were sold, especially when Woodson told them about his plans to expand into the Caribbean—a topic close to the "Jafrican" AJ's heart. Woodson said he was planning a satellite campus in Haiti that would cater to the children of the Caribbean's elite but also be a center for charitable outreach and building of connections between the islands and the United States. Basketball could be a bridge between peoples, nations, and communities. Players at Utah Prep would visit the United Nations and take classes in "human flourishing," as Woodson called it. Utah Prep workers were gathering a large collection of shelter tents, intended for distribution in Haiti, near one of the school's buildings. "I like what they are building. That's why I am here," AJ told a reporter. "I believe in Brent."[39]

So the Dybantsas signed. Utah Prep gave them an undisclosed

amount of NIL money and Ace Dybantsa a share in ownership. The school seemed to offer the best of both worlds that AJ was raised in—the commitment to doing things the right way, giving back, and taking family and community seriously, while as scrupulously and fairly as possible making it big.

It may not be entirely surprising that Brent Woodson did not last. His enthusiasm and plans spiraled to the point that Ace Dybantsa and some of his new partners, like the school's headmaster, Adam Cheney, grew worried. Woodson was looking for partnerships to build campuses in the Caribbean and planning exchange programs to get Utah Prep students to the Vatican, all while the school was having trouble paying its rent and utility bills. In February 2024 the *Daily Beast* reported that Woodson had gotten entangled in a series of legally dubious financial ventures. He had received payments from a Utah-based Ponzi schemer who spent years in federal prison. Later Woodson pled ignorance when Utah state authorities investigated how he ended up in possession of tens of thousands of dollars of raw diamonds from an apparent fraudster from Saudi Arabia. And even as he was talking about expanding Utah Prep to international campuses, he was getting involved in an odd scheme masterminded by operatives with Operation Underground Railroad, a controversial nonprofit that claimed to be devoted to rescuing children from child trafficking. In this case, though, OUR officials appeared to be collaborating with the profoundly corrupt government of Haiti to build a luxury resort on the island. Woodson was acting as the chief financier for the project, which never materialized.[40] As August turned into September 2024 and Utah Prep's first school year began, Ace, Adam Cheney, and others of the Utah Prep leadership told Woodson he'd have to go.

He did. Cheney and the others had moments of panic, fearing that the Dybantsas would leave the school too. After all, Woodson's plans for Haiti seemed to be taking on a much different cast than what the Dybantsas were hoping for. The shelter tents were moldering in storage on campus. But the Dybantsas stuck to their word. Before he left, Woodson had recruited an inaugural class of thirty-eight students—fewer than he had hoped for but enough to assemble a legitimate basketball team. It was led by Dybantsa but included other top AAU players who were attracting interest from major college programs. And finally before his exit, Woodson got Utah Prep into an August 2024 tournament in Shanghai. Dybantsa's team defeated teams from Canada, China, and Serbia. In October 2024, and again in January 2025, Utah Prep played on ESPN—the second game against Montverde Academy, the Florida powerhouse school Dybantsa had turned down. Utah Prep became part of a group of elite basketball schools called the "Grind Session," which toured the country playing each other at various sites happy to host them.

The school also succeeded at building connections to the NBA. In January 2025, Utah Prep brought in Keith Smart to be head coach, replacing Justin Yamzon. Yamzon was a thirty-year-old former college player and private trainer, the sort of coach who would thrive at most high schools in the country. But Keith Smart was sixty years old and a former head coach for three NBA franchises, including a brief stint coaching Jimmer Fredette in Sacramento. Smart was an assistant coach to Kevin Young's old nemesis Eric Musselman at the University of Arkansas when Utah Prep's team approached him. The Dybantsas were thrilled. AJ and Ace crafted a statement included in the press release. "Keith Smart is a game-changer. Having someone with his experience and knowledge is incredible."[41]

By then, AJ was consorting more and more with NBA players. Before he joined Utah Prep, Ace took him to a Boston Celtics game a few days after he turned seventeen. The Los Angeles Lakers were in town. When the game was over (a surprising Lakers victory) Dybantsa received an invitation. He and Ace left their seats and headed to the visiting team's locker room. Lakers' star LeBron James came out to welcome the high school player. All the Lakers greeted AJ. "They knew him by name," Ace proudly told a reporter.[42]

The previous summer, AJ Dybantsa worked out with Chris Paul shortly after the Phoenix Suns traded the aging star. Paul was in Los Angeles for the summer, and the Dybantsas were there for a little while too. Hearing of this, Paul reached out to AJ to say that he'd be at the gym at six the next morning. He asked AJ to join him.

Ace told his son that they should get there early. But when they arrived at five-thirty, Paul was already drenched with sweat.

Ace told reporters this story because, in all its brevity, it captured a great deal about the complicated world that AJ Dybantsa lived in. For one thing, Ace immediately took from it a lesson in the virtues of discipline and hard work. He believed those virtues had taken him from Brazzaville to Boston to Los Angeles, and a point where he had the telephone numbers of NBA agents and Nike representatives stored in his cell phone. So when Ace saw Chris Paul was already in the gym, Ace was impressed. "See, AJ, that's why he has nineteen years in the league," Ace recalled telling his son.[43]

But at the same time, Ace and AJ both relished knowing Chris Paul, relished the influence and attention and money that was flowing their way. A few months later, Ace Dybantsa would call Stephen A. Smith and ask if they'd be interested in having AJ announce where he'd be going to college on *First Take*. "I was happy to do it," Smith told Kevin Reynolds of *The Salt Lake Tribune*.[44] Ace had come a long way from Brazzaville.

KYU

In some ways, AJ Dybantsa is the culmination of the trajectory of BYU basketball that began when Stan Watts began pestering Ernest Wilkinson to allow him to grant players scholarships, or even when Eugene Roberts and his successors began entering BYU in tournament play—small, incremental steps toward prioritizing winning, prestige, and the benefits that derive from them. Dybantsa chose BYU because he was satisfied that the university had completed that transition while still clinging to certain parts of its legacy.

The Dybantsas first set foot on BYU campus the last full week of April 2024. Brent Woodson and the other Utah Prep Academy leadership took Ace and Chelsea to the university as part of their tour—the idea was to sell the Dybantsas not only on the school but also on the state. A number of Utah Prep backers had ties to the athletic department at BYU, and they tipped off Kevin Young that the Dybantsas would be passing through. Young was in Minneapolis, wrapping up his job with the Phoenix Suns, trying to figure out how to win a first-round playoff series, and also preparing to move to Provo. He put together a pitch on the plane and later got the chance to refine it. In June 2024, Ace and Chelsea brought AJ to Provo to meet Young. In October the Dybantsas returned to campus yet again for a formal recruiting visit.

Young put his finger on what the Dybantsas were looking for. The money was a given. Ace Dybantsa wanted it, and a lot of it. Reporters from CBS and *The Boston Globe* pegged the NIL deal the Dybantsas were looking for at $5 million. The Dybantsas asked every one of the four final schools AJ was considering—Kansas, Alabama, North Carolina, and BYU—for the same amount and told them they would not accept more. "Everyone met it, and we didn't ask for an extra penny," Ace told a reporter for *The Boston Globe*. But it's easy to imagine him smiling when he followed that with an acknowledgment that if they'd wanted more, "We would've gotten more. Way more."[45]

To keep AJ focused on the things his parents thought were important, Ace and Chelsea didn't tell AJ how much money the schools were offering. "There's a lot more to an offer than just money. People only see the money part of it, but it's not just about money," AJ told a reporter. It was not until AJ had made his final decision and signed off on the paperwork that Ace told his son how much he had brought to the family. "Wow," said AJ.[46]

Beyond the cash, certain things would set a school apart for the Dybantsas. Leonard Armato, the family's business adviser, counseled them through the decision. "The decision wasn't a money decision as much as it was a culture fit, a decision for the family, basketball, all those things that should be the determining factors," Armato told reporter Matt Norlander. AJ Dybantsa wanted to become a great NBA player. He wanted a program that would train him, not one that would simply cater to what it thought a teenage star would want.

So Young mattered. "Kevin Young comes from the NBA and they run NBA-style practices and NBA-style offense and they pattern their play after the NBA," Armato said.[47] Young had emphasized this in his meetings with the Dybantsas. He described what it was like to coach against Paul George and told them that AJ's play reminded him of the All-Star. He outlined BYU's offense and described how it resembled how the Philadelphia 76ers and the Phoenix Suns played. But he went deeper than that. In October 2024 Kevin Young introduced AJ to the sort of staff members for a major basketball team that the general public barely thinks about. Young had hired developmental coaches who focused on single skills like shooting, analytics experts who crunched the numbers on player performance, and even dietitians. Many of them had come with him from the Suns. "This stuff doesn't resonate with all players," Young told a reporter. "But a guy like AJ" cared because he was focused not simply on a good college experience but on where his career was headed.[48]

And then, of course, Kevin Young called in favors. He told *The Salt Lake Tribune* that when the NBA players he had worked with heard about his courtship of the Dybantsas, they wanted to help. "The cool thing is, those guys will hit me. They hear about it and say, 'Hey, you need me to do anything?'" Young would say, "Yes." Ace Dybantsa, who was building a contact list of his own, was impressed at how many NBA veterans were willing to vouch for Young. By the 2020s Danny Ainge was working for the Utah Jazz organization in Salt Lake City but managed to be in Provo when the Dybantsas stopped at BYU campus. AJ had grown up a Boston Celtics fan and knew Ainge both from his career in a Celtics uniform and his long stint as the general manager of the Celtics organization. Phoenix Suns star Devin Booker met with AJ after the Dybantsas attended a Suns game and "swore by Young's coaching acumen." Booker let loose with his favorite acronym. BYU was now KYU, he happily told everybody who would listen. Kevin Young was in the house.

To cap it off, when the Dybantsas were on campus, Young took out his cell phone and called Kevin Durant. Then he handed the phone to AJ. Durant "had high praise" for his former coach, AJ said afterward.[49]

The money and the career path looked good. But the Dybantsas wanted their son to learn what they thought of as character, too. Some things still mattered to the parents that had kept their son doing chores even after he was making six figures playing basketball, as well as to the son who insisted he wasn't interested in video games or late nights. "He's not a party kid, he's not interested in distractions. He wants to play basketball, have his family and keeps to himself," Armato told CBS.[50]

AJ decided he wanted to go to BYU in mid-November 2024. After telling his parents, the family went back to Provo to watch the team play a game in the Marriott Center. AJ signed the paperwork then, but Ace kept the news quiet. He wanted to give AJ time to

The Dybantsa family in Provo, Utah, August 2025. *Courtesy Dybantsa family. Madisson White, photographer.*

ponder his decision in private and reverse it if he had regrets. He also wanted to prime the media a bit more. He and AJ went to Chapel Hill, North Carolina, to watch UNC play, too. Then he reached out to Stephen A. Smith at ESPN.

After the news broke on *First Take,* Ace told a reporter that his family would be moving to Provo for Dybantsa's year at BYU (except for AJ's sister Samarra, who was already in college herself). AJ was looking forward to eating his mother's Jamaican cooking again. Because of BYU policy, AJ planned to live in the dorms, but once he was drafted, the family planned to move in with him. "Next year will be like old times," AJ said, "just better."[51]

CONCLUSION

Perhaps to the surprise of the national audience and assuredly to the delight of BYU fans, the Cougars controlled the game for most of the night. It was March 22, 2025, the second round of the NCAA tournament. BYU was poised to upset the University of Wisconsin, a perennial powerhouse. Wisconsin had played in the tournament's championship game ten years before, had regularly received a top-five seed in the tournament since then, and came into this tournament as a third seed. BYU was seeded sixth for its third appearance in the tournament in a row. In the Cougars' previous appearances in 2024 and 2021, they were upset by a lower seed in the first round. This time, though, was Kevin Young's first tournament as head coach, and the Cougars easily dispatched their first-round opponent. But now came Wisconsin—probably the strongest team BYU had faced in the tournament since the University of Florida team that had ended Jimmer Fredette's college career in 2011.

And the Cougars were hanging in.

A few minutes in, the game was tied 2–2, but after that Wisconsin trailed the entire night. Not that it was easy for BYU. At one point, the Cougars extended the lead to 11, but Wisconsin simply wouldn't go away. Their surprising star, John Tonje, had begun his college career at Colorado State University. Then he transferred to University of Missouri, where a foot injury ended his season. In 2024 he entered the NCAA's transfer portal again, an unheralded journeyman of a college player. When Wisconsin picked him up, he suddenly exploded. In his fourth game he scored 41 points in a victory over the highly ranked University of Arizona. At the end of the season Tonje was named a second team All-American, one of the ten best college players in the country. And he would not let Wisconsin lose without a fight.

With a minute and a half left in the game, BYU was up 8, 91–83.

But then Tonje hit a 3-pointer. And then with one minute left he drove between two BYU players and sank a layup. He was fouled on the play and got a free throw on top of the basket. Suddenly BYU was up by only 2. In twenty-four seconds, Tonje had single-handedly taken what looked like a sure victory for BYU and turned it into a coin toss.

Kevin Young called for a time out.

* * *

The Cougars had enjoyed a surprising season, their second as a member of the Big 12 conference. There had been worry about how BYU would be able to handle the strong teams in the Big 12 since before the Cougars joined it. In 2023–24, the last year that Mark Pope coached the team and the team's first as a member of the Big 12, an anonymous poll of its coaches predicted BYU would end up with the thirteenth-best record out of the fourteen teams in the conference. Pope managed to tie for fifth, beating conference titans Baylor and Kansas en route to a 10–8 record against conference opponents.

A year later the same poll predicted the first year of Kevin Young's tenure to be little more successful. The coaches voted BYU ninth out of sixteen teams. The media predicted the same mediocrity. BYU had lost one of its best players in Jaxson Robinson, an excellent shooter and slithery guard who followed Mark Pope to Kentucky. Several other players Pope relied on had either graduated or transferred when he left. It appeared Kevin Young would have to lean on very green players. "Relying on freshmen can be a challenge," *Sports Illustrated* reporter Kevin Sweeney wrote. He pegged BYU at ninth in the conference.[1]

But Young managed to plug a few of the holes in the dike. As soon as he was hired he rushed to contact the sophomores Richie Saunders and Dallin Hall. Saunders was a fan-favorite swingman, a scrappy and smooth-shooting bench player. Hall had been Pope's starting point guard, the engine of the team. Both had submitted their names to the NCAA's transfer portal when Pope left, signaling their openness to other universities. Some journalists suspected they were going to follow Pope to Kentucky. Saunders visited Lexington, and Pope personally picked him up from the airport. "It really does feel like Saunders will choose to follow Coach Pope," wrote Andrew Stefaniak of *Sports Illustrated*.[2] But Kevin Young called both players and asked Danny Ainge to call them, too, and managed to persuade them to stay. "He's as talented as any wing in the country," Young said of Saunders. "I really believe that."[3]

Young also believed he had a few tricks up his sleeve. He thought people were underestimating Egor Demin, the Russian point guard he had recruited. "Not a lot of people know much about him, and even if they did, how is that going to translate?" Young said.[4] He persuaded Kanon Catchings, a highly touted prospect out of Indiana, to commit to BYU too. Catchings's aunt was a star in the WNBA, and his grandfather was an eleven-year NBA veteran. Catchings told reporters that—as with so many other players—it was Young who attracted him. "Coach Young emphasizes building relationships and I have complete trust in him," Catchings said.[5] Young also signed Brody Kozlowski and Elijah Crawford, two other highly touted recruits. Unlike Saunders and Hall, none of these players were LDS. By the end of the summer, the media was projecting that BYU would be starting Hall, Saunders, Demin, and Catchings, along with, perhaps, Mawot Mag, a transfer from Rutgers University. Only the first two had played under Mark Pope, and neither had been a star.[6]

Young's instincts proved reliable. In the game against Wisconsin, Richie Saunders scored twenty-five points before John Tonje made his run. This wasn't unusual for Saunders, who had broken out that year. He went from averaging nine points per game under Mark Pope to eighteen points per game under Young. He became the second-leading scorer in the Big 12 conference and one of the best three-point shooters in the country. Young said that when they were scrambling to keep Saunders in Provo both he and Danny Ainge had told the young man that they believed he could take more of a role in the offense and become one of the leaders of the team. "He does what he's good at," Young told reporters. "That sounds easy, but I think there's a real skill to just doing what you're good at."[7]

Saunders surprised people, and BYU did, too. They closed out the season with an eight-game winning streak, went 14–6 against teams from the Big 12, and ended up ranked third in the conference. By the time the NCAA tournament rolled around, the Associated Press marked BYU the thirteenth-best team in the country. Overall for the season, BYU went 26–10. They had earned that sixth seed in the tournament.

* * *

After Kevin Young's timeout, the team ran a play for Demin. He missed a three-point shot. Young forgave him because Demin had carried the team to that point. He had scored eleven points, grabbed eight rebounds, and passed eight assists—leading the team in the last two categories. This was Egor Demin's game, and Young recognized it. The Russian was doing a bit of everything.

During the fight for the rebound off of Demin's miss, the ball went out of bounds with 30.3 seconds left in the game. After an official review verifying whether Richie Saunders or Wisconsin's John Blackwell knocked the ball off the court, the referees gave possession back to BYU. Dallin Hall drove to the rim and threw up a difficult shot that missed badly. Wisconsin's Carter Gilmore leapt onto the floor to secure the rebound and managed to call a timeout before any Cougars could reach him. There were thirteen seconds left. BYU was up by two, Wisconsin had the ball, and, of course, John Tonje would get the last shot of the game.

BYU had not won a game in the NCAA tournament since 2012. And no BYU coach had ever won a tournament game in his first year as head coach. So, it's understandable that Cougar Nation was hoping to extend the good feelings a bit longer, to have their faith in Young's vision for the future of BYU basketball strengthened just a bit more. All the men in blue had to do was hold on for thirteen seconds.

They did.

Young kept the message simple during the team's huddle. "Just go out there and get the stop. Get the job done."[8]

After the timeout Tonje took the ball and went directly at Mawot Mag, who was guarding the basket. Later Wisconsin's coach said that he was hoping for a better play but ultimately shrugged. "I put the ball in my best player's hands," he said. "You trust your players. We're not in this position without John Tonje."[9] After several pump fakes, Tonje attempted a ten-foot fadeaway shot that ended up being an airball. BYU was on its way to the Sweet Sixteen for the first time since Jimmer Fredette led the team there in 2011.

The University of Alabama hammered BYU in the Sweet Sixteen, 113–88. BYU was overmatched in this game in just about every way. Still, fans and writers considered BYU's season a triumph.

Jackson Payne of the *Deseret News* wrote, "Despite the finish, both BYU's NCAA tournament run, and season as a whole were tremendous successes. Cougar fans may not want to hear it right now, but Young's first season with the program went about as well as anyone could have hoped for a year ago when Mark Pope bolted for Kentucky."[10] Casey Lundquist of *Sports Illustrated* said, "Young has exceeded expectations in every way."[11]

* * *

Young—as a representative of BYU and the church behind it—presented this success as being primarily about character. The team had nine players who had served a mission for the LDS Church. The *Church News* reported that under Mark Pope, the team regularly held devotional events for young people when the team was on the road. In Oklahoma, Richie Saunders told a crowd of youth that his faith in God helped him succeed on the court. "God cares about the things we care about," Saunders said. "While I don't know if, in the grand scheme of things, He cares about me air-balling a shot or us winning a game, I do know that He cares about the things that we're passionate about."[12] Young himself said that the team's success in the tournament "speaks to the character of the guys we have in our locker room, and in our program."[13]

Other observers credited BYU's success to Young's recruiting, which itself grew from a host of economic and cultural developments that extend far beyond how BYU administration might think about the relationship between character and basketball.

The sportswriter Rodger Sherman observed that since "hiring Young from the Suns last April, BYU has emerged as a recruiting powerhouse, almost overnight."[14] Sherman noted, comically, that there were three possible reasons for this sudden change. First, "the Mormon population of America has suddenly started producing loads of 5-star Brigham Ballers." Second, "Young is simply the single greatest recruiter in the history of college sports." And third, "There are some rich Mormons out there. Like, *RICH* rich." Given the legal transformations around the NCAA, the revolution in finances and player subsidies, those wealthy Mormons "can give their money to elite athletes to get them to play at BYU."

Sherman believed that the answer was a mixture of the last two reasons. He is probably correct.[15] Sherman also speculated that what was happening at BYU was the future of college basketball, a sign of what would matter to players in the years to come: money and a plausible pathway to the NBA.

If Sherman is correct, Kevin Young was a savvier hire than perhaps even BYU leadership understood at the time. Other players joining AJ Dybantsa on campus in fall 2025 testified to that. Nate Pickens, a junior guard from the University of California, Riverside, announced his intention to transfer to BYU in May 2025. "I had some options, but I just came to the conclusion that BYU was probably the best place for me in order to get to the next level, which is my ultimate goal—to play professional basketball," he said. "I feel like BYU puts me in the best position to do that." Kevin Young gave Pickens the same tour he gave the Dybantsas. Pickens said that Young introduced him to the staff he brought with him from the Phoenix Suns. "They showed me all the resources they had and the NBA backgrounds they all had," he said. "If you want to be a pro, I just felt like this was the best place to be, with just the resources and what they know."[16]

At the same time, the financial engine behind BYU's NIL collective is formidable to an extent that many American basketball fans, accustomed to not paying much attention to a mid-level program like BYU, have probably not noticed. In April 2025 reporter Ricky O'Donnell reported that the University of Kentucky and BYU had the largest NIL budgets of all the universities in the country. According to O'Donnell, the NIL money being funneled to the men's basketball teams at the two schools was roughly equal—around $12 million.[17]

In February 2025, Paul Liljenquist, the CEO of the $500 million outsourcing company, Focus Services, had lunch with ESPN reporter Myron Medcalf in Provo. According to Medcalf, when he asked Liljenquist about his commitment to securing the money to bring players like AJ Dybantsa to BYU, the CEO took a sip of water, set down the glass, and said, "You're not going to outbid us."

Liljenquist is one of the most active organizers of The Royal Blue, the leading NIL collective behind BYU sports. The Royal Blue, like all NIL collectives, is technically unaffiliated with the university it supports, but it has a board of directors and an accounting firm and submitted the paperwork to register as a public charity with the IRS for tax purposes. The Royal Blue coordinates booster donations and helps BYU athletes find NIL licensing opportunities. A lot of money flows through the organization. Liljenquist pointed to the rapid expansion of Utah tech companies like his own and Ryan Smith's Qualtrics in the 2010s and 2020s. Thanks to that boom, organizations like The Royal Blue "have the donor base now" to compete with schools like Kentucky that have national basketball reputations. Liljenquist made it clear to wealthy BYU fans who want to pitch in that million-dollar checks are expected.[18]

But as Liljenquist was insisting that The Royal Blue would win any bidding war for a player, other leaders at BYU worried that such steely-eyed transactionalism might hurt what BYU was really about. Part of the worry on the part of BYU and LDS Church leaders was the perception that church members' tithing money might be funneled to athletes. Though tithing money is used to support BYU's budget, BYU leaders made clear that, as the university's vice president Keith Vorkink put it, "there is absolutely no church or university financial support of any student-athlete agreements. Tithing will never be used to support our athletics department in any way, including revenue sharing with student-athletes."[19]

Even beyond tithing, BYU and church leaders have consistently sought to downplay and even dispute reports about the amount of money players have received. They would prefer to redirect the conversation to how sports can support the university's professed values.

In June 2025, a television station in Waco, Texas, home of Baylor University, reported that Baylor men's basketball coach Scott Drew believed his star guard Rob Wright left Baylor in the spring of 2025 for financial reasons. Baylor "lost him to BYU, which reportedly offered Wright a deal worth $3.5 million," a reporter wrote. Baylor could simply not match that sum.[20]

When asked how BYU managed to recruit Wright, Vorkink said "the numbers that are thrown around are not correct. It is hard for me to say on every single case, but what I have been seeing recently would not reflect the accurate situation for at least our participation in trying to recruit student-athletes to come to BYU."[21] As with his reaction to reports about Kevin Young's contract, Vorkink's careful wording—the "our" referring to the university itself—does foreclose BYU directly paying athletes in the millions of dollars but does not preclude, for instance, the money The Royal Blue could offer.

Rather, Vorkink and other church leaders want to emphasize a much older story about basketball at BYU. Vorkink insisted that non–Latter-day Saint athletes like Egor Demin, AJ Dybantsa, and Robert Wright come to BYU not for the money but because BYU basketball is invested with moral meaning. "We don't want to be a school where a student-athlete is choosing to come here predominantly because of the compensation," Vorkink said. "We want that choice to be driven by our distinctive mission and culture."[22]

Clark Gilbert, the church's commissioner of education, agreed. "We will lay out some principles. We can never become a place where the culture is pay to play," he told a reporter. "We would undermine everything at BYU if that wins out." For Gilbert, recruitment should be based on the appeal of BYU's unique culture rather than simply outbidding everybody else. He pointed to Jake Retzlaff, the Jewish quarterback who helmed the BYU football team in 2023 and 2024. "Authentically, his experience around faith here has been transformational," Gilbert said. And that was worth more than dollars.[23]

This story of BYU sports had its successes. After the 2025 tournament, Richie Saunders declared that he was grateful he stayed. Kevin Young "believes in me and he knows and can help me to reach higher," he told a reporter. "Super grateful for this season."[24]

But BYU's commitment to values beyond winning could also collide with other goals. In May 2025, a Utah woman filed a civil suit accusing Retzlaff of sexual assault, battery, and infliction of emotional distress. Retzlaff admitted to a sexual encounter but claimed it was consensual. The next month his attorneys and those of the accuser agreed to jointly dismiss the case, but Retzlaff's admission drew him a seven-game suspension from BYU's Honor Code office. That, in turn, prompted Retzlaff to announce he would transfer to another university to finish his college career. The university's athletics department issued a statement that "BYU athletics understands and respects Jake's decision to withdraw from BYU, and we wish him all the best."[25]

The case points to the continuing complications that the Honor

Code holds for non-LDS athletes at the school, even as the university touts its benefits. The sordidness of the whole situation also shows that the virtues athletics might impart are not so easily conveyed as coaches and athletic directors often imply.

None of this, of course, means that the non-material reasons the Dybantsas and Wrights of the world chose BYU are meaningless. Over and over again, recruits cite Kevin Young as a reason for signing up. Young's appeal is indeed partly cultural—namely, his gifts as a teacher and his ability to build a community around basketball that the Dybantsas loved. But to players, his appeal is also professional. His NBA connections and authority and the promise that he can teach young players what they need to eventually make it as professionals is a powerful asset. And while these gifts are hardly untouched with financial incentive as BYU administrators might hope, they are also not so simply mercenary as the financial reservoirs of The Royal Blue might imply.

The energies of basketball at BYU are as complex and maddening as they were for James Naismith, who was so dismayed at seeing players in that Kansas City game fouling to steal the ball. The sport is the tensions between finance and character, between professionalism and amateurism, between self-aggrandizement and community. They were all present at the birth of basketball, were present in the first NCAA tournament, are present at Utah Prep and Oak Hill Academies, and will remain at Brigham Young University so long as there are hoops on campus.

NOTES

Preface

1. Kevin Reynolds, "The 'Crazy Story' of How the Best Basketball Recruit in the Country Decided to Play at BYU," *Salt Lake Tribune*, Dec. 12, 2024, sltrib.com.

2. Kevin Reynolds, "The No. 1 High School Basketball Recruit in the Country Visits BYU on Monday," *Salt Lake Tribune*, June 3, 2024, sltrib.com.

3. Jackson Payne, "Egor Demin Becomes BYU's First 5-star Prospect in Program History," *Deseret News*, Aug. 2, 2024, deseret.com.

4. Kelsey Mae Nield, "Nonmember Students Face Challenges at BYU," *Daily Universe*, Oct. 26, 2021, universe.byu.edu.

5. Gordon Monson, "BYU Continues to Move Further into the Bright Spotlight of College Sports," *Salt Lake Tribune*, Apr. 25, 2025, sltrib.com.

6. Jordan Burke, "BYU Says Tattoos Were Not 'Erased,'" *Deseret News*, Jan. 15, 2004, deseret.com.

7. Jim Donaldson, "One and Done Is Latest Woe for the College Game," *Minneapolis Star-Tribune*, Apr. 19, 2008, startribune.com.

8. Sara Coello, "What Is NIL in College Sports?" *ESPN*, Mar. 24, 2025, espn.com.

9. Ernest G. Wilkinson, *Brigham Young University: The First Hundred Years*, 4 vols. (Brigham Young University Press, 1975), 2:513.

10. Wilkinson, *Brigham Young University*, 2:422.

11. Marissa Liu, "BYU Football Puts Faith First with Fireside Tradition," *Daily Universe*, Oct. 28, 2015, universe.byu.edu; Dick Harmon, "Mendenhall Tweaks Things in Quest for Perfection," *Deseret News*, July 27, 2008, deseret.com.

12. Kevin Reynolds, "BYU's Tom Holmoe and Kalani Sitake Have Focus on Big 12 During Final Media Day as a Football Independent," *Salt Lake Tribune*, June 22, 2022, sltrib.com.

13. Kevin Reynolds, "BYU Head Coach Mark Pope Says He's Losing Out on Recruits," *Salt Lake Tribune*, Mar. 16, 2023, sltrib.com.

14. Jared Weiss, "Meet AJ Dybantsa," *New York Times*, Jan. 7, 2025, nytimes.com; Matt Norlander, "BYU to Hire Kevin Young as Coach," *CBS Sports*, Apr. 16, 2024, cbssports.com.

15. Tad Walch, "How BYU Benefits from Upheaval in Business of College Sports," *Deseret News*, July 16, 2025, deseret.com; Jon Conahan, "BYU Looking to Become a Powerhouse in NIL Era," *Sports Illustrated*, Dec. 16, 2024, si.com

16. Adam Zagoria, "No. 1 Hoops Prospect AJ Dybantsa Already Eyeing NBA Teams," *Forbes*, Dec. 13, 2024, forbes.com.

17. Walch, "How BYU Benefits from Upheaval in Business of College Sports."

18. Tad Walch, "The Lord's Timing: The Inside Story of How Kevin Young Landed at BYU," *Deseret News*, Apr. 22, 2024, deseret.com.

19. Armand Mauss, *The Angel and the Beehive: The Mormon Struggle with Assimilation* (University of Illinois Press, 1994).

20. Onaje Woodbine, *Black Gods of the Asphalt: Religion, Hip-Hop, and Street Basketball* (Columbia University Press, 2016); other competing meanings of the sport are discussed in Craig Forney, *The Holy Trinity of American Sports: Civil Religion in Football, Baseball, and Basketball* (Mercer University Press, 2010), 84–100.

21. Quentin L. Cook, "Preparing Students for Eternity," address at BYU University Conference, Aug. 28, 2023, speeches.byu.edu.

22. McKenna Park, "Henry J. Eyring to Replace Clark Gilbert as BYU-Idaho President," *Daily Universe*, Feb. 8, 2017, universe.byu.edu.

23. Clark Gilbert, "Dare to Be Different," *Deseret News*, Sep. 14, 2022, deseret.com.

24. Dave McCann, "The 2 Sides of AJ Dybantsa," *Deseret News*, May 6, 2025, deseret.com.

25. Dave McCann, "AJ Dybantsa's Journey to BYU Began with His Parents," *Deseret News*, Dec. 11, 2024, deseret.com.

Chapter 1

1. Eric Jackson, "Shaq Assists as No. 1 Recruit AJ Dybantsa Eyes Off-Court Riches," *Sportico*, Mar. 5, 2025, sportico.com.

2. Tom Friend, "How Shaq Cashed In," *Sports Business Journal*, Feb. 10, 2025, sportsbusinessjournal.com.

3. Jackson, "Shaq Assists."

4. Theodore Roosevelt, "Professionalism in Sports," *North American Review*, Aug. 1890, 190–91.

5. Kyle Tucker, "AJ Dybantsa Is One of High School Basketball's Top Players—Thanks to Spider-Man," *New York Times*, Sep. 22, 2023, nytimes.com.

6. Thomas Neumann, "Michigan's Fab Five in Their Own Words," *ESPN*, Mar. 11, 2011, espn.com.

7. Chad Millman, "Fab Friend," *ESPN*, June 18, 2002, espn.com.

8. The somewhat confusing sequence of events is broken down in Jimmy Sanderson, *Corruption and Scandal in American Sports* (Bloomsbury Press, 2023), 131–37.

9. Jerry Parkinson, *Infractions: Rule Violations, Unethical Conduct, and Enforcement in the NCAA* (University of Nebraska Press, 2019) argues that the committee ultimately strives for fairness; the journalists Joe Nocera and Ben Strauss, in *Indentured: The Inside Story of the Rebellion Against the NCAA* (Penguin, 2016), maintain that the NCAA's investigative arm is mainly concerned with protecting the NCAA itself from lawsuits and preventing players from claiming a piece of the revenue from college sports.

10. Kevin Blackistone, "The Impact of Michigan's 'Fab 5' on the Social Milieu of College Sports," *NPR Morning Edition*, Oct. 12, 2016, npr.org.

11. Ronald A. Smith, *Pay to Play: A History of Big-Time College Athletic Reform* (University of Illinois, 2010), 44.

12. Allan Sack and Ellen Staurowsky, *College Athletes for Hire: The Evolution and Legacy of the NCAA's Amateur Myth* (Praeger Publishers, 1998), 33–34.

13. Howard Savage et al., *American College Athletics* (Carnegie Foundation for the Advancement of Teaching, 1929), 259.

14. Savage et al., 262.

15. Taylor Branch, "The Shame of College Sports," *The Atlantic*, Oct. 2011, 86.

16. Jack McCallum, "In the Kingdom of the Solitary Man," *Sports Illustrated*, Oct. 6, 1986, 66.

17. James Bolin, *Adolph Rupp and the Rise of Kentucky Basketball* (University Press of Kentucky, 2019), 155–56.

18. Bolin, 181.

19. Bolin, 192.
20. Ronald Smith, *Walter Byers and the NCAA: Power, Amateurism, and Growing Controversy in Big-Time College Sport* (University of Tennessee Press, 2025), 155–66.
21. Seth Davis, *When March Went Mad: The Game that Transformed Basketball* (Henry Holt, 2009), 244.
22. Davis, 8–9.
23. Ronald A. Smith, *The Myth of the Amateur: A History of College Athletic Scholarships* (University of Texas Press, 2021), 147–51.
24. Walter Byers, *Unsportsmanlike Conduct: Exploiting College Athletes* (University of Michigan Press, 2014), 69.
25. Branch, "Shame of College Sports," 89.
26. Byers, *Unsportsmanlike Conduct*, 371.
27. Smith, *Myth of the Amateur*, 116.
28. "Ivy Group Agreement," *Dartmouth Alumni Magazine*, Oct. 1952, 17.
29. Diane Pucin, "As Good as It Got," *Los Angeles Times*, Mar. 14, 2005, 16.
30. Nocera and Strauss, *Indentured*, 162.
31. Nocera and Strauss, 267–68.
32. Helen Christophi, "Student Athletes Say NCAA 'Exploited' Them in Antitrust Trial," *Courthouse News Service*, Sep. 7, 2018, courthousenews.com.
33. Troutman Pepper Locke, "From 'Student-Athletes' to 'Players': A Review of the 2021 Legal Developments Shaping a New Reality of College Sports," *JD Supra*, Jan. 6, 2022, jdsupra.com.
34. Albert Samaha et al., "The Hidden NIL Economy of College Sports," *Washington Post*, Oct. 21, 2024, washingtonpost.com.
35. Dan Murphy, "Universities, NCAA See Pros and Cons of New State NIL Laws," *ESPN*, July 1, 2023, espn.com.
36. Charlie Baker, "A Letter from NCAA President Charlie Baker," June 6, 2025, ncaa.org.
37. Ralph Russo and Justin Williams, "DOE Memo Says NIL Payments Must Be Proportionate Between Male, Female Athletes, But Guidance Could Be Short-Lived," *New York Times*, Jan. 17, 2025, nytimes.com.
38. Byers, *Unsportsmanlike Conduct*, 5.
39. Byers, 65, 70.
40. Byers, 5–6.
41. Nicole Aurbach and Manny Navarro, "Miami's Isaiah Wong Won't Enter Transfer Portal After Threatening Move Over NIL Compensation," *New York Times*, Aug. 31, 2022, nytimes.com.
42. PJ Pfeiffer, "'A Bad System': Tom Izzo Delivers a Harsh Truth About the Transfer Portal Era," *State News*, Apr. 17, 2025, statenews.com.
43. "NIL Marketing Partnerships, 2023–2024," *SponsorUnited*, Mar. 20, 2024, sponsorunited.com.
44. Thilo Kunkel, "Is NIL a Good Thing or a Bad Thing," *Temple Now*, June 25, 2024, news.temple.edu.
45. Charlie Parent, "Number 1 Recruit AJ Dybantsa Talks Recruitment and Red Bull NIL Deal," *ZagsBlog*, Oct. 16, 2024, zagsblog.com.

Chapter 2

1. Brigham Henry Roberts, "Sphere of YMMIA Activities," *Improvement Era*, Jan. 1913, 191, 193.
2. James Naismith, *Basketball: Its Origins and Development* (Association Press, 1941), 23.

3. Oliver Wendell Holmes, *The Autocrat of the Breakfast-Table: Every Man His Own Boswell* (Lupton Publishing Company, 1858), 177.

4. Naismith, *Basketball*, 35.

5. Cited in Rob Rains, *James Naismith: The Man who Invented Basketball* (Temple University Press, 2009), 32.

6. James Naismith, "The Fundamentals of Basketball" (1910), in Douglas Stark, ed., *The James Naismith Reader* (University of Nebraska Press, 2021), 160–62.

7. "A New Game of Ball," *New York Times*, Apr. 26, 1892, 2.

8. "Hamilton School Won," *Salt Lake Tribune*, Feb. 6, 1897, 7.

9. Chester Ames, "To the Basket-Ball Girls (At Resting Time)," *Daily Utah Chronicle*, May 25, 1897, 9.

10. Art Remillard, *Bodies in Motion: A Religious History of Sports in America* (Oxford University Press, 2025), 127–29.

11. Clifford Putney, *Muscular Christianity: Manhood and Sports in Protestant America* (Harvard University Press, 2009), 71–73.

12. Cited in Rains, *James Naismith*, 73–74.

13. Cited in Rains, 91.

14. "Over the Pioneer Trail," *Improvement Era*, Aug. 1912, 933.

15. "President Heber J. Grant's Conference Message," *Improvement Era*, Apr. 1926, 682.

16. "Game of Basketball," *Deseret News*, Feb. 22, 1900, 5.

17. E.J. Milne, "Ward and Gymnasium Hall," *Improvement Era*, Dec. 1908, 162–63.

18. Joseph F. Smith, "Amusements," *Improvement Era*, May 1911, 638–39.

19. Levi Edgar Young, "Sociological Aspects of Mormonism," *Improvement Era*, July 1920, 829.

20. L.R. Martineau, "Some Problems in Athletics," *Improvement Era*, Oct. 1912, 1139; L.R. Martineau, "Mutual Work," *Improvement Era*, July 1910, 858.

21. "Basket Ball," *Improvement Era*, May 1908, 562.

22. Statistics and the stories of Paul Hansen, Larry Schlappi, and the Cincinnati Stake, reported in Jessie Embry, *Spiritualized Recreation: Mormon All-Church Athletic Tournaments and Dance Festivals* (Brigham Young University, 2008), 59–69.

23. George Durrant, *A Dad, a Boy, and a Ball* (Bookcraft, 1988), 46.

24. "A Report of M-Men Basketball, 1949–1950," *Improvement Era*, Apr. 1950, 281.

25. Les Goates, "Ten in Ten Thousand," *Improvement Era*, June 1936, 484.

26. Cited in Embry, *Spiritualized Recreation*, 44.

27. Cited in Richard Ian Kimball, *Sports in Zion: Mormon Recreation, 1890–1940* (University of Illinois, 2003), 101.

28. "Missionary Attention Getters," *Improvement Era*, Sep. 1936, 571.

29. J. Paul Vorkink and Joseph Lambert, "Our Friend-Making Missionaries in the Netherlands," *Improvement Era*, July 1938, 412.

30. Parry D. Sorensen, "Building Good Will in Britain Through Sports," *Improvement Era*, Feb. 1938, 117; Parry D. Sorensen, "Mormon Missionaries Under the Union Jack," *Improvement Era*, Aug. 1938, 476, 501.

31. Jessie L. Embry and John H. Brambaugh, "Preaching Through Playing: Using Sports and Recreation in Missionary Work, 1911–64," *Journal of Mormon History* 35, no. 4 (Fall 2009): 73–74; Donald Brown, "Pres. Matis Receives Finnish Silver Cross," *Deseret News*, Aug. 15, 1951, 40.

32. Fred Woods, "Mormon Missionaries and Mid-Twentieth Century Basketball in Australia: Religion Through Sport as a Vehicle to Reach Secular Society," *Journal for the Academic Study of Religion* 29, no. 1 (2016): 77–93.

33. Both William and Larson cited in Ryan A. Davis, "Mormon Missionaries and

the Emergence of Modern Argentine Sport, 1938–1943," *International Journal of the History of Sport* 35, no. 1 (2018), 67–68; see also Frederick G. Williams and Frederick Salem Williams, *From Acorn to Oak Tree: A Personal History of the Establishment and First Quarter Century Development of the South American Missions* (Et Cetera Graphics Press, 1987), 140–45.

34. Davis, "Mormon Missionaries," 64.

35. Davis, "Mormon Missionaries," 78.

36. Lerone Martin, *The Gospel of J. Edgar Hoover: How the FBI Aided and Abetted the Rise of White Christian Nationalism* (Princeton University Press, 2023), 33–67.

37. Embry and Brambaugh, "Preaching Through Playing," 79–84.

38. Richard D. Poll and Stan Larson, *Working the Divine Miracle: The Life of Apostle Henry D. Moyle* (Signature Books, 1999), 203; D. Michael Quinn "I-Thou vs. I-It Conversions: The Mormon 'Baseball Baptism' Era," *Sunstone*, Dec. 1993, 30–44.

39. Quinn, "I-Thou vs. I-It Conversions," 40.

40. Cited in Embry and Brambaugh, "Preaching Through Playing," 83.

41. Melissa Inouye, "A Tale of Two Chapels," *Rational Faiths*, Aug. 9, 2014, rationalfaiths.com.

42. "Best High School Basketball Player Since Lebron James Is Mormon Seminary Student," *LDS Church Newsroom*, news-ph.churchofjesuschrist.org.

43. Nick Newman, "Gospel Teachings Apply in Games," *Deseret News*, Oct. 22, 2009.

44. "Church Balls Are Gold and Green—and Now Orange," *Sunstone*, Oct. 2004, 18.

45. Rich Johnson, "Carpet Burns and Whistles," *University Journal*, Nov. 25, 2002, 18.

46. J.J. Jackson, "Athletic High Councilman Lets Sports Help with Religion," *Daily Spectrum*, Mar. 4, 1983, 25.

47. "Thurl Bailey Speaks to Crowd," *Emery County Progress*, Dec. 2, 2003, 6.

48. Dennis Romboy, "Church Ball Takes to a New Court: The Utah Supreme Court," *Deseret News*, July 15, 2019.

49. Judd Nixon v. Edward Clay, 2019 UT 32.

50. Kristine Haglund, "Why Mormon Men Love Church Ball and Fear Homosexuality," *Arc*, Sep. 10, 2012, arcmag.org.

Chapter 3

1. C.W. Whitney, "Investigation," in *Football Facts and Figures*, Walter Camp, ed. (Harper and Brothers, 1894), 33–34.

2. Michael Weinraub, "As Mass Plays Threatened the Future of Football in the 1890s, a Fluke Pass Showed a Path Forward," *New York Times*, Feb. 25, 2019, nytimes.com.

3. "LDS Board Ends Football," *Salt Lake Herald*, Oct. 11, 1901, 7, suggests—incorrectly—that trustee John Nicholson's son had died in a game. J. Marinus Jensen et al., *History of Brigham Young University* (Brigham Young University, 1942), 287, speculates about a death in an unspecified football game.

4. "Football Contest," *Ogden Standard Examiner*, Nov. 24, 1885, 1.

5. Ernest L. Wilkinson, *Brigham Young University: The First Hundred Years* (Brigham Young University Press, 1973), 1:283.

6. Cited in Hunter M. Hampton, "Saints Embrace Savagery: BYU Football and the Making of Modern Mormonism," in *The History of American College Football: Institutional Policy, Culture and Reform*, eds. Christian K. Anderson and Amber C. Fallucca (Routledge, 2021), 113–14.

7. "College Football," *Provo Daily Enquirer*, Apr. 12, 1896, 2.

8. "LDS Board Ends Football," *Salt Lake Herald*, Oct. 11, 1901, 7.

9. "Opposed to the Game of Football," *Deseret News*, Dec. 8, 1905, 2.

10. Wilkinson, *Brigham Young University*, 1:483.
11. Jensen et al., *History of Brigham Young University*, 287.
12. "Athletic Association Officers," *Utah County Democrat*, Oct. 5, 1898, 1.
13. "Basketball," *Utah County Democrat*, Apr. 1, 1903, 1.
14. Jensen et al., *History of Brigham Young University*, 288.
15. "A Great Event," *Utah County Democrat*, May 3, 1899, 1.
16. Cited in Axel Bundgaard, *Muscle and Manliness: Sport in American Boarding Schools* (Syracuse University Press, 2005), 30.
17. Paul Putz, *The Spirit of the Game: American Christianity and Big-Time Sports* (Oxford University Press, 2024).
18. Elwin Garfield, "The Word of Wisdom," *Improvement Era*, January 1933, 165.
19. Quoted in Wilkinson, *Brigham Young University*, 1:505.
20. Theodore Roosevelt, *The Winning of the West* (New York: Putnam, 1889–96), 4:1.
21. Eugene Roberts, "Men Are That They Might Have Joy," *Improvement Era*, Feb. 1929, 324.
22. "Credit Due," *White and Blue*, Mar. 5, 1912, 2.
23. Richard Dahl, *BYU's Stan Watts: The Man and his Game* (Horizon Publishers, 1976), 92.
24. Hy Turkin, "Mormons Choice Over Dayton," *New York Daily News*, Mar. 17, 1951, 31.
25. Hack Miller, "Cougars Should Win NIT," *Deseret News*, Mar. 17, 1951, 4A.
26. Dahl, *Stan Watts*, 96.
27. Sara Lenz, "Former Miss America Vandeweghe Left Legacy of Family, Faith," *Deseret News*, Apr. 6, 2010, www.deseretnews.com.
28. Bergera and Priddis indicate it dropped by half in these years. Gary Bergera and Ron Priddis, *Brigham Young University: A House of Faith* (Signature Books, 1985), 383.
29. Dahl, *Stan Watts*, 113.
30. Dahl, *Stan Watts*, 114.
31. Thomas G. Alexander had access to the General Priesthood Committee's attendance records from the mid-1910s; cited and discussed in his *Mormonism in Transition: A History of the Latter-day Saints, 1890–1930* (University of Illinois Press, 1996), 114; for early twenty-first-century survey results, see the discussion in Jana Riess, *The Next Mormons: How Millennials Are Changing the LDS Church* (Oxford University Press, 2019), 155–56.
32. Kurt Kemper, *Before March Madness: The Wars for the Soul of College Basketball* (University of Illinois Press, 2020), 69–107.
33. John A. Widtsoe, *Priesthood and Church Government* (Deseret Book, 1939), 204.
34. Quoted in Wilkinson, *Brigham Young University*, 3:422.
35. Ronald Smith, *The Myth of the Amateur: A History of College Athletic Scholarships* (University of Texas Press, 2021), 91–94.
36. Wilkinson, *Brigham Young University*, 3:423.
37. "Coach Watts Knows the Value of Life," *Deseret News*, Mar. 18, 1972, 44.
38. Stan Watts, *Developing an Offensive Attack in Basketball* (Prentice Hall, 1959), 97, 99.
39. Watts, *Offensive Attack*, 104.
40. Stan Watts, *Brigham Young University Basketball* (Brigham Young University Press, 1972), 2–3.
41. Watts, *Brigham Young University Basketball*, 3, 5–6; Stan Watts, "If I Were You," in *If I Were You*, ed. Victor L. Brown (Bookcraft, 1975), 118–19.
42. Boyd Jay Petersen, *Hugh Nibley: A Consecrated Life* (Kofford Books, 2002), 341.

See also Beverly Campbell, *Krešimir Ćosić: One Man's Spiritual Journey* (Y Mountain Press, 2014), 33–35.

43. Petersen, *Hugh Nibley*, 341–42.

44. Dick Harmon, "Superstar Kresimir Cosic: His Trek from Atheist to Partner with God," *Deseret News*, Apr. 25, 2020, 7.

45. Dick Harmon, "Kresimir Cosic: The Passionate Gamesman, His Mark and Legacy," *Deseret News*, Apr. 24, 2020, 7.

46. Gary Roe, "A Long Way from Basketball Star to Diplomat," *Davis County Clipper*, Apr. 5, 1993, 20; Bob Ryan, "Inductee Cosic Was Europe's First Great Basketball Import," *Boston Globe*, May 8, 1996, 14.

47. Bruce R. McConkie, *Mormon Doctrine*, 2nd ed. (Deseret Book, 1966), 83, 245.

48. Cited in Gary James Bergera, "'This Time of Crisis': The Race-Based Anti-BYU Athletic Protests of 1968–1971," *Utah Historical Quarterly* 81, no. 3 (Summer 2013): 205.

49. Bob Williams, "Bobbin Around," *Salt Lake Tribune*, Feb. 13, 1961, 23.

50. Bergera, "'This Time of Crisis,'" 206.

51. "Negros to Boycott BYU Meet," *Salt Lake Tribune*, Apr. 12, 1968, 54.

52. Joe Watts, "Three Touchdown Explosion Boosts San Jose," *Provo Sunday Herald*, Dec. 1, 1968, 14.

53. Bergera, "'This Time of Crisis,'" 212.

54. Pete Erickson, "Cats Enter WAC Cage War Under Protest," *Tucson Daily Citizen*, Jan. 8, 1970, 32; Abe Chanin, "Black UA Cagers Will Play," *Arizona Daily Star*, Jan. 8, 1970, 1D.

55. "Protests Not Against Y—Watts," *Daily Universe*, Mar. 11, 1970, 1.

56. Joe Watts, "First Black Basketball Player Quits BYU Team," *Provo Daily Herald*, Dec. 17, 1974, 6.

57. Grace Soelberg, "Peculiar Students of a Peculiar Institution: A Historical Analysis of Racial Minority Students and Race Relations at Brigham Young University Presented in the Banyan from 1911–1985," honors thesis (Brigham Young University, 2021), 29–30.

58. Doug Robinson, "Blessing in Disguise," *Deseret News*, Aug. 31, 2011, deseretnews.com.

Chapter 4

1. Steve Cameron, "There's a Lesson in This," *Provo Daily Herald*, Dec. 20, 1996, C2.

2. Austin Murphy, "Stormin' Mormons: Coach Roger Reid and Sons Randy and Robbie Have Made BYU Basketball a Family Affair," *Sports Illustrated*, Feb. 20, 1995, 153.

3. Jerry Tipton, "UK Basketball Notebook," *Lexington Herald Leader*, Nov. 17, 1996, C3.

4. "Hoops for Heaven's Sake," *Salt Lake Tribune*, Nov. 21, 1996, 16.

5. Patrick Kinahan, "Reid Makes Amends with Burgess Family," *Salt Lake Tribune*, Nov. 20, 1996, 29.

6. Dick Rosetta, "Dumping Reid a No-Brainer for Cougars," *Salt Lake Tribune*, Dec. 18, 1996, 41.

7. Peter May, *The Last Banner: The Story of the 1985–1986 Celtics, The NBA's Greatest Team of All Time* (Simon and Schuster, 1996), 87.

8. May, *The Last Banner*, 88.

9. Dick Harmon, "Who Was the Better Player at BYU?" *Deseret News*, Apr. 5, 2020, 5.

10. Steve Wilson, "Ainge Leads Cougar Win," *Salt Lake Tribune*, Dec. 24, 1978, 2C.

11. Bob Hudson, "Rocky Mountain Cage Outlook," *Provo Daily Herald*, Nov. 28, 1978, 10.

12. Marion Dunn, "Clemson Chains Cougars," *Provo Daily Herald*, Mar. 9, 1980, 6.

13. Dick Rosetta, "Clemson Tigers Roar to 71–66 Upset over BYU," *Salt Lake Tribune*, Mar. 9, 1980, D2.

14. Rosetta, "Clemson Tigers Roar," D2

15. Jeff Call, "Danny Ainge on Legacy of Elite Eight Team," *Deseret News*, Jan. 26, 2022, 3.

16. Marion Dunn, "Cougars Make Impression," *Daily Herald*, Mar. 15, 1981, 6.

17. Max Stultz, "Irish Battling BYU in East," *Indianapolis Star*, Mar. 19, 1981, 35; Ray Herbat, "Ainge Could Be BYU's Edge," *Salt Lake Tribune*, Mar. 19, 1981, K1.

18. Michael Coffey, *Echoes on the Hardwood: 100 Seasons of Notre Dame Basketball* (Taylor Trade Publishing, 2004), 179.

19. Marion Dunn, "Ainge, Cougars Topple Irish 51–50," *Daily Herald*, Mar. 20, 1981, 6.

20. Ray Herbat, "Sampson Stymies Cougars as Virginia Wins Regional," *Salt Lake Tribune*, Mar. 22, 1981, D1; "Ainge Talks About Technical," *Daily Spectrum*, Mar. 22, 1981, 12.

21. The discussion about Stern's career draws on Pete Croatto, *From Hang Time to Prime Time: Business, Entertainment, and the Birth of the Modern-Day NBA* (Atria Books, 2020); David Halberstam, *Playing for Keeps: Michael Jordan and the World He Made* (Random House, 1999), 109–35; Joshua Mendelsohn, *The Cap: How David Stern and Larry Fleisher Built the Modern NBA* (University of Nebraska Press, 2020).

22. Halberstam, *Playing for Keeps*, 20.

23. Krista Jahnke, "A Coach for the Ages," *Detroit Free Press*, May 10, 2009, 6C.

24. May, *Last Banner*, 183.

25. Bob Snyder, "Three Sport Star to Plug Shortstop," *Syracuse Herald Journal*, Apr. 16, 1978, 7.

26. Alan Greenberg, "Second Baseman Will Finish Playing at BYU," *Los Angeles Times*, June 8, 1979, 12.

27. May, *Last Banner*, 183.

28. Pat Forde, *The Contract: The Journey of Jimmer Fredette from the Playground to the Pros* (Shadow Mountain Press, 2012), 28.

29. Forde, *Contract* 40, 63.

30. Jason Franchuk, "BYU Tries to See Positives After First Round Exit," *Daily Herald*, Mar. 18, 2007, D5.

31. Darnell Dickson, "BYU Leaves Tourney with Heartache Once Again," *Daily Herald*, Mar. 16, 2007, C1.

32. Forde, *Contract*, 65–66.

33. Forde, *Contract*, 70–71.

34. Forde, *Contract*, 76.

35. Darnell Dickson, "Questions Persist After Another Quick NCAA Exit," *Daily Herald*, Mar. 23, 2008, D5.

36. Darnell Dickson and Jason Franchuk, "Fredette Gives Fans, Team Glimpse of Future," *Daily Herald*, Mar. 21, 2008, C4.

37. Carmelo Anthony with D. Watkins, *Where Tomorrows Aren't Promised: A Memoir of Survival and Hope* (Gallery Books, 2021), 128.

38. Dick Weiss, "Back on Campus, Melo in Rare Class," *New York Daily News*, Feb. 24, 2013, 80.

39. Anthony, *Where Tomorrows Aren't Promised*, 169.

40. Forde, *Contract*, 9.

41. Jason Franchuk, "Family Push," *Daily Herald*, Mar. 11, 2009, C4.

42. Franchuk, "BYU Men Earn Tough Victory," *Daily Herald*, Mar. 1, 2009, D8.

43. Franchuk, "Assessing Credit and Debit," *Daily Herald*, Mar. 30, 2009, D4.

44. Paul Delos Santos, "Trio of Teams Highlight Mountain West," *Daily Spectrum*, Nov. 2010, D5.

45. Jay Drew, "Cougars Raise Bar, Look to Future," *Salt Lake Tribune*, Mar. 21, 2010, 11.

46. Drew, "Cougars Raise Bar."

47. Jay Drew, "Fredette's 37-Point Game Reignites NBA Talk," *Salt Lake Tribune*, Mar. 19, 2010, 10.

48. Lynn DeBruin, "Frenzied over Fredette," *Port Charlotte Sun*, Jan. 28, 2011, 3.

49. DeBruin, "Frenzied over Fredette."

50. Kate Fagan, "The Name Is Jimmer," *Philadelphia Inquirer*, Mar. 15, 2011, E2.

51. Todd Shanesy, "Mission Impossible?" *The State* (Columbia, South Carolina), Mar. 17, 2011, C1.

52. *Sports Illustrated*, Mar. 16, 2011.

53. Jim Meehan, "Manic No More," *Spokane Spokesman-Review*, Mar. 20, 2011, C3.

54. Kelli Anderson, "Balanced Gators Too Much for the Jimmer Show," *Sports Illustrated*, Mar. 24, 2011, 55.

55. John Blanchette, "This Loss Wasn't All About the Jimmer," *Spokane Spokesman-Review*, Mar. 20, 2011, C9.

56. Jesse Hyde, "The Lonely Master: From March Madness to Shanghai, the Unlikely Journey of Jimmer Fredette," *Deseret News*, Mar. 18. 2018, deseret.com.

57. Chris Mannix, "The Jimmer Dilemma," *Sports Illustrated*, June 20, 2011, 46.

58. Ailene Voisin, "Kings Chat," *Sacramento Bee*, June 30, 2011, C3; Ailene Voisin, "Jimmermania to Test Kings," *Sacramento Bee*, June 24, 2011, C7.

59. Jason Jones, "Playoffs a Memory, Future a Guess," *Sacramento Bee*, Apr. 26, 2011, C2.

60. Jason Jones, "Good Mix at Point Guard," *Sacramento Bee*, Oct. 5, 2012, C4.

61. Matt Kawahara, "Buyout Done: Fredette No Longer a King," *Sacramento Bee*, Feb. 27, 2014, C4.

62. Hyde, "Lonely Master."

63. Hyde, "Lonely Master."

64. Jay Drew, "BYU's Brandon Davies Apologizes to Teammates," *Salt Lake Tribune*, Mar. 3, 2011, sltrib.com.

65. Dick Harmon, "Dave Rose Praises His 32–5 Team's Toughness in NCAA Tournament," *Deseret News*, Mar. 24, 2011, deseret.com.

66. Matthew Piper, "The History of BYU's Honor Code," *Salt Lake Tribune*, Oct. 31, 2016, sltrib.com.

67. Mike Lopresti, "At BYU, Honor Not Just from Winning," *Town Talk*, Mar. 5, 2011, 11.

68. Lopresti, "At BYU, Honor Not Just from Winning."

69. John Jeansonne, "Like Accountability? Join the BYU Club," *Newsday*, Mar. 6, 2011, A62.

70. Luke O'Brien and Darron Smith, "The Truth About Race, Religion, and the Honor Code at BYU," *Deadspin*, Apr. 13, 2011, deadspin.com; Darron T. Smith, *Where Race, Religion, and Sport Collide: Black Athletes at BYU and Beyond* (Rowman and Littlefield, 2016).

71. Brian Maffly, "BYU Honor Code Enforcers Are Tougher on Blacks, Critics Say," *Salt Lake Tribune*, Apr. 24, 2011, archive.sltrib.com.

72. Ebenezer Samuel, "Amar'e Stoudemire Takes BYU to Task," *New York Daily News*, Mar. 4, 2011, nydailynews.com.

73. Jason Horowitz, "The Genesis of a Church's Stand on Race," *Washington Post*, Feb. 28, 2012, washingtonpost.com.

74. Kate Bennion, "Washington Post Article on Black Priesthood Ban Spurs Concern, Outrage," *Daily Universe*, Mar. 1, 2012, universe.byu.edu.

75. O'Brien and Smith, "Truth about Race."

76. O'Brien and Smith, "Truth about Race"; Smith, *Where Race, Religion, and Sport Collide*, 111–13.

77. Maffly, "BYU Honor Code Enforcers."

78. Dick Harmon, "Arrest Ends Broadus's BYU Career," *Deseret News*, Jan. 7, 2007, deseret.com.

79. Dave McCann, "How BYU Basketball Quietly Made History," *Deseret News*, Dec. 2, 2022, deseret.com; Trent Toone, "The Experience of 3 Muslim Basketball Players at BYU," *Church News*, Mar. 21, 2024, thechurchnews.com.

Chapter 5

1. Dick Harmon, "NCAA Penalizes BYU Men's Basketball Program," *Deseret News*, Nov. 9, 2018, deseret.com.

2. Jay Drew, "An Emotional Dave Rose Steps Down After Fourteen Years," *Salt Lake Tribune*, Mar. 26, 2019, sltrib.com.

3. Francis Cullen et al, "Assessing the Extent and Sources of NCAA Rule Infractions: A National Self-Report Study of Student-Athletes," *Criminology and Public Policy* 11, no. 4 (Nov. 2012): 665–66.

4. Doug Lederman, "The Rule Breakers," *Inside Higher Ed*, Jan. 10, 2016, insidehighered.com.

5. Casey Lundquist, "The Kevin Young Hire Is Proof of Change in the BYU Athletic Department," *Sports Illustrated*, Apr. 17, 2024, si.com.

6. Jay Drew, "Analysis: Mark Pope Wasn't Perfect at BYU, but His Departure Could Leave Program Hurting for Awhile," *Deseret News*, Apr. 12, 2024, deseret.com.

7. Drew, "Analysis: Mark Pope."

8. Kevin Reynolds, "Who Could Replace Mark Pope at BYU? A Few Coaching Candidates Stand Out Early," *Salt Lake Tribune*, Apr. 12, 2024, sltrib.com.

9. Jay Drew, "Hiring of NBA Assistant Kevin Young Shows BYU Is Serious About Paying for Top-Flight Talent," *Deseret News*, Apr. 16, 2024, deseret.com.

10. Dave McCann, "Steve Young Is Happy to Make Room for Another Young at BYU," *Deseret News*, Apr. 16, 2024, deseret.com.

11. Mitch Harper, "Social Media Reacts to BYU Basketball Hiring Kevin Young," *KSL Sports*, Apr. 16, 2024, kslsports.com.

12. Harper, "Social Media Reacts."

13. Jay Drew, "Kevin Young's High School Coach Has Become One of His Biggest Fans," *Deseret News*, Mar. 21, 2025, deseret.com.

14. Drew, "Kevin Young's High School Coach."

15. Doug Haller, "How Kevin Young Rose from Irish Super League to Suns's Head Coach Finalist," *New York Times*, May 25, 2023, nytimes.com.

16. "Utah Flash Set Local Player Tryouts," *Provo Daily Herald*, Sep. 5, 2007, 14.

17. Tad Walch, "The Lord's Timing: The Inside Story of How Kevin Young Landed at BYU," *Deseret News*, Apr. 22, 2024, deseret.com.

18. Haller, "How Kevin Young Rose."

19. Kevin Reynolds, "New BYU Coach Kevin Young's Path to Provo Included Irish Sea Plunges, Driving Buses, and Subbing Out Chris Paul," *Salt Lake Tribune*, Apr. 2, 2025, sltrib.com.

20. Walch, "Lord's Timing."

21. Darnell Dickson, "Ties That Bind: Kevin Young and Ingle Family Have Long History Together," *Provo Daily Herald*, Apr. 19, 2024, heraldextra.com.

22. Reynolds, "New BYU Coach Kevin Young's Path."

23. John Gale, "Jones, Fredman Bring Wealth of Experience to Team," *Deseret News*, Nov. 25, 2007, deseret.com.

24. Reynolds, "New BYU Coach Kevin Young's Path."

25. Reynolds, "New BYU Coach Kevin Young's Path."

26. "Catching Up with Kevin Young, Assistant Coach for NBA's Philadelphia 76ers and Former Clayton State Laker," *Clayton State Sports*, Feb. 1, 2017, claytonstatesports.com.

27. Scott Schroeder, "Eric Musselman and Kevin Young Went Toe-to-Toe," *SB Nation*, Mar. 13, 2011, ridiculousupside.com.

28. Dan Hinxman, "Intensity and Drive Are in Musselman's DNA," *Reno Gazette-Journal*, Mar. 20, 2011, 5C.

29. Bryan Chu, "A Coach for All Seasons," *San Francisco Chronicle*, June 7, 2008, sfgate.com.

30. Hinxman, "Intensity and Drive"; Haller, "How Kevin Young Rose."

31. Brian Smith, "Utah Flash for Sale; Won't Play This Season," *Salt Lake Tribune*, June 19, 2011, 6.

32. Haller, "How Kevin Young Rose."

33. Gina Mizell, "BYU Coach Learned a Lot as a Sixers Assistant," *Philadelphia Inquirer*, Mar. 25, 2025, C7.

34. Walch, "Lord's Timing."

35. Haller, "How Kevin Young Rose."

36. Haller, "How Kevin Young Rose."

37. Mizell, "BYU Coach Learned a Lot."

38. Mizell, "BYU Coach Learned a Lot."

39. Duane Rankin, "Suns Add Battle Tested Assistant Kevin Young to Coach's Staff," *Arizona Republic*, Oct. 16, 2020, B5.

40. Kent Somers, "Can Suns Get Thunder's Paul at Right Price," *Arizona Republic*, Nov. 12, 2020, B1.

41. Duane Rankin, "Pros, Cons, of Trading for Chris Paul," *Arizona Republic*, Nov. 17, 2020, B3.

42. "Chris Paul Tells Jim Conlan That Kevin Young Is an Amazing Coach," press conference excerpt, *YouTube*, Dec. 30, 2021, youtube.com.

43. Duane Rankin, "Williams Should Be Coach of the Year," *Arizona Republic*, Apr. 3, 2021, B1.

44. Kent Somers, "The Way Suns Lost Will Hurt for a While," *Arizona Republic*, July 21, 2021, S2.

45. Duane Rankin, "Suns Look to Learn from Close Loss to Kings," *Arizona Republic*, Nov. 10, 2021, C8; Duane Rankin, "Suns Elevate Young to Associate Head Coach," *Arizona Republic*, Aug. 8, 2021, C6.

46. Duane Rankin, "Suns' Ayton, Crowder, McGee Available vs Heat," *Arizona Republic*, Jan. 8, 2022, B5; Duane Rankin, "Suns Welcome Back Williams," *Arizona Republic*, Jan. 5, 2022, C3.

47. Duane Rankin, "Suns' Payton Has Wild Week in, Out of Virus Protocols," *Arizona Republic*, Jan. 6, 2022, B3.

48. Reynolds, "New BYU Coach Kevin Young's Path."

49. Rankin, "Suns Welcome Back Williams."

50. Duane Rankin, "Nurse, Rivers Lead List," *Arizona Daily Star*, May 25, 2023, B6.

51. Greg Moore, "Suns Coach Hire Ratchets Up Pressure," *Arizona Republic*, June 3, 2023, B1.

52. Duane Rankin, "Why Vogel Was Suns' First Choice as Head Coach," *Arizona Republic*, June 4, 2023, C3.

53. Walch, "Lord's Timing."

54. Walch, "Lord's Timing."

55. Duane Rankin, "Suns Icon Paul Westphal Dies at 70 of Cancer," *Arizona Republic*, Jan. 3, 2021, A13.

56. Kelley D. Evans, "God Makes Me Look Much Better than I Deserve," *Andscape*, Dec. 9, 2018, andscape.com.

57. Duane Rankin, "Paul Learned About Trade on Plane Ride," *Arizona Republic*, June 20, 2023, B7.

58. Walch, "Lord's Timing"; on the new policies around hiring implemented at BYU in the 2020s, see Peggy Fletcher Stack, "New Rules Have BYU Professors Running Scared," *Salt Lake Tribune*, Jan. 6, 2025, sltrib.com.

59. Matt Norlander, "BYU to Hire Kevin Young as Coach," *CBS Sports*, Apr. 16, 2024, cbssports.com.

60. Jay Drew, "Hiring of NBA Assistant Kevin Young Shows BYU Is Serious About Paying for Top-Flight Talent," *Deseret News*, Apr. 16, 2024, deseret.com.

61. "Men's Basketball Head Coach Salaries," *USA Today*, Mar. 13, 2025, sportsdata.usatoday.com.

62. Frank Josza, *College Sports, Inc: How Commercialism Influences Intercollegiate Athletics* (Springer, 2012), 51.

63. Howard Nixon, *The Athletic Trap: How College Sports Corrupted the Academy* (Johns Hopkins University Press, 2014), 70–71.

64. Casey Lundquist, "Can BYU Afford $20 million Annually in Athlete Revenue Share?" *Sports Illustrated*, May 24, 2024, si.com; Nate Carlisle, "Here's the Money Utah, BYU, and Big 12 Schools Have Been Making," *Fox 13*, Aug. 7, 2023, fox13now.com.

65. Casey Lundquist, "The Kevin Young Hire Is Proof of Change in the BYU Athletic Department," *Sports Illustrated*, Apr. 17, 2024, si.com.

66. Gordon Monson, "In Hiring Kevin Young, BYU Is Doing Something It's Never Done Before," *Salt Lake Tribune*, Apr. 17, 2024, sltrib.com.

67. Walch, "Lord's Timing."

68. Walch, "Lord's Timing."

69. Kevin Reynolds, "When It Comes to Recruiting at BYU, Kalani Sitake Says, We Are Never Going to Be a Program Focused on the Money," *Salt Lake Tribune*, Dec. 20, 2023, sltrib.com; Monson, "In Hiring Kevin Young."

70. Reynolds, "When It Comes to Recruiting."

71. Shyler Johnson, "The Experience of BYU's Religiously Diverse Student Athletes," *Daily Universe*, Feb. 2, 2022, universe.byu.edu.

72. Jay Drew, "'I Know My Voice': New BYU Basketball Coach Kevin Young Displays Blend of Confidence, Humility," *Deseret News*, Apr. 18, 2024, deseret.com.

73. Casey Lundquist, "Devin Booker Wishes He Could Have Played College Basketball for BYU's Kevin Young," *Sports Illustrated*, Apr. 17, 2024, si.com.

74. Jackson Payne, "Egor Demin Becomes BYU's First 5-star Prospect in Program History," *Deseret News*, Aug. 2, 2024, deseret.com.

75. Jason Christensen, "How Does Freshman Egor Demin Compare with BYU's past NBA Draft 1st Round Prospects?" *Daily Universe*, Apr. 10, 2025, universe.byu.edu.

76. Dave McCann, "The Egor Demin Effect," *Deseret News*, Nov. 26, 2024,

deseret.com; Jay Drew, "Egor Demin's BYU Experience Shows Kevin Young's Rising Program Anchored in Culture and Family," *Deseret News*, Apr. 9, 2025, deseret.com.

Chapter 6

1. Krysten Peek, "AJ Dybantsa, The Projected No. 1 Pick in 2026 NBA Draft," Yahoo Sports, Oct. 21, 2024, sports.yahoo.com. Erikas Polockas, "AJ Dybantsa: Future NBA Star, Relentless Journey," Talk Basket, Dec. 25, 2024, talkbasket.net.
2. Dave McCann, "The 2 Sides of AJ Dybantsa," Deseret News, May 6, 2025, deseret.com.
3. Marcus Hartman, "Stephen A. Smith's Latest Take," Dayton Daily News, Dec. 8, 2016, daytondailynews.com.
4. Scoop Jackson, "Stephen A. Smith Got a Five-Year, $100M Deal from ESPN, and He Just Might Be Underpaid," Chicago Sun-Times, Mar. 14, 2025, chicago.suntimes.com.
5. "No. 1 Overall Recruit AJ Dybantsa Announces Commitment to BYU Cougars," YouTube, Dec. 10, 2024, youtube.com.
6. McCann, "2 Sides of AJ Dybantsa."
7. Adam Himmelsbach, "The Making of AJ Dybantsa," Boston Globe, Feb. 26, 2025, bostonglobe.com.
8. Luke Akinsola, "Inside the Rise of AJ Dybantsa," NBA, Nov. 1, 2023, nba.com.
9. Ran Abramitzky and Leah Boustan, Streets of Gold: America's Untold Story of Immigrant Success (Public Affairs Press, 2022); Jared Weiss, "2026 NBA Draft Potential No. 1 Pick Reshaping NIL, Basketball: Meet AJ Dybantsa," New York Times, Dec. 24, 2024, nytimes.com.
10. Himmelsbach, "Making of AJ Dybantsa."
11. Weiss, "2026 NBA Draft."
12. Himmelsbach, "Making of AJ Dybantsa."
13. Abramitzky and Boustan, Streets of Gold, 87.
14. Weiss, "2026 NBA Draft."
15. "Top-Ranked US High School Basketballer Heads to Jamaica," Jamaica Gleaner, May 7, 2025, jamaica-gleaner.com.
16. Tim Reynolds, "With Eyes on 2026 Draft, Touted Prospect AJ Dybantsa Watches Spurs-Pacers in Paris," Jan. 25, 2025, kslsports.com.
17. Akinsola, "Inside the Rise of AJ Dybantsa."
18. Weiss, "2026 NBA Draft."
19. Weiss, "2026 NBA Draft."
20. David Halberstam, Playing for Keeps: Michael Jordan and the World he Made (Random House, 1999), 18–19; Robert Novak, "Riding the Air," Washington Post, Jan. 31, 1999, X3.
21. Kobe Bryant, The Mamba Mentality: How I Play (FSG, 2018), 4.
22. Hank Hersh, "Miles from Nowhere," Sports Illustrated, Feb. 16, 1987, 78–80.
23. "History," Oak Hill Academy, oakhillhoops.com, accessed May 12, 2025.
24. Carmelo Anthony and D. Watkins, Where Tomorrows Aren't Promised: A Memoir of Survival and Hope (Gallery Books, 2021), 139.
25. Alejandro Danois, "The Oak Hill Basketball Family," Bleacher Report, June 8, 2018, bleacherreport.com.
26. Danois, "Oak Hill Basketball Family."
27. Gregg Doyel, "Prep Players Still Consider Going to Diploma Mills," Gainesville Sun, July 8, 2006, gainesville.com.

28. Mark Schlabach, "Recruits from Dubious Prep Schools Allowed to Play," Washington Post, July 5, 2006, washingtonpost.com.

29. Armen Keteyian, Money Players: Inside the New NBA (Pocket Books, 1997), 124–25.

30. Arash Markazi, "Kobe: Europe's Players are More Skillful," ESPN, Jan. 3, 2015, espn.com.

31. Baxter Holmes, "These Kids Are Ticking Time Bombs: The Threat of Youth Basketball," ESPN, July 11, 2019, espn.com.

32. "David Stern Wants Change to Age Rule," ESPN, Apr. 3, 2012, espn.com.

33. Kevin Reynolds, "The Crazy Story of How the Best Basketball Recruit in the Country Decided to Play at BYU," Salt Lake Tribune, Dec. 12, 2024, sltrib.com.

34. Himmelsbach, "Making of AJ Dybantsa."

35. Weiss, "2026 NBA Draft."

36. Kevin Reynolds, "Crazy Story."

37. Kevin Reynolds, "New Utah Academy Is a Basketball Powerhouse," Salt Lake Tribune, Dec. 2, 2024, sltrib.com.

38. Reynolds, "New Utah Academy."

39. Reynolds, "New Utah Academy."

40. William Bredderman, "How Ex-SEAL on Child Rescue Mission Became Island Kingpin," Daily Beast, Feb. 16, 2024, thedailybeast.com.

41. Ryan McDonald, "AJ Dybantsa Will Have a Coach with NBA Experience for the Rest of His Time at Utah Prep," Deseret News, Jan. 13, 2025, deseret.com.

42. Reynolds, "Crazy Story."

43. Reynolds, "Crazy Story."

44. Reynolds, "Crazy Story."

45. Himmelsbach, "Making of AJ Dybantsa"; Matt Norlander, "Court Report: The Details on Why AJ Dybantsa Chose BYU and How Much NIL Money the No. 1 Recruit Is Set to Make," CBS Sports, Dec. 11, 2024, cbssports.com.

46. Weiss, "2026 NBA Draft."

47. Norlander, "Court Report."

48. Himmelsbach, "Making of AJ Dybantsa."

49. Reynolds, "Crazy Story."

50. Norlander, "Court Report."

51. Himmelsbach, "Making of AJ Dybantsa."

Conclusion

1. Kevin Sweeney, "Big 12 Men's Basketball Preview," *Sports Illustrated*, Oct. 14, 2024, si.com.

2. Andrew Stefaniak, "Kentucky Has Received a Crystal Ball to Land a Talented Guard in the Transfer Portal," *Sports Illustrated*, Apr. 22, 2024, si.com.

3. Mitch Harper, "Kevin Young on Richie Saunders," *KSL Sports*, Jan. 13, 2025, kslsports.com.

4. Jay Drew, "Can the Revamped, but Talented, Cougars Make an Impact in Big 12?" *Deseret News*, Nov. 1, 2024, deseret.com.

5. Brandon Judd, "BYU Signs 4-Star Talent Kanon Catchings," *Deseret News*, June 18, 2024, deseret.com.

6. Drew, "Revamped Cougars."

7. Jackson Payne, "Why Richie Saunders Should Be a First Team All-Big 12 Selection," *Deseret News*, Mar. 3, 2025, deseret.com.

8. Mitch Harper, "BYU's Mawot Mag Explained Final Defensive Stand to Defeat Wisconsin," *KSL Sports*, Mar. 23, 2025, kslsports.com.

9. Mike Hall, "What Greg Gard and John Tonje Said About Wisconsin's Final Play, Shot Selection vs. BYU," *Badger's Wire*, Mar. 23, 2025, sports.yahoo.com.

10. Jackson Payne, "3 Takeaways from BYU's Sweet 16 Loss Against Alabama," *Deseret News*, Mar. 27, 2025, deseret.com.

11. Casey Lundquist, "Fans Welcome BYU Basketball Home after NCAA Tournament Win," *Sports Illustrated*, Mar. 23, 2025, si.com.

12. Trent Toone, "Latter-day Saints to Watch During NCAA Basketball's March Madness," *Church News*, Mar. 12, 2024, thechurchnews.com.

13. Jay Drew, "The Man Behind BYU's Rise: How Kevin Young's NBA Methods Turned the Season Around," *Deseret News*, Mar. 12, 2025, deseret.com.

14. Rodger Sherman, "BYU Basketball Has Activated the Mormon Money Cannon," *Rodger Sherman*, Feb. 2, 2025, rodgersherman.substack.com.

15. Sherman, "BYU Basketball."

16. Jay Drew, "'I Just Felt Right at Home': Why Transfer Guard Nate Pickens Picked BYU and Coach Kevin Young," *Deseret News*, May 23, 2025, deseret.com.

17. Ricky O'Donnell, "2 College Basketball Teams Are Out-Spending the Field in Men's Transfer Portal, and the Numbers Are Wild," *SBNation*, Apr. 22, 2025, sbnation.com.

18. Myron Medcalf, "How BYU and Its Big-Money Booster Are Going All-In on Men's Basketball," *ESPN*, Feb. 5, 2025, espn.com.

19. Jay Drew, "Egor Demin's BYU Experience Shows Kevin Young's Rising Program Anchored in Culture and Family," *Deseret News*, Apr. 9, 2025, deseret.com.

20. Sydney Wicker and Michael Mazzuca, "Baylor Men's Basketball Feels Impact of NCAA Settlement," *KCEN TV*, June 11, 2025, kcentv.com.

21. Drew, "Egor Demin's BYU Experience."

22. Drew, "Egor Demin's BYU Experience."

23. Dave McCann, "Commissioner of Church Education: BYU Sports Can't Drift From Core Principles," *Deseret News*, Oct. 23, 2024, deseret.com.

24. Mitch Harper, "BYU's Richie Saunders on When He Connected with Kevin Young's Scheme," *KSL Sports*, Mar. 25, 2025, kslsports.com; Jay Drew, "BYU's Richie Saunders Has Turned Himself into a Future Pro," *Deseret News*, Mar. 28, 2025, deseret.com.

25. Kevin Reynolds, "BYU QB Jake Retzlaff Officially Leaves Football Team," *Salt Lake Tribune*, July 11, 2025, sltrib.com.

INDEX

C

D

E

F

N

X

Y

Z

ABOUT THE AUTHORS

Matthew Bowman is the Howard W. Hunter Chair of Mormon Studies and professor of religion and history at Claremont Graduate University. He is the author of *The Mormon People: The Making of an American Faith* (Random House, 2012) and *Christian: The Politics of a Word in America* (Harvard, 2018). He played church ball until his knees began protesting during the second Obama administration.

Wayne LeCheminant is a hoops aficionado, writer, and academic. He earned a PhD from the University of Southern California and a BA from Brigham Young University. He lives with his family in Claremont, California.